Femi & Dotun Oyewopo

LIGHT OF LIFE

Daily Devotional Guide

Femi & Dotun OYEWOPO

Copyright

LIGHT OF LIFE
A Daily Devotional Guide
Copyright 2024 by Femi & Dotun Oyewopo

Published by:
Achievers World Publishing House
Perth - Western Australia

All Rights Reserved
This book, or parts thereof, may not be reproduced, stored in a retrieval system, or transmitted in any form or by any means, electronic, mechanical, photocopying, recording or otherwise, without the written permission of the publisher.

Requests for information should be addressed to:
achieversworld100@gmail.com
ISBN: 978-0-6489792-5-8

PRESENTED TO:

_____

FROM:

_____

DATE:

_____

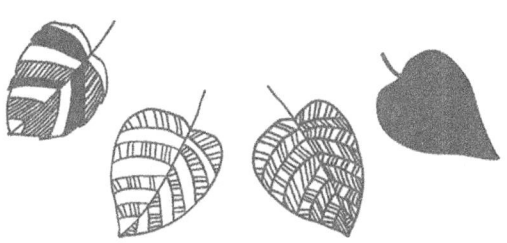

LIGHT OF LIFE

Daily Devotional Guide

Introduction

Welcome to "The Light of Life" Daily Devotional, a 365-day journey designed to illuminate your path in 2024 with the enduring light of God's Word. This devotional is not just a book; it's a transformative experience, a daily meeting place with God, and a guide for living a life that is rich in faith, hope, and love.

Imagine starting each day with a moment of reflection, inspiration, and spiritual nourishment. "The Light of Life" offers this and so much more. It's an invitation to explore the depths of God's wisdom, to find comfort in His promises, and to grow in your relationship with Him. Each day's devotion includes a carefully selected scripture, a thought-provoking reflection, and a prayer to guide you closer to the heart of God.

But "The Light of Life" is not meant to be a solitary journey. It is a gift of love, a tool for transformation that you can share with friends, loved ones, and colleagues. Imagine the impact of gifting this devotional to someone. You are not just giving them a book; you are sharing a year-long adventure in faith, a daily reminder of God's presence in their lives, and an endless source of hope and encouragement.

For families, this devotional is a priceless treasure in a world where time is often scarce and many distractions; "The Light of Life" offers a daily opportunity for families to come together in God's presence. As Joshua 1:8 urges, meditating on God's Word day and night brings prosperity and success.

This devotional helps families imbibe this powerful habit, promising to strengthen bonds, enrich conversations, and bring God's wisdom into everyday decisions and challenges.

Furthermore, Psalm 1:1-3 paints a vivid picture of the blessings that come from delighting in the law of the Lord. "The Light of Life" helps individuals and families to be like trees planted by streams of water, yielding fruit in season and prospering in all they do. It is a tool for grounding your life and your family's life in the nourishing soil of God's truth.

For married couples, this devotional serves as a beacon of light, guiding through the complexities of shared life. It offers wisdom for building a marriage that is not only enduring but also flourishing. Each devotional provides insights for nurturing love, understanding, patience, and, above all, a shared faith that can weather any storm.

"The Light of Life" Daily Devotional is more than just a daily reading; it's a lifestyle, a commitment to continual growth and learning. It's an acknowledgment that every day is a gift from God, filled with new opportunities to learn, love, and live out His calling on your life.

As you embark on this journey, may you find in these pages light for your path, strength for your trip, and joy in your walk with God. Let "The Light of Life" Daily Devotional be your daily companion in 2024, transforming your life and those around you.

Blessing

Pastor Femi & Pastor Dotun Oyewopo

Inspiring Books by Pastor Femi & Pastor Dotun OYEWOPO

Get your copy on Amazon TODAY! Looking for life transforming gift ideas? Get copies and give as gifts to bless other.

Scan QR Code to buy book on Amazon.

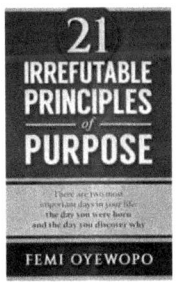

Scan QR Code to buy book on Amazon.

Scan QR Code to buy book on Amazon.

Scan QR Code to buy book on Amazon.

Scan QR Code to buy book on Amazon.

Scan QR Code to buy book on Amazon.

Monday January 01

Topic: Embracing New Beginnings with God

Memory Verse: "See, I am doing a new thing! Now it springs up; do you not perceive it? I am making a way in the wilderness and streams in the wasteland." - Isaiah 43:19

Bible Reading: Lamentations 3:22-23

Read & Learn:

The story of Noah and the ark in Genesis 8-9 symbolises new beginnings and God's faithfulness. After the flood, Noah stepped out into a world that had been cleansed and renewed. God's covenant with Noah, marked by the rainbow, was a promise of new beginnings and hope. This story reminds us that, no matter the challenges of the past, God offers us a fresh start. As we step into the New Year, we can do so with the assurance of God's presence and His promises, ready to embrace the new things He has in store for us.

The start of a new year is a time for reflection, renewal, and anticipation of what God will do. Isaiah 43:19 encourages us to look forward to the new things God is doing. It's a reminder that God can create pathways in our wilderness and bring life to desolate areas. Lamentations 3:22-23 speaks of God's mercies being new every morning, symbolising continual renewal and hope. As we enter 2024, let us embrace it with faith, open to the changes and opportunities God brings, trusting in His unfailing love and faithfulness to guide us through the year.

Prayer Point:
Heavenly Father, as I step into this new year, help me to perceive and embrace the new things You are doing in my life.

Tuesday January 02

Topic: Aligning Our Goals with Faith and Determination

Memory Verse: "Trust in the Lord with all your heart and lean not on your own understanding; in all your ways submit to him, and he will make your paths straight." **- Proverbs 3:5-6**

Bible Reading: Matthew 17:14-21

Read & Learn:

The biblical account of Nehemiah rebuilding the walls of Jerusalem (Nehemiah 2:1-20) is a powerful example of aligning goals with faith. Faced with the daunting task of reconstruction amidst opposition and ridicule, Nehemiah's planning and goal-setting were deeply rooted in prayer and reliance on God. Despite numerous challenges, his unwavering faith and strategic planning led to the successful rebuilding of the walls in just 52 days. Nehemiah's story illustrates the importance of coupling faith with action, demonstrating that with God's guidance, even seemingly insurmountable goals can be achieved.

As we step into a new year, setting goals and planning are essential, but aligning these with faith is crucial. Matthew 17:14-21 highlights the power of faith, even as small as a mustard seed, in overcoming challenges. Like Nehemiah, believers today can draw inspiration from this passage. It teaches that faith, coupled with action, is vital in achieving our objectives. Whether it's personal aspirations, professional goals, or spiritual growth, the key is to trust in God's power and guidance while actively working towards these goals. This approach helps in overcoming obstacles and realising the plans we set forth, just as Nehemiah did in his time.

Prayer Point:
Heavenly Father, as we set our goals for this year, help us to trust in Your guidance and align our efforts with steadfast faith.

Wednesday January 03

Topic: The Power of Prayer and Fasting

Memory Verse: "However, this kind does not go out except by prayer and fasting." **- Matthew 17:21**

Bible Reading: Isaiah 58:6-11

Read & Learn:

The biblical account of Esther calling for a fast in Esther 4:16 powerfully illustrates the power of prayer and fasting. Facing the threat of genocide against her people, Esther, though queen, recognised her own limitations and the need for divine intervention. She called for all the Jews in Susa to fast for three days before she approached the king to plead for her people. This act of humility and dependence on God through fasting and prayer led to a remarkable turnaround in the situation, showcasing God's power and faithfulness in response to earnest seeking and obedience.

Prayer and fasting are spiritual disciplines that demonstrate our dependence on and trust in God. They are means through which believers can intensify their focus on God, seek His guidance, and express earnestness in their petitions. Isaiah 58:6-11 reveals that true fasting is not merely a ritualistic act but a sincere expression of humility and a desire for God's will. It involves a commitment to justice and compassion. The power of prayer and fasting lies not in the acts themselves but in the God to whom they are directed. These practices can lead to spiritual breakthroughs, deeper understanding, and alignment with God's purposes.

Prayer Point:
Lord, in times of prayer and fasting, draw me closer to You, deepening my understanding and reliance on Your power and wisdom.

Thursday January 04

Topic: The Motive Behind Your Prayers

Memory Verse: "When you ask, you do not receive, because you ask with wrong motives, that you may spend what you get on your pleasures." - **James 4:3**

Bible Reading: Matthew 6:5-15

Read & Learn:

In the early 20th century, a renowned preacher named Charles Spurgeon told a story of a man who prayed fervently for the ability to preach so that he could be famous. Despite his prayers, he never received the gift he sought. Years later, he realised that his motive was self-centred, not God-centred. Once he shifted his focus to wanting to serve God and others, his prayers were answered in unexpected ways. Spurgeon's story serves as a timeless reminder to align our desires with God's will.

Prayer is a powerful tool in the Christian faith, a direct line to God. But have you ever stopped to consider why you're praying for what you're praying for? The Bible teaches us that the motive behind our prayers is just as important, if not more so, than the actual requests we make.

The Bible is replete with examples that emphasise the importance of the heart's condition when approaching God. In the Old Testament, King David prayed, "Create in me a pure heart, O God" (Psalm 51:10). Jesus Himself taught us to pray for God's will to be done (Matthew 6:10). When our motives align with God's will, our prayers become powerful conduits for His work in our lives and the lives of others.

Prayer Point:
Lord, please help me to examine the motives behind my prayers. Create in me a pure heart that seeks your will above all else. Amen.

Friday January 05

Topic: Trusting God in the Waiting Seasons

Memory Verse: "But those who hope in the Lord will renew their strength. They will soar on wings like eagles; they will run and not grow weary, they will walk and not be faint." - **Isaiah 40:31**

Bible Reading: John 11:1,6, 17-25, 38-44

Read & Learn:

We all experience seasons of waiting in our lives—waiting for answers, waiting for change, or waiting for a breakthrough. It's easy to grow impatient and question God's timing. How can we trust God in these periods of delay?

Waiting is a common theme in the Bible. Abraham waited for a son, Joseph waited in prison, and the Israelites waited 40 years to enter the Promised Land. Waiting is not a sign of God's absence or disinterest; rather, it's often a period of preparation and growth. Isaiah 40:31 assures us that those who place their hope in God will find renewed strength. The verse emphasises that waiting on God is not passive but a time of spiritual renewal and empowerment.

James 1:4 says, "Let perseverance finish its work so that you may be mature and complete, not lacking anything." Waiting seasons are opportunities for us to grow in faith, character, and reliance on God. It's essential to remember that God's timing is perfect, even when it doesn't align with ours.

Prayer Point:

Lord, in my seasons of waiting, help me to trust in Your perfect timing. Renew my strength as I place my hope in You. Amen.

Saturday January 06

Topic: Making the Best Use of Your Life

Memory Verse: "Be very careful, then, how you live - not as unwise but as wise, making the most of every opportunity, because the days are evil." **- Ephesians 5:15-16**

Bible Reading: 1 Samuel 2:12-17, 27-30

Read & Learn:

Life is a precious gift, but it's easy to get caught up in the busyness and lose sight of our true purpose. How can we ensure that what we're doing is the best use of our lives, especially in the context of our Christian faith? Ephesians 5:15-16 advises us to live wisely and make the most of every opportunity. The passage emphasises the urgency of living a purposeful life, especially in a world filled with challenges and distractions.

The Bible is filled with examples of individuals who made the best use of their lives by aligning their actions with God's will. Think of Esther, who risked her life to save her people, or Paul, who spread the Gospel despite facing numerous hardships. Living a life of purpose doesn't necessarily mean doing something grandiose. It means aligning your daily actions, no matter how small, with God's will. Colossians 3:23 says, "Whatever you do, work at it with all your heart, as working for the Lord, not for human masters."

Remember, time is a non-renewable resource. James 4:14 reminds us that we do not know what tomorrow will bring. Therefore, let's strive to make the most of today, for the glory of God.

Prayer Point:

Lord, help me to live each day with purpose, aligning my actions with Your will. Grant me the wisdom to make the most of every opportunity. Amen.

Sunday January 07

Topic: The Ripple Effect: How Your Decisions Affect Others

Memory Verse: "Be careful, however, that the exercise of your rights does not become a stumbling block to the weak." **- 1 Corinthians 8:9**

Bible Reading: Joshua 7:1-12

Read & Learn:

Every decision we make creates ripples that extend beyond ourselves, affecting the people around us in ways we may not even realise. The Bible is filled with stories of individuals whose decisions had far-reaching consequences. For example, Esther's choice to approach the king saved an entire nation. Conversely, Jonah's initial decision to flee from God's call led to turmoil for him and those around him.

Being mindful of how our decisions affect others is an essential aspect of Christian living. Philippians 2:4 says, "Let each of you look not only to his own interests but also to the interests of others." This doesn't mean we should live our lives solely to please people, but rather, we should aim to honour God in a way that also edifies others. 1 Corinthians 8:9 warns us to be mindful of how our actions and decisions can impact others, especially those who are spiritually or emotionally vulnerable. It calls us to exercise our freedoms responsibly, considering the well-being of others. Romans 14:13 advises us to "make up our minds not to put any stumbling block or obstacle in the way of a brother or sister." This involves being sensitive to how our actions could be interpreted or how they might influence someone else's faith journey.

As believers, our decisions should be guided by love, wisdom, and a consideration for the collective well-being of the community, just as Christ considered us in His ultimate decision to go to the cross.

Prayer Point:
Lord, help me to be mindful of how my decisions affect those around me. May I exercise my freedoms responsibly and lovingly. Amen.

Monday January 08

Topic: The Consequences of Doing What You Know is Wrong

Memory Verse:

"Do not be deceived: God cannot be mocked. A man reaps what he sows." **- Galatians 6:7**

Bible Reading:

Read & Learn:

We've all been there - facing a decision where we know what the right thing to do is, but are tempted to choose otherwise. What happens when we give in to that temptation and do what we know is wrong? Galatians 6:7 serves as a stern warning that our actions have consequences. It emphasises the principle of sowing and reaping: what we put into our lives is what we'll get out of them. God's moral laws cannot be bypassed.

The Bible is filled with stories that illustrate the consequences of doing what is wrong. Adam and Eve's disobedience led to the fall of humanity. King David's affair with Bathsheba led to a series of tragic events, including the death of their child. On the other hand, choosing to do what is right, even when it's difficult, brings blessings and favour. Joseph resisted temptation and was eventually elevated to a position of authority in Egypt. James 1:15 says, "Then, after desire has conceived, it gives birth to sin; and sin, when it is full-grown, gives birth to death." This doesn't necessarily mean physical death but can refer to the death of relationships, opportunities, and even our spiritual vitality.

It's crucial to remember that while God is merciful and forgiving, His grace doesn't negate the natural consequences of our actions.

Prayer Point:
Lord, give me the strength to choose what is right, even when it's difficult. Help me to remember that my actions have consequences. Amen.

Tuesday January 09

Topic: Aligning Decisions with God's Word

Memory Verse: "Your word is a lamp for my feet, a light on my path." - **Psalm 119:105**

Bible Reading: Psalm 1: 1- 6

Read & Learn:

During the American Civil Rights Movement, Martin Luther King Jr. faced numerous challenges and decisions that carried significant risks. He often turned to the Bible for guidance and inspiration. His famous "I Have a Dream" speech was deeply rooted in Biblical principles of justice and equality. By aligning his decisions with God's Word, King was able to lead a movement that brought about transformative social change.

Life is a series of decisions, some trivial and some monumental. Psalm 119:105 tells us that God's Word serves as both a lamp and a light, guiding us through the complexities of life. It illuminates our path, helping us make decisions that are in line with God's will.

The Bible is more than just a historical document or a collection of moral teachings; it is the inspired Word of God, meant to guide us in all aspects of life. Proverbs 3:5-6 says, "Trust in the Lord with all your heart and lean not on your own understanding; in all your ways submit to him, and he will make your paths straight."

When we align our decisions with God's Word, we invite His wisdom and guidance into the process. Colossians 3:17 says, "And whatever you do, whether in word or deed, do it all in the name of the Lord Jesus, giving thanks to God the Father through him." So, the next time you're faced with a decision, big or small, turn to God's Word for guidance. It's the best way to ensure that your choices are not just good but godly.

Prayer Point:
Lord, guide me in aligning my decisions with Your Word. May it be a lamp to my feet and a light to my path. Amen.

Wednesday January 10

Topic: The Power of Commitment in Building Connections

Memory Verse:

"Commit to the Lord whatever you do, and he will establish your plans."
- Proverbs 16:3

Bible Reading: Matthew 21:28-32

Read & Learn:

Mother Teresa, a Catholic nun known for her work in Calcutta, India, exemplified commitment in her lifetime. Despite facing numerous challenges, including limited resources and harsh conditions, she remained committed to serving the poor and sick. Her unwavering commitment not only deepened her connection with God but also inspired millions to commit to causes greater than themselves.

In a world that often values convenience over commitment, it's easy to overlook the importance of fully committing to relationships, endeavours, and most importantly, our faith.

Commitment is a recurring theme in the Bible. Jesus calls us to commit to Him wholeheartedly, as seen in Matthew 16:24: "Then Jesus said to his disciples, 'Whoever wants to be my disciple must deny themselves and take up their cross and follow me.'" This level of commitment is not just about following rules; it's about establishing a deep, meaningful relationship with God.

The Biblical call to commitment stands as a counter-cultural directive. It challenges us to look beyond ourselves and to invest in relationships and causes that have eternal significance.

So, whether it's your relationship with God, your family, or a cause you believe in, remember that true connection is rooted in commitment.

Prayer Point:
Lord, help me to commit my plans and actions to You, trusting that You will guide me according to Your will. Amen.

Thursday January 11

Topic: The Destructive Power of Gossip in Relationships

Memory Verse: "A perverse person stirs up conflict, and a gossip separates close friends." - **Proverbs 16:28**

Bible Reading: James 3:1-6

Read & Learn:

Gossip is often dismissed as harmless chatter, but the Bible warns us of its destructive power, especially in relationships. Proverbs 16:28 warns that gossip has the power to separate close friends and stir up conflict. It identifies gossip as a form of perversion that disrupts harmony and trust within relationships.

The Bible is clear about the dangers of gossip. James 3:5-6 compares the tongue to a small spark that can set an entire forest on fire. Similarly, gossip can start as a small act but lead to devastating consequences, affecting not just the subject but also the integrity of those who spread it. Ephesians 4:29 advises, "Do not let any unwholesome talk come out of your mouths, but only what is helpful for building others up according to their needs, that it may benefit those who listen." This verse challenges us to use our words to uplift rather than tear down.

Gossip not only harms others but also distances us from God. Psalm 34:13-14 says, "Keep your tongue from evil and your lips from telling lies. Turn from evil and do good; seek peace and pursue it." When we engage in gossip, we are not seeking peace but sowing discord. Therefore, let's be vigilant about the words we speak, ensuring they align with God's will and contribute to building up others in love and truth.

Prayer Point:

Lord, help me to guard my tongue and refrain from gossip. May my words be pleasing to You and beneficial to those around me. Amen.

Friday January 12

Topic: Using Words to Build Others Up

Memory Verse: "Do not let any unwholesome talk come out of your mouths, but only what is helpful for building others up according to their needs, that it may benefit those who listen." - **Ephesians 4:29**

Bible Reading: 2 Samuel 16:5-13

Read & Learn:

Words have the power to either build up or tear down. In a world where negative talk often prevails, how can we use our words to encourage and uplift others, especially in the context of our Christian faith? Ephesians 4:29 instructs us to be mindful of the words we speak, emphasising that they should serve to build others up. It calls for a shift from unwholesome talk to words that meet the needs and benefit those who listen.

The Bible is replete with guidance on how to use our words wisely. Proverbs 18:21 says, "The tongue has the power of life and death," highlighting the significant impact our words can have. James 3:9-10 warns against using the same mouth to praise God and curse people, pointing out the inconsistency and urging us to do better. In the New Testament, Jesus Himself sets an example by using words to heal, to forgive, and to impart wisdom.

Using words to build others up is not just a good social practice; it's a Christian duty. It reflects the character of God, who spoke the world into existence and whose Word brings life and hope. When we use our words to encourage and uplift, we are participating in God's creative work, bringing light into someone's darkness and potentially changing the course of their life.

Prayer Point:
Lord, help me to use my words to build others up, reflecting Your love and grace in all that I say. Amen.

Saturday January 13

Topic: The Impact of Fear on Relationships

Memory Verse:

"There is no fear in love. But perfect love drives out fear, because fear has to do with punishment. The one who fears is not made perfect in love." - **1 John 4:18**

Bible Reading: Genesis 3:1-10

Read & Learn:

Fear is a powerful emotion that can significantly affect our relationships. It can lead to mistrust, isolation, and even the breakdown of connections. 1 John 4:18 teaches that fear and love are incompatible. Fear is rooted in the expectation of punishment or negative outcomes, while love seeks the best for others. Perfect love, therefore, has the power to drive out fear and its damaging effects on relationships.

Fear can have a crippling effect on relationships. It can lead to defensiveness, as we try to protect ourselves from perceived threats. Proverbs 29:25 says, "Fear of man will prove to be a snare, but whoever trusts in the Lord is kept safe."

Fear can also lead to isolation. Just like Adam and Eve hid from God out of fear (Genesis 3:10), we too may withdraw from relationships when we are afraid. However, the Bible offers a solution: perfect love. Romans 8:15 tells us, "The Spirit you received does not make you slaves, so that you live in fear again; rather, the Spirit you received brought about your adoption to sonship. And by him we cry, 'Abba, Father.'" Through Christ, we are adopted into a relationship of love, not fear. Therefore, let us strive to replace fear with love in our relationships, trusting that God's perfect love will guide us into healthier, more fulfilling connections.

Prayer Point:
Lord, help me to replace fear with love in my relationships. May Your perfect love drive out all forms of fear and mistrust. Amen.

Sunday January 14

Topic: Recognising the World Doesn't Revolve Around Us

Memory Verse: "Do nothing out of selfish ambition or vain conceit. Rather, in humility value others above yourselves." **- Philippians 2:3**

Bible Reading: Acts 12:21-23

Read & Learn:

George Washington, the first President of the United States, is often remembered for his leadership during the American Revolution. However, one of his most commendable acts was his decision to step down from the presidency after two terms, setting a precedent for future leaders. Despite having the power and opportunity to remain in office, Washington chose the path of humility, believing that the young nation's future was more important than any one individual's ambition.

In a world that often promotes self-centeredness, it's easy to fall into the trap of believing everything revolves around us. Philippians 2:3 calls believers to act without selfish motives or pride. Instead, it encourages a heart of humility, where we recognise the worth of others and prioritise their needs and feelings above our own. Jesus, our ultimate example, "did not come to be served, but to serve, and to give his life as a ransom for many" (Mark 10:45). He put the needs of humanity above His own, demonstrating the depth of His love and humility.

In today's culture, where individual achievements and personal branding are highly valued, it's easy to become self-focused. Recognising that the world doesn't revolve around us is not about diminishing our value but understanding our role in the larger picture. It's about building meaningful relationships, serving others, and reflecting Christ's love in our interactions.

Prayer Point:
Lord, cultivate in me a heart of humility. Help me to see the value in others and to serve them selflessly, just as You did. Amen.

Monday January 15

Topic: Your Significance in the Body of Christ

Memory Verse:

"Now you are the body of Christ, and each one of you is a part of it." - **1 Corinthians 12:27**

Bible Reading: 1 Samuel 17:26-33

Read & Learn:

In the early days of the civil rights movement, Rosa Parks, a seamstress, refused to give up her seat to a white man on a segregated bus. Rosa Parks showed that one individual, standing firm in their convictions, can make a significant impact. Her story reminds us that we all have a role to play in larger narratives.

The Bible uses the metaphor of a body to describe the Church, highlighting the interdependence of its members. Romans 12:4-5 says, "For just as each of us has one body with many members, and these members do not all have the same function, so in Christ we, though many, form one body, and each member belongs to all the others." This concept is not just theological; it's practical. It means that your gifts, talents, and even your limitations have a purpose. You are not an accident; you are intentionally designed by God to fulfil a specific role in His kingdom.

Feeling insignificant often stems from comparing ourselves to others. Your significance in the Body of Christ is not determined by how you measure up to others but by how you serve God and others with the gifts you've been given.

Prayer Point:
Lord, help me to recognise my unique role in the Body of Christ. Grant me the wisdom to use my gifts for Your glory and the betterment of others. Amen.

Tuesday January 16

Topic: Finding Peace by Relinquishing Control

Memory Verse:

"Trust in the LORD with all your heart and lean not on your own understanding; in all your ways submit to him, and he will make your paths straight." **- Proverbs 3:5-6**

Bible Reading: Mark 4:35-40

Read & Learn:

Stress often arises from our desire to control situations, outcomes, or even people. The Bible, however, offers a different approach: relinquishing control and placing our trust in God. Proverbs 3:5-6 encourages us to trust God wholeheartedly, without relying on our own limited understanding. By submitting to God's guidance in every aspect of our lives, we can experience peace and direction, alleviating stress.

The Bible is filled with examples and teachings that emphasise the importance of trusting God rather than trying to control everything ourselves. Jesus Himself said, "Come to me, all you who are weary and burdened, and I will give you rest" (Matthew 11:28). This invitation is an antidote to stress, offering us the peace that comes from surrendering control to Him. Philippians 4:6-7 advises, "Do not be anxious about anything, but in every situation, by prayer and petition, with thanksgiving, present your requests to God. And the peace of God, which transcends all understanding, will guard your hearts and your minds in Christ Jesus."

When we try to control everything, we carry a burden that we were never meant to bear. By trusting God and giving up control, we can experience a peace that surpasses all understanding, reducing stress and increasing our faith.

Prayer Point:
Lord, help me to trust You with all aspects of my life. Relieve me of the stress that comes from trying to control everything. Amen.

Wednesday January 17

Topic: The Power of Choice in Personal Transformation

Memory Verse: "But if serving the LORD seems undesirable to you, then choose for yourselves this day whom you will serve." **- Joshua 24:15**

Bible Reading: Ruth 1:6-17

Read & Learn:

Change is a constant part of life, but meaningful transformation often starts with a conscious choice. The Bible emphasises the power of choice in shaping our lives and our relationship with God. Joshua 24:15 challenges us to make a deliberate choice about whom we will serve. It underscores the idea that our choices have consequences, not just for us but also for our relationship with God and others.

The Bible is replete with stories and teachings about the power of choice. Adam and Eve's choice to eat the forbidden fruit had consequences that affected all of humanity (Genesis 3). Conversely, Ruth's choice to stay with Naomi led to her becoming an ancestor of Jesus (Ruth 1:16-17). Deuteronomy 30:19 says, "This day I call the heavens and the earth as witnesses against you that I have set before you life and death, blessings and curses. Now choose life, so that you and your children may live."

Choices are not just about following rules; they're about shaping our character and destiny. When we choose to serve God, to love others, and to live righteously, we set ourselves on a path of blessing and purpose. The New Testament also emphasises choice. Jesus often gave people options, like when He asked the blind man, "What do you want me to do for you?" (Mark 10:51). Our choices reveal our desires, priorities, and ultimately, our hearts.

Prayer Point:

Lord, help me to make choices that honour You and lead me on a path of transformation. Give me the wisdom to discern what is right. Amen.

Thursday January 18

Topic: Letting Go of the Past

Memory Verse: "Brothers and sisters, I do not consider myself yet to have taken hold of it. But one thing I do: Forgetting what is behind and straining toward what is ahead, I press on toward the goal to win the prize for which God has called me heavenward in Christ Jesus." - **Philippians 3:13-14**

Bible Reading: Isaiah 43:18-19

Read & Learn:

The story of the woman caught in adultery in John 8:1-11 illustrates the power of letting go of the past. When the religious leaders brought her to Jesus, they wanted to condemn her for her sinful past. Jesus responded with compassion, saying, "Let any one of you who is without sin be the first to throw a stone at her." As the crowd dispersed, Jesus forgave her and encouraged her to go and sin no more. This story reminds us that Jesus offers forgiveness and a fresh start, allowing us to let go of our past mistakes and sins.

The Bible teaches us the importance of letting go of our past, which may include regrets, mistakes, and sins. Philippians 3:13-14 encourages us to focus on what lies ahead rather than dwelling on the past. God's promise in Isaiah 43:18-19 reminds us that He is doing a new thing in our lives, even in the midst of our past failures.

Letting go of the past doesn't mean denying our mistakes but acknowledging them, seeking God's forgiveness, and allowing His grace to enable us to move forward. It's about embracing the hope and transformation found in Christ.

Prayer Point:
Father, thank you for your forgiveness and grace that enable me to move forward. Help me to release the past and embrace the newness of life in Christ. Guide me in making choices that honour God's plan for my future.

Friday January 19

Topic: A Tree by the River

Memory Verse: "They will be like a tree planted by the water that sends out its roots by the stream. It does not fear when heat comes; its leaves are always green. It has no worries in a year of drought and never fails to bear fruit." - **Jeremiah 17:8**

Bible Reading: Psalm 1:1-3

Read & Learn:

In Luke 19:1-10, we find the story of Zacchaeus, a tax collector who climbed a sycamore-fig tree to see Jesus. This tree played a crucial role in Zacchaeus' encounter with Jesus. When Jesus saw Zacchaeus, He called him by name and said He must stay at his house. Zacchaeus welcomed Jesus joyfully and pledged to give half of his possessions to the poor and pay back four times what he had cheated from others. This story illustrates how encountering Jesus can transform a person's life, making them like a tree by the river, bearing fruit and prospering.

Being like a tree by the river symbolises spiritual strength, stability, and fruitfulness. Jeremiah 17:8 and Psalm 1:1-3 remind us that those who delight in God's Word and stay rooted in Him will flourish even in challenging circumstances. Just as a tree by the river is nourished, Christians who meditate on God's Word and seek His guidance will find sustenance, peace, and fruitfulness in their lives.

Prayer Point:

Father, help me to stay rooted in You and bear fruit in every season. Guide me to delight in your Word and be like trees planted by the water.

Saturday January 20

Topic: Discovering the Peace of God

Memory Verse: "And the peace of God, which transcends all understanding, will guard your hearts and your minds in Christ Jesus." - **Philippians 4:7**

Bible Reading: Isaiah 26:3-4

Read & Learn:

In Mark 4:35-41, we find the story of Jesus calming the storm while He and His disciples were in a boat. As a furious storm raged, the disciples were filled with fear, but Jesus was asleep in the boat. When they woke Him, Jesus rebuked the storm, and it immediately became calm. Jesus then asked them why they were so afraid and had so little faith. This story illustrates how, even in the midst of life's storms, we can discover the peace of God through unwavering faith in Jesus.

Discovering the peace of God means experiencing a deep and abiding sense of tranquillity that transcends all human understanding. Philippians 4:7 assures us that this peace will guard our hearts and minds when we place our trust in Christ. Isaiah 26:3-4 emphasises the importance of steadfast trust in God, describing it as the key to perfect peace. In the midst of life's challenges and storms, we can find peace by placing our faith and trust in Jesus, the eternal Rock.

Prayer Point:

Father, help me to trust in You unwaveringly and discover Your peace in all circumstances. Calm the storms in my life and grant me Your peace. Guide me to place my complete trust in Christ, the eternal Rock.

Sunday January 21

Topic: The Crossroads of Life

Memory Verse: "In all your ways submit to him, and he will make your paths straight." - **Proverbs 3:6**

Bible Reading: Psalm 32:8, Jeremiah 6:16

Read & Learn:

In Genesis 22:1-18, we find the story of Abraham at a significant crossroads of life. God called him to offer his son Isaac as a sacrifice. Abraham faced a difficult decision but chose to obey God in faith. At the last moment, God provided a ram for the sacrifice instead of Isaac. This story illustrates the importance of trusting God and obeying His guidance when we find ourselves at life's crossroads.

Life often presents us with crossroads - moments when we must make significant decisions that shape our future. Proverbs 3:6 encourages us to submit to God in all our ways, trusting that He will make our paths straight. Psalm 32:8 reminds us that God instructs, teaches, and counsels us in the way we should go. When we face important decisions, we can seek God's guidance, trust His wisdom, and choose obedience, even when it seems difficult. Just as God provided for Abraham, He guides and cares for us at our crossroads.

Prayer Point:

Father, guide me at the crossroads of life, and grant me the wisdom to make decisions that honour You. Lead me in the way I should go, and counsel me with Your loving presence. Help me to trust and obey even when the path seems uncertain.

Monday January 22

Topic: Prayer Works

Memory Verse: "The prayer of a righteous person is powerful and effective." - **James 5:16**

Bible Reading: Matthew 7:7-8

Read & Learn:

In Acts 12:1-17, we find a powerful story of prayer in action. Peter was imprisoned by King Herod, and the church fervently prayed for his release. An angel of the Lord appeared to Peter in prison, and his chains fell off. When Peter reached the house where the believers were praying, a servant girl named Rhoda was so amazed that she forgot to open the door. The story illustrates how God responds to the earnest prayers of His people. Sometimes, like Rhoda, we may be surprised by God's swift answers to our prayers.

The Bible is filled with examples of prayer's effectiveness. James 5:16 reminds us that the prayer of a righteous person is powerful and effective. In Matthew 7:7-8, Jesus encourages us to ask, seek, and knock in prayer, with the assurance that God responds. The story of Peter's miraculous release demonstrates that God hears and answers the heartfelt prayers of His people. Prayer is not just a religious ritual; it is a powerful means of communicating with God and seeing His work in our lives.

Prayer Point:

Father, I thank You for the gift of prayer and for hearing my petitions. Help me to approach You with faith and persistence in prayer. Teach me to pray in alignment with Your will and to trust in the effectiveness of prayer.

Tuesday January 23

Topic: God's Ways are Higher

Memory Verse: "As the heavens are higher than the earth, so are my ways higher than your ways and my thoughts than your thoughts." - **Isaiah 55:9**

Bible Reading: Isaiah 55:6-11

Read & Learn:

In the book of Job, we find the story of a man named Job who faced unimaginable suffering and loss. Job was a righteous man who loved and feared God. Despite his devotion, he experienced a series of tragic events that left him in despair. Throughout his ordeal, Job questioned God's ways and sought understanding for his suffering. In the end, God revealed Himself to Job and reminded him of His sovereignty and wisdom. Job's story teaches us that even in times of great confusion and suffering, we must trust that God's ways are higher, and His plans are beyond our comprehension. Isaiah 55:9 reminds us that God's ways and thoughts are infinitely higher than ours. Human understanding is limited, but God's wisdom is boundless. The passage from Isaiah encourages us to seek the Lord, turn from our sinful ways, and trust in His mercy, love and faithfulness. Just as rain and snow bring life to the earth, God's Word accomplishes His purposes and does not return empty. Job's story illustrates the importance of maintaining faith in God's wisdom and unfailing love even in the midst of life's trials and questions.

Prayer Point:

Father, I acknowledge that Your ways are higher than my ways, and Your thoughts are beyond my understanding. Help me to trust in Your wisdom, especially when I face trials and questions in life.

Wednesday January 24

Topic: Building Your Future on a Solid Foundation

Memory Verse: "Therefore, everyone who hears these words of mine and puts them into practice is like a wise man who built his house on the rock. The rain came down, the streams rose, and the winds blew and beat against that house; yet it did not fall because it had its foundation on the rock." **- Matthew 7:24-25**

Bible Reading: Matthew 7:24-27

Read & Learn:

In the Bible, Jesus told a parable about two builders - one who built his house on a rock and another who built his house on sand. When the storms came, the house built on the rock stood firm, while the one built on sand collapsed. This story illustrates the importance of building our lives and futures on the solid foundation of God's Word and obedience to His teachings. It teaches us that challenges and trials will come, but when we anchor ourselves in God's truth, we can withstand the storms of life.

The passage from Matthew 7:24-27 emphasises the significance of not only hearing God's words but also putting them into practice. It's not enough to merely know God's truth; we must apply it in our lives. When we build our future on the solid foundation of God's Word, prayer, and obedience, we can have confidence that our lives will be able to withstand the challenges that come our way. The parable reminds us that a life built on worldly values and wisdom is like a house built on sand, easily shaken by life's storms.

Prayer Point:

Father, I thank You for the wisdom found in Your Word. Help me to build my life and future on the solid foundation of Your truth and teachings. Guide me in discerning and avoiding the traps of building my life on worldly values and wisdom. Grant me the strength to put Your words into practice, especially in challenging times.

Thursday January 25

Topic: Don't be Unequally Yoked

Memory Verse: "Do not be yoked together with unbelievers. For what do righteousness and wickedness have in common? Or what fellowship can light have with darkness?" - **2 Corinthians 6:14**

Bible Reading: 2 Corinthians 6:14-18

Read & Learn:

The story of Solomon's later years serves as a cautionary tale about being unequally yoked. Despite his great wisdom, Solomon's heart turned away from God due to his many foreign wives who worshipped other gods. These wives led him into idolatry, causing him to compromise his faith. It teaches us the importance of choosing a life partner who shares our faith and values to avoid spiritual compromise and heartache. 2 Corinthians 6:14-18 warns against being unequally yoked with unbelievers. This principle applies not only to marriage but also to various relationships in our lives. It reminds us that our faith is central to our identity as Christians, and aligning ourselves with those who do not share our faith can lead to spiritual compromise and hinder our growth in Christ. While we can befriend and show God's love to unbelievers, entering into partnerships or close relationships with those who do not share our faith may lead us away from God's path.

Prayer Point:

Father, grant me wisdom in my relationships, that I may not be unequally yoked with unbelievers. Guide me to be lights in the lives of unbelievers, showing them Your love and truth.

Friday January 26

Topic: Importance of Budgeting

Memory verse: "The plans of the diligent lead surely to abundance, but everyone who is hasty comes only to poverty." - **Proverbs 21:5**

Bible Reading: Luke 14:28-30

Read & Learn:

In the Bible, we find a story that illustrates the importance of budgeting and financial planning. It's the story of the man who wanted to build a tower. He didn't rush into construction without counting the cost first. He knew that without proper planning and budgeting, he might not have enough resources to complete the project. This principle applies to our lives today. Just as wise builders count the cost before building a tower, we should carefully plan and budget our finances to avoid falling into financial hardship or debt.

Budgeting is a practical and biblical principle that helps us manage our finances wisely. It's not about restricting our spending but about being intentional with our money. The Bible encourages us to be diligent and plan ahead, just as the man in the story considered the cost of building the tower. Through budgeting, we can ensure that our financial resources are used wisely and that we are prepared for unexpected expenses. Proverbs 21:5 reminds us that diligent planning leads to abundance, while being hasty can lead to financial difficulties. Budgeting allows us to allocate funds for giving, saving, and spending, aligning our financial decisions with our values and priorities. It empowers us to be good stewards of the resources God has entrusted to us, honouring Him with our finances.

Prayer Point:

Father, grant me the discipline and wisdom to budget my finances wisely. Help me to be good stewards of the resources You provide and to make responsible financial choices. Guide me in honouring You with my financial decisions and using my resources for Your glory.

Saturday January 27

Topic: Bible Wisdom on Debt

Memory verse: ""The rich rule over the poor, and the borrower is slave to the lender." - Proverbs 22:7**

Bible Reading: 2 Kings 4:1-7

Read & Learn:

Consider the story of the widow and Elisha in 2 Kings 4:1-7. The widow, burdened with debt after her husband's death and facing the loss of her sons to slavery, turned to the prophet Elisha for help. Elisha instructed her to gather empty jars and fill them with oil, which miraculously multiplied, allowing her to sell the oil, pay off her debts, and live on what was left. This story not only highlights God's provision but also illustrates the stress and bondage that debt can bring, and the relief and freedom that come with its resolution.

The Bible offers practical wisdom on managing finances, including the topic of debt. Proverbs 22:7 warns of the bondage that debt can create, likening the borrower to a slave of the lender. Romans 13:8 encourages believers to owe nothing to anyone except the ongoing debt to love one another. While the Bible doesn't explicitly prohibit borrowing, it advises caution, urging believers to avoid being enslaved by debt and to live within their means. It also emphasizes the importance of integrity in repaying debts. Managing debt wisely involves careful planning, living responsibly, and trusting in God's provision, while also striving to be generous and to help others in need.

Prayer Point:

Heavenly Father, grant me wisdom to manage my finances responsibly, avoiding the bondage of debt and trusting in Your provision. Help me to honour my financial commitments with integrity and to live within my means, reflecting Your wisdom in my stewardship.

Sunday January 28

Topic: Directing Your Finances with Intention

Memory Verse: "Be sure you know the condition of your flocks, give careful attention to your herds; for riches do not endure forever, and a crown is not secure for all generations." **- Proverbs 27:23-24**

Bible Reading: Genesis 41:14 - 37

Read & Learn:

Managing finances can often feel overwhelming, but the Bible provides wisdom on how to take control. Instead of letting your money control you, you can direct it purposefully.

In the Bible, Joseph's story of financial management stands out. During seven years of abundance in Egypt, Joseph didn't squander the resources; instead, he stored grain for the seven years of famine that followed. His foresight not only saved Egypt but also his own family from starvation. Joseph's story exemplifies the principle of directing resources with intention. Proverbs 27:23-24 advises us to be aware of our assets, symbolised by "flocks and herds." The passage emphasises the transient nature of wealth and suggests that careful management is essential for long-term security. It reminds us that wealth is not permanent. Therefore, we must manage it wisely while we have it. This involves budgeting, saving, and giving - all actions that require us to direct our money intentionally.

When we manage our finances with purpose, we honour God. We also create opportunities to be generous, to invest in things of eternal value, and to provide for our needs and those of our families. In doing so, we align ourselves with biblical principles, build generational wealth and find peace in our financial lives.

Prayer Point:

Father, thank You for the resources You have entrusted to me. grant me the wisdom to manage my finances intentionally, in a way that honours You and provides for my needs and those of others.

Monday January 29

Topic: Setting Goals for Your Future

Memory Verse:

"Commit to the Lord whatever you do, and he will establish your plans." - Proverbs 16:3

Bible Reading: Philippians 3:13-14

Read & Learn:

In the book of Genesis, we encounter the story of Joseph, who had dreams and set goals for his future (Genesis 37:5-11). These dreams were given to him by God and revealed a great destiny. Despite facing trials, setbacks, and even betrayal by his brothers, Joseph held onto his dreams and remained faithful to God. Through unwavering determination and faith, he eventually became a ruler in Egypt, fulfilling the very dreams he had as a young man. Joseph's story teaches us the importance of setting godly goals for our future. Just as Joseph's dreams were a part of God's plan, our goals should align with God's purpose for our lives. With faith and perseverance, we can overcome obstacles and see God's plans fulfilled in our journey.

Setting goals for your future is a valuable practice. It allows you to focus your efforts and make intentional strides toward a purposeful life. The Apostle Paul's words in Philippians 3:13-14 remind us to press on toward the goal and not dwell on past failures or accomplishments. Our journey with God is a forward-looking one, filled with hope and anticipation. As we set goals that reflect our faith and values, we can experience growth, transformation, and God's blessings.

Prayer Point:

Father, guide us as we set goals for our future, and help us align them with Your purpose. We commit our plans to You, trusting that You will establish them. Grant us the faith and perseverance to pursue our dreams, even in the face of challenges.

Tuesday January 30

Topic: Biblical Perspective on Time Management

Memory Verse: "Teach us to number our days, that we may gain a heart of wisdom." - **Psalm 90:12**

Bible Reading: Luke 10:38-42

Read & Learn:

In the book of Luke, we find the story of Mary and Martha (Luke 10:38-42). Jesus visited their home, and Martha was busy with preparations, while Mary sat at Jesus' feet, listening to His teachings. Martha became frustrated and asked Jesus to tell Mary to help her. Jesus gently replied, "Martha, Martha, you are worried and upset about many things, but few things are needed - or indeed only one. Mary has chosen what is better, and it will not be taken away from her."

This story illustrates the importance of time management from a biblical perspective. While tasks and responsibilities are essential, spending time with the Lord and prioritising spiritual growth is of greater significance. It reminds us to balance our busyness with moments of quietness and reflection at the feet of Jesus. Prioritising spiritual growth, prayer, and studying God's Word are crucial. Balancing our responsibilities with moments of reflection and connection with God helps us to build our faith, grow spiritually and manage our time effectively from a biblical perspective.

Prayer Point:
Father, teach me to number my days and use them for Your glory. Help me manage my time wisely and seek Your guidance in my daily routines. Grant me the wisdom to prioritise spending time with You amidst my busy life.

Wednesday January 31

Topic: Discovering Your Real Identity in Christ

Memory Verse: "Therefore, if anyone is in Christ, the new creation has come: The old has gone, the new is here!" - **2 Corinthians 5:17**

Bible Reading: Romans 8:14-16

The story of the prodigal son in Luke 15:11-32 is a powerful illustration of discovering one's true identity in Christ. The younger son, after squandering his inheritance in a far-off country, returns home in shame and repentance. His father, filled with compassion, welcomes him with open arms, not as a servant but as a beloved son. This story reminds us that even when we wander from God, our true identity is found in His unwavering love and grace.

Discovering your real identity in Christ is a transformational journey. 2 Corinthians 5:17 highlights that in Christ, we are made new creations. Our past mistakes and sins do not define us; our identity is now rooted in Christ's redemption. Romans 8:14-16 emphasises that through the Holy Spirit, we become God's children, adopted into His family. Our identity is no longer one of fear and shame but of love and sonship.

The story of the prodigal son illustrates that our true identity is not determined by our past or our failures. It is defined by God's unconditional love and acceptance when we return to Him in repentance.

Prayer Point:

Father, thank You for adopting me as Your child and freeing me from fear and shame. Help me discover my real identity in Christ and embrace the new creation I am in You. Help me live daily in the awareness of my identity as Your beloved child.

Thursday February 01

Topic: The Impact of Love on Identity

Memory Verse: "See what great love the Father has lavished on us, that we should be called children of God! And that is what we are! The reason the world does not know us is that it did not know him." **- 1 John 3:1**

Bible Reading: Luke 8:1-3, Ephesians 2:4-5

Read & Learn:

The story of Mary Magdalene in the Bible is a powerful illustration of the impact of love on one's identity. Mary, once possessed by seven demons, encountered Jesus' love and forgiveness. This encounter transformed her from a woman plagued by darkness to a devoted follower of Christ. Mary's identity shifted from being defined by her past struggles to being known as one deeply loved by Jesus.

Love has a profound impact on our identity. 1 John 3:1 reminds us that the Father's great love has lavished upon us the identity of being called children of God. We are deeply loved and cherished by our Heavenly Father, and this love transforms how we see ourselves. Ephesians 2:4-5 emphasises that God's love and mercy make us alive in Christ, even when we were lost in sin. Our identity is no longer defined by our past mistakes but by God's grace and love.

Mary Magdalene's story illustrates that encountering the love and forgiveness of Christ can radically change our identity. She went from darkness to light, from bondage to freedom, and from being known by her demons to being known as a beloved disciple of Jesus.

Prayer Point:

Father, thank You for lavishing Your great love upon me and calling me Your child. Remind me daily of my identity as deeply loved and cherished by God. Help me to experience the transforming power of Your love on my identity.

Friday February 02

Topic: AGAPE: The God Kind of Love

Memory Verse: "Dear friends, let us love one another, for love comes from God. Everyone who loves has been born of God and knows God. Whoever does not love does not know God, because God is love." - **1 John 4:7-8**

Bible Reading: 1 Corinthians 13:4-7

Read & Learn:

The story of the Good Samaritan in the Bible exemplifies AGAPE love. In Luke 10:25-37, Jesus tells the parable of a Samaritan who showed compassion and selfless love to a wounded man left for dead on the side of the road. Despite their cultural and religious differences, the Samaritan went above and beyond to care for the injured traveler. This parable illustrates the sacrificial and compassionate nature of AGAPE love.

AGAPE is the highest form of love, representing the unconditional, selfless, and sacrificial love of God. 1 John 4:7-8 tells us that God is love, and those who truly know Him will demonstrate this AGAPE love in their lives. 1 Corinthians 13:4-7 provides a comprehensive description of AGAPE love, highlighting its patience, kindness, humility, forgiveness, and enduring qualities.

The story of the Good Samaritan demonstrates how AGAPE love transcends cultural, social, and religious barriers. The Samaritan's actions reflect the heart of God, who loves unconditionally and calls us to do the same.

Prayer Point:

Father, help me to understand and practice AGAPE love in my daily life. Teach me to love others as You have loved me. Empower me to demonstrate selfless and sacrificial love in all my relationships.

Saturday February 03

Topic: Love Cannot Fail

Memory Verse: "Love never fails. But where there are prophecies, they will cease; where there are tongues, they will be stilled; where there is knowledge, it will pass away." - **1 Corinthians 13:8**

Bible Reading: Romans 8:38-39

Read & Learn:

The story of the Prodigal Son in Luke 15:11-32 beautifully illustrates how love cannot fail. Despite the younger son's rebellion, selfishness, and poor choices, his father's love remained unwavering. When the prodigal son returned home, expecting judgment, he was met with his father's open arms and love. This parable reveals the relentless and unconditional love of our Heavenly Father. The Bible teaches that love, particularly God's love, is unshakable and enduring. Romans 8:38-39 reassures us that nothing in all creation can separate us from God's love. 1 Corinthians 13:8 reminds us that love never fails. The story of the Prodigal Son illustrates how love can withstand even the most challenging circumstances.

In our human relationships, love can be tested by various trials and conflicts, but true love, modelled after God's love, perseveres and overcomes. When we choose to love others unconditionally, we reflect the love of Christ, which cannot fail.

Prayer Point:

Father, thank you for your unfailing love that holds me close. Help me to reflect your love in all our relationships. Teach me to love others with the same love you have shown me.

Sunday February 04

Topic: Building a Firm Foundation in Faith

Memory Verse: "Therefore everyone who hears these words of mine and puts them into practice is like a wise man who built his house on the rock." - **Matthew 7:24**

Bible Reading: Luke 6:47-49

Read & Learn:

The parable of the two builders in Luke 6:47-49 teaches us about the importance of building our faith on a solid foundation. When the storms come, the house on the rock stands firm, but the one without a foundation collapses. This story illustrates that hearing God's words and putting them into practice is akin to building our faith on a strong foundation. It reminds us that a steadfast faith is built on obedience to God's teachings and is unshaken by life's challenges.

Building a firm foundation in faith involves more than just hearing God's word; it requires putting that word into action. The parable illustrates that obedience to God's teachings is the key to a resilient faith. Just like a house built on a solid rock can withstand storms, a faith grounded in obedience to God's word can endure trials and tribulations. To build a strong foundation in faith, we must not only read and hear the Scriptures but also apply them to our lives. This means aligning our actions, attitudes, and choices with God's principles. As we do so, our faith becomes unshakeable, and we can weather life's challenges with confidence.

Prayer Point:
Father, grant us the wisdom and determination to build our faith on a solid foundation of obedience to Your word. Help us put Your teachings into practice daily, so our faith may withstand the storms of life.

Monday February 05

Topic: Letting Go of What Slows You Down

Memory Verse: "Therefore, since we are surrounded by such a great cloud of witnesses, let us throw off everything that hinders and the sin that so easily entangles. And let us run with perseverance the race marked out for us." **- Hebrews 12:1**

Bible Reading: Philippians 3:12-14

Read & Learn:

In Philippians 3:12-14, the apostle Paul uses the analogy of a race to convey the idea of letting go of what slows us down. Just as a runner must shed unnecessary weight and distractions to race effectively, we too must release the burdens and sins that hinder our spiritual journey. Imagine a runner carrying a heavy backpack; it would impede their progress. Similarly, holding onto past regrets, grudges, or worldly attachments can hinder our spiritual growth and slow us down in our walk with Christ. Paul encourages us to forget what is behind, focus on what lies ahead, and press on toward the goal of knowing Christ more deeply.

Letting go of what slows us down is essential for spiritual growth and progress in our Christian journey. The Bible emphasises the importance of shedding burdens, distractions, and sin. Hebrews 12:1 urges us to throw off everything that hinders and the sin that entangles us, enabling us to run the race with perseverance. It's about recognising that we cannot move forward effectively if we are weighed down by past mistakes, unforgiveness, or worldly attachments. Just as an athlete prepares and conditions themselves, we must prepare our hearts and minds to follow Christ wholeheartedly. By doing so, we can focus on the ultimate goal: knowing and serving Christ more fully.

Prayer Point:
Father, grant us the strength and wisdom to let go of anything that hinders our walk with You. Help us release past regrets, worldly distractions, and sinful entanglements that slow us down.

Tuesday February 06

Topic: The Importance of Community for Spiritual Reset

Memory Verse: "And let us consider how we may spur one another on toward love and good deeds, not giving up meeting together, as some are in the habit of doing, but encouraging one another - and all the more as you see the Day approaching." - **Hebrews 10:24-25**

Bible Reading: Acts 2:42-47

Read & Learn:

The early Christian community described in Acts 2:42-47 provides a powerful example of the importance of community for spiritual reset. These believers devoted themselves to various practices, including the apostles' teaching, fellowship, breaking of bread, and prayer. They shared their lives and resources, supporting one another in times of need. This vibrant and close-knit community not only experienced the favour of God but also drew others to Christ through their unity and love. In times of spiritual dryness or struggle, having a community of fellow believers to lean on, pray with, and grow alongside can be a source of renewal and reset.

The importance of community for a spiritual reset cannot be overstated. In today's fast-paced world, it's easy to become spiritually drained or distracted. Having a community that encourages and supports your spiritual journey can provide the reset needed to refocus on Christ. Together, you can spur one another toward love and good deeds, sharing both joys and challenges. As Hebrews 10:24-25 reminds us, gathering with fellow believers should be a priority, especially as we anticipate Christ's return.

Prayer Point:

Father, thank You for the gift of our Christian community. Help me to prioritise gathering with fellow believers for spiritual renewal. Grant us the wisdom to spur one another on toward love and good deeds as we share life's journey.

Wednesday February 07

Topic: Freeing Your Mind from Destructive Thoughts

Memory Verse: "Finally, brothers and sisters, whatever is true, whatever is noble, whatever is right, whatever is pure, whatever is lovely, whatever is admirable—if anything is excellent or praiseworthy - think about such things." - **Philippians 4:8**

Bible Reading: Romans 12:2

Read & Learn:

The story of King David and his battle against destructive thoughts provides insight into freeing one's mind. In 1 Samuel 30:1-6, when David and his men returned to their camp in Ziklag, they found it burned, and their families taken captive. In his distress, the people talked of stoning David. "But David found strength in the Lord his God" (1 Samuel 30:6, NIV). Instead of succumbing to self-destructive thoughts or blame, David turned to God, sought His guidance, and regained his strength. This story teaches us that even in dire situations, turning our thoughts to God can bring renewal and empowerment.

Freeing your mind from destructive thoughts is crucial for a healthy Christian life. Romans 12:2 emphasises the importance of renewing our minds to discern God's will. In a world filled with negativity and distractions, we must guard our minds and focus on thoughts that align with God's Word, as stated in Philippians 4:8. Destructive thoughts can lead to anxiety, despair, and ungodly actions. By intentionally replacing negative thoughts with those that are true, noble, right, pure, lovely, admirable, excellent, and praiseworthy, we can experience transformation and peace.

Prayer Point:

Father, help us in recognising and releasing destructive thoughts that hinder our spiritual growth. Grant us the strength to replace negative thoughts with those that are true and praiseworthy, keeping our minds focused on You.

Thursday February 08

Topic: Spirit-Led Thinking for a Fulfilling Life

Memory Verse: "Those who live according to the flesh have their minds set on what the flesh desires; but those who live in accordance with the Spirit have their minds set on what the Spirit desires." - **Romans 8:5**

Bible Reading: Galatians 5:22-23

Read & Learn:

The story of the Apostle Paul's transformation illustrates the power of Spirit-led thinking. Paul, formerly known as Saul, persecuted Christians zealously until he encountered Jesus on the road to Damascus (Acts 9:1-19). After his conversion, Paul's thinking was radically transformed by the Holy Spirit. He went on to become one of the most influential figures in the early Christian church, authoring numerous epistles that continue to guide believers today. Paul's life demonstrates that when we allow the Holy Spirit to lead our thoughts, our entire trajectory can change, leading to a fulfilling life centred on God's purposes.

Spirit-led thinking is essential for a fulfilling life as a Christian. Romans 8:5 contrasts the mind set on the flesh with the mind set on the Spirit. When our thoughts align with the desires of the Holy Spirit, we produce the fruit of the Spirit, as described in Galatians 5:22-23. These attributes, such as love, joy, peace, and self-control, not only bring fulfilment but also reflect the character of Christ. Cultivating Spirit-led thinking involves surrendering our will and seeking God's guidance in every aspect of life. It allows us to navigate challenges with faith and trust, maintain inner peace, and experience the joy that comes from living in alignment with God's purposes.

Prayer Point:

Father, guide our thoughts by the Holy Spirit, that we may bear the fruit of Your Spirit in our lives. Help us to discern when our thinking is led by the flesh and grant us the wisdom to surrender it to Your Spirit.

Friday February 09

Topic: The Battle for Your Mind: Choosing Godly Thoughts Over Worldly Distractions

Memory Verse: "Do not conform to the pattern of this world, but be transformed by the renewing of your mind. Then you will be able to test and approve what God's will is- his good, pleasing and perfect will." - **Romans 12:2**

Bible Reading: Philippians 4:8

Read & Learn:

The story of Jesus' temptation in the wilderness (Matthew 4:1-11) demonstrates the battle for the mind. Satan tempted Jesus with worldly distractions, offering Him power, wealth, and glory. However, Jesus resisted by anchoring His thoughts in God's Word. Each time Satan tempted Him, Jesus responded with Scripture. This event illustrates the importance of filling our minds with God's truth to resist worldly distractions. By choosing godly thoughts and aligning our minds with Scripture, we can overcome the temptations and distractions that seek to lead us away from God's plan for our lives.

Our minds are battlegrounds where worldly distractions and God's truth vie for supremacy. Romans 12:2 urges us not to conform to the patterns of this world but to be transformed by renewing our minds. Philippians 4:8 provides guidance on the kind of thoughts we should cultivate. Choosing godly thoughts over worldly distractions involves intentionally focusing on what is true, noble, right, pure, lovely, and admirable. By doing so, we allow God to transform our thinking, making it align with His will. This transformation empowers us to discern and reject worldly distractions, leading to a life centered on God's purpose and peace.

Prayer Point:

Father, renew our minds and help us resist worldly distractions that pull us away from Your truth. Guide us in the battle for our minds, empowering us to choose Your wisdom over worldly distractions.

Saturday February 10

Topic: Turning Your Pain into a Testimony

Memory Verse: "And we know that in all things God works for the good of those who love him, who[a] have been called according to his purpose." - **Romans 8:28**

Bible Reading: Genesis 45:1-14

Read & Learn:

The story of Joseph in the book of Genesis (Genesis 37-50) is a powerful illustration of turning pain into testimony. Joseph faced betrayal, slavery, false accusations, and imprisonment. However, through God's providence and Joseph's unwavering faith, he eventually rose to a position of great authority in Egypt. Joseph's suffering wasn't in vain; it was part of God's plan to save his family and many others from famine. Joseph forgave his brothers and acknowledged that what they meant for evil, God used for good. His life serves as a testament to the idea that God can bring purpose and redemption out of our most painful experiences.

Suffering is an inevitable part of life, but as Christians, we can find purpose in our pain. Romans 8:28 assures us that God can work all things, including our suffering, for our good and His glory. When we face trials, we have an opportunity to experience God's comfort and to later comfort others who are going through similar difficulties. Our pain can become a testimony of God's faithfulness, love, and transformative power. Just as Joseph's suffering ultimately led to the salvation of his family, our trials can be the catalyst for God's redemptive work in our lives and in the lives of those around us.

Prayer Point:

Father, give us the faith to believe that You are always working for our good and Your glory, even in the midst of trials. Use our experiences of suffering to bring comfort and hope to others who are hurting.

Sunday February 11

Topic: ZOE: The God Kind of Life

Memory Verse: "The thief comes only to steal and kill and destroy; I have come that they may have life, and have it to the full." - **John 10:10**

Bible Reading: John 10:7-18

Read & Learn:

The concept of ZOE, the God-kind of life, is central to understanding the Christian faith. In John 10, Jesus describes Himself as the Good Shepherd who came to give us abundant life. He contrasts His mission with that of the thief, who seeks to steal, kill, and destroy. The story of the prodigal son in Luke 15 is a powerful illustration of ZOE. The son who squandered his inheritance experienced spiritual death and famine in a distant land. However, when he returned to his father, he found full restoration and abundant life. This story reflects God's desire to bring us back to Himself, offering us the richness of His grace and love.

ZOE, often translated as "eternal life," means more than just living forever; it signifies the God-kind of life. This life is characterised by an intimate relationship with God, purpose, fulfilment, and overflowing joy. Jesus came to give us this ZOE, to rescue us from spiritual death and to restore us to the Father. It is a life that transcends earthly circumstances and is marked by deep peace and contentment. By believing in Jesus, we enter into this abundant life, and it is a life that begins now and continues into eternity. We are called to live in the fullness of this ZOE, enjoying the presence and provision of our Good Shepherd.

Prayer Point:

Father, thank You for the ZOE life You offer through Your Son, Jesus Christ. Help us to embrace and live in the fullness of this abundant life. Empower us to overcome the thief who seeks to steal, kill, and destroy, and help us live victoriously in ZOE life.

Monday February 12

Topic: Great Dreams Require Great Faith

Memory Verse: "Now faith is confidence in what we hope for and assurance about what we do not see." - **Hebrews 11:1**

Bible Reading: Genesis 15:1-6

Read & Learn:

The story of Abraham (originally Abram) and God's promise of descendants as numerous as the stars in the sky is a remarkable example of great faith and a dream fulfilled. God made this promise to Abram when he and his wife Sarai were already well advanced in age, and they had no children. Despite the seemingly impossible circumstances, Abram believed God's promise and had faith that it would come to pass. This faith in God's word and dream led to a covenant between God and Abram, and eventually, the birth of his son Isaac. Abram's faith, even when facing impossibility, serves as an inspiring reminder that great dreams require great faith in God's promises.

Great dreams often appear unattainable, and achieving them may demand unwavering faith. Hebrews 11:1 defines faith as confidence in what we hope for and assurance about what we do not see. In the case of Abram, his dream of becoming the father of a great nation was rooted in God's promise. Despite the natural obstacles and human doubts, Abram held fast to his faith in God's ability to fulfil the dream. Likewise, our dreams may require us to trust in God's promises even when circumstances seem impossible. By doing so, we align our dreams with God's purposes, allowing Him to work in and through us to bring about great outcomes.

Prayer Point:

Father, thank You for the dreams and visions You have placed in our hearts. Help us to believe in the impossible and have unwavering faith in pursuing the dreams You've given us.

Tuesday February 13

Topic: Making Intentional Decisions in Pursuit of God's Dream

Memory Verse: "Trust in the Lord with all your heart and lean not on your own understanding; in all your ways submit to him, and he will make your paths straight." - **Proverbs 3:5-6**

Bible Reading: Jeremiah 29:11-13

Read & Learn:

The life of Joseph in the book of Genesis is a compelling example of making intentional decisions in pursuit of God's dream. Joseph had dreams of greatness from a young age, but he faced many trials and challenges along the way, including betrayal by his brothers, slavery, and imprisonment. Throughout his journey, Joseph remained faithful to God and consistently made choices that aligned with God's plan for his life. He resisted temptation, interpreted dreams, and ultimately rose to a position of authority in Egypt. His intentional decisions, rooted in trust in God, led to the fulfilment of God's dream for him and the salvation of many during a time of famine.

Making intentional decisions in pursuit of God's dream involves seeking His guidance and aligning our choices with His will. God often places dreams and plans in our hearts, but it requires intentional steps and unwavering trust to see them come to fruition. Proverbs 3:5-6 reminds us to trust in the Lord with all our hearts and acknowledge Him in all our ways. By doing so, He directs our paths toward the realisation of His purpose. Just as Joseph remained faithful in the face of adversity, we must intentionally choose obedience, integrity, and faithfulness as we journey toward the fulfilment of God's dream for our lives.

Prayer Point:

Father, thank You for the dreams and purposes You have for each of us. Grant us wisdom to make intentional decisions that honour Your plan. Empower us to resist temptation and choose integrity and faithfulness in all our decisions on the journey toward fulfilling God's dream.

Wednesday February 14

Topic: Love as Defined by God

Memory Verse: "My command is this: Love each other as I have loved you. Greater love has no one than this: to lay down one's life for one's friends." - **John 15:12-13**

Bible Reading: 1 Corinthians 13:4-7

Read & Learn:

On Valentine's Day, the story of Ruth and Boaz offers a beautiful depiction of godly love. Ruth, a Moabite widow, chose to stay with her Israelite mother-in-law, Naomi, out of love and loyalty. Boaz, recognising Ruth's devotion, acted with kindness and integrity, eventually marrying her. Their story is not just a romantic tale but a portrayal of selfless love, commitment, and God's providence. It reminds us that true love is about more than feelings; it's about actions, choices, and a commitment to the well-being of others, reflecting the love that God has for us.

Valentine's Day often focuses on romantic love, but it's also an opportunity to reflect on the broader, deeper love that God calls us to. 1 Corinthians 13:4-7 defines love not by fleeting emotions but by enduring qualities like patience, kindness, and truth. John 15:12-13 emphasises the sacrificial nature of love, as exemplified by Jesus. This day can be a reminder to express and embody this kind of love in all our relationships, whether romantic, familial, or platonic. It's a call to love as God loves us - unconditionally, sacrificially, and wholeheartedly.

Prayer Points:

Father, thank You for the perfect example of love shown in Jesus Christ. Help me to understand and practice Your definition of love in all my relationships. Fill my heart with Your love, that I may be a source of kindness, patience, and truth to those around me.

Thursday February 15

Topic: Waiting Patiently on God's Timing

Memory Verse: "Wait for the Lord; be strong and take heart and wait for the Lord." - **Psalm 27:14**

Bible Reading: Isaiah 40:28-31

Read & Learn:

The story of Abraham and Sarah waiting for the birth of their promised child, Isaac, illustrates the concept of waiting patiently on God's timing. God had given them a specific promise, but they grew impatient and took matters into their own hands by having a child through Sarah's maidservant, Hagar. However, this decision led to strife and complications. It was only when Abraham and Sarah patiently waited for God's appointed time that Isaac, the child of promise, was born. This story reminds us that God's timing is perfect, and our impatience can lead to unnecessary challenges. Waiting on the Lord with trust and patience is the path to receiving His best blessings.

Waiting patiently on God's timing is a significant aspect of the Christian journey. Isaiah 40:28-31 assures us that God is the everlasting, all-powerful Creator who provides strength to the weary and hope to those who trust in Him. Impatience often stems from our desire for immediate gratification, but God's ways and timing are higher than ours. Waiting patiently requires faith and trust in His plans, even when they seem delayed. During these times, we can draw closer to God, seeking His wisdom, and allowing Him to strengthen us. By waiting on God, we position ourselves to receive His best blessings and to walk in His perfect will.

Prayer Point:

Father, grant us the wisdom to recognise Your timing and the patience to wait for Your best in our lives. Strengthen us when we are weary and renew our hope as we trust in You.

Friday February 16

Topic: Don't Settle for Less than God's Best

Memory Verse: "Now to him who is able to do immeasurably more than all we ask or imagine, according to his power that is at work within us."

— **Ephesians 3:20**

Bible Reading: Numbers 13:16-33

Read & Learn:

The story of Caleb in the Bible exemplifies not settling for less than God's best. In Numbers 13, when the Israelites sent spies to scout the Promised Land, most of them returned with a fearful report. However, Caleb, full of faith, declared that they could conquer the land because God was with them. Despite the majority's doubts, Caleb refused to settle for less than the promise God had given. As a result, he, along with Joshua, was the only one of that generation to enter the Promised Land. Caleb's unwavering faith and refusal to settle for less serve as an inspiring example for us. We are reminded that God's best often requires courage, faith, and a determination to pursue His promises.

Settling for less than God's best can be a common temptation in life. It often happens when we compromise our values, accept mediocrity, or allow fear to hinder us from pursuing God's promises. We should be like Caleb, who believed in the greatness of God's promises and was willing to step out in faith to claim them, regardless of the obstacles. Don't settle for less; pursue God's best with unwavering faith and determination.

Prayer Point:
Father, grant us the faith and determination to press on toward the goals and dreams You have placed in our hearts, knowing that Your best awaits us.

Saturday February 17

Topic: In Your Delay, Remember God's Faithfulness

Memory Verse: "Because of the Lord's great love we are not consumed, for his compassions never fail. They are new every morning; great is your faithfulness." - **Lamentations 3:22-23**

Bible Reading: Genesis 18:1-15

Read & Learn:

The story of Abraham and Sarah waiting for the birth of their promised son, Isaac, is a powerful reminder of God's faithfulness in delays. God had given them a remarkable promise, but as years passed, their faith was tested. In their old age, when it seemed impossible, God fulfilled His promise, and Sarah bore a son. This delay in receiving God's promise allowed them to witness His faithfulness in an extraordinary way. It reminds us that God's timing is perfect, even when it seems delayed. We can trust in His faithfulness to fulfil His promises, no matter how long we wait.

Waiting for God's promises to come to fruition can be challenging, and delays may lead to doubt and discouragement. However, Lamentations 3:22-23 reminds us of God's unwavering faithfulness. His love and compassion are renewed daily, and His timing is always perfect. Psalm 27:14 encourages us to wait for the Lord with strength and courage. Instead of becoming disheartened in the delay, we can choose to remember God's faithfulness in our past and believe that He will fulfil His promises in His perfect time. Waiting can be a season of growth, faith-building, and an opportunity to witness God's faithfulness firsthand.

Prayer Point:

Father, help us to remember Your faithfulness, especially in times of waiting. Grant us the strength and courage to trust in Your perfect timing and unwavering love.

Sunday February 18

Topic: The Power of Gentleness in Resolving Conflict

Memory Verse: "A gentle answer turns away wrath, but a harsh word stirs up anger." - **Proverbs 15:1**

Bible Reading: John 8:1-11

Read & Learn:

The story of Jesus encountering the woman caught in adultery (John 8:1-11) illustrates the power of gentleness in conflict resolution. When religious leaders brought the woman to Jesus, they sought to trap Him with a difficult question. Instead of responding with anger or condemnation, Jesus responded with gentleness. He stooped down to write on the ground and then said, "Let any one of you who is without sin be the first to throw a stone at her." His gentle response disarmed the accusers, and they left one by one. Jesus then spoke to the woman with compassion, encouraging her to go and sin no more. His gentleness transformed a potentially explosive situation into a moment of grace and reconciliation.

Conflict is an inevitable part of life, but how we respond to it can make a significant difference. Proverbs 15:1 reminds us that a gentle response can defuse anger and tension. As Christians, we are called to be peacemakers (Matthew 5:9), and one powerful way to do this is through gentleness. Gentleness involves responding to conflict with kindness, patience, and humility. It means seeking to understand others, listening carefully, and speaking with respect. Gentleness doesn't mean avoiding difficult conversations but approaching them with a heart of love and a desire for reconciliation. When we respond to conflict with gentleness, we reflect the character of Christ and open the door to healing and restoration.

Prayer Point:
Father, grant us the wisdom to respond to conflict with gentleness and grace. Empower us to be peacemakers in our relationships and communities.

Monday February 19

Topic: Loving the Imperfect Church

Memory Verse: "Be completely humble and gentle; be patient, bearing with one another in love." - **Ephesians 4:2**

Bible Reading: 1 Corinthians 3:1-10

Read & Learn:

The early Christian church in Corinth faced numerous challenges and imperfections. The Apostle Paul wrote multiple letters to address these issues, highlighting divisions, immorality, and misuse of spiritual gifts among believers. Yet, Paul's letters were filled with love and a desire for unity. He didn't abandon the Corinthian church because of its imperfections; instead, he addressed their issues with grace and truth. Paul's example teaches us that loving the imperfect church involves bearing with one another's faults, extending grace, and working towards unity, even when disagreements and shortcomings exist.

Every church, no matter how wonderful, is composed of imperfect people. Conflict, differences of opinion, and shortcomings are inevitable. However, as Ephesians 4:2 reminds us, we are called to be completely humble, gentle, patient, and to bear with one another in love. Loving the imperfect church means recognising that it will have flaws and imperfections, just as we do. It means extending grace to fellow believers and seeking unity even when differences arise. When we love the imperfect church, we honour Christ's body, and we become part of the solution, working toward reconciliation and growth.

Prayer Point:

Father, grant us the humility to love our imperfect churches as You do. Help us to extend grace and work toward unity within our church community. Guide us in being part of the solution and agents of love and reconciliation.

Tuesday February 20

Topic: Filling Your Life with Peace through Trust in God

Memory Verse: "You will keep in perfect peace those whose minds are steadfast because they trust in you." - Isaiah 26:3

Bible Reading: Psalm 42:1-11

Read & Learn:

The story of King David, especially during his time as a shepherd and his encounter with Goliath, illustrates the concept of filling your life with peace through trust in God. As a young shepherd, David faced many trials and dangers while caring for his flock. He knew that his trust in God was essential to protect and provide for the sheep entrusted to him. When he faced the giant Goliath, David's trust in God's power and faithfulness enabled him to step forward with courage and peace, even in the face of overwhelming odds. This story reminds us that trusting in God can bring us a deep sense of peace, enabling us to face life's challenges with confidence and reliance on Him.

The key to filling your life with peace is to trust in God wholeheartedly. Isaiah 26:3 assures us that when our minds are steadfastly fixed on God through trust, He will grant us perfect peace. In Psalm 37:3-7, we find a roadmap for achieving this peace. It begins with trusting in the Lord, delighting in Him, and committing our ways to Him. As we do so, God promises to fulfil the desires of our hearts and shine His light on our paths. Importantly, we are encouraged to be still before the Lord and wait patiently, refusing to fret or be anxious when we see others succeed through unrighteous means. Trusting God fills our lives with peace as we surrender control, find joy in His presence, and confidently rely on His faithfulness.

Prayer Point:

Father, help us to commit our ways to You and find delight in Your love and guidance. Let our lives be filled with Your calming presence as we place our trust in Your unwavering faithfulness.

Wednesday February 21

Topic: Feeding Your Mind with Truth

Memory Verse: "Your word is a lamp for my feet, a light on my path."
               - Psalm 119:105

Bible Reading: John 8:31-32

Read & Learn:

In 2 Timothy 3:16-17, we are reminded that all Scripture is God-breathed and useful for teaching, rebuking, correcting, and training in righteousness. The story of the Berean Jews in Acts 17:11 beautifully illustrates the importance of feeding our minds with truth. These Bereans were commended for their noble character because, when they heard the teachings of the apostle Paul, they didn't simply accept them blindly. Instead, they examined the Scriptures daily to see if what Paul said was true. Their commitment to searching the Scriptures allowed them to discern truth from error and grow in their faith. It shows us the power of engaging with God's Word to find truth, discern falsehood, and strengthen our spiritual journey.

In a world filled with information and competing ideas, it's crucial for Christians to feed their minds with truth. Jesus, in John 8:31-32, highlights the relationship between His teachings, knowing the truth, and experiencing freedom. When we immerse ourselves in the Scriptures, we align our thoughts with God's truth. God's Word serves as a guide, providing light for our path and helping us distinguish right from wrong. It equips us for every aspect of life, nurturing our faith and enabling us to live in accordance with God's will. By feeding our minds with truth, we become better disciples of Christ, walking in the freedom and wisdom that only His truth can bring.

Prayer Point:

Father, help us hold fast to Your teachings and know the truth that sets us free. Let Your Word be a guiding light in our lives, illuminating our path.

Thursday February 22

Topic: Changing Your Life by Changing Your Thoughts

Memory Verse: "Do not conform to the pattern of this world, but be transformed by the renewing of your mind. Then you will be able to test and approve what God's will is - his good, pleasing and perfect will."

- Romans 12:2

Bible Reading: Philippians 4:8-9

Read & Learn:

In the book of Numbers, chapters 13 and 14, we read about the Israelites who had been delivered from Egypt but faced challenges when approaching the Promised Land. Twelve spies were sent to explore the land, but ten of them returned with a negative report, instilling fear and doubt in the hearts of the people. However, Joshua and Caleb had a different mindset. They believed that, with God's help, they could overcome any obstacles and inherit the land. Their positive and faith-filled thoughts set them apart, and they were the ones who eventually entered the Promised Land. This story emphasises the power of our thoughts in shaping our destiny.

The Bible repeatedly emphasises the importance of our thoughts in shaping our lives. Romans 12:2 encourages us not to conform to worldly patterns but to be transformed by renewing our minds. Our thoughts influence our attitudes, decisions, and actions. By changing our thoughts and aligning them with God's Word, we can change our lives for the better. This transformation begins with filling our minds with positive, God-honouring thoughts and taking action accordingly. As we think differently, we start to live differently, reflecting God's will and experiencing His peace.

Prayer Point:

Father, help us renew our minds with Your Word and transform our lives. Grant us the wisdom to focus on thoughts that align with Your will. Let our minds be filled with thoughts that bring honour to You.

Friday February 23

Topic: Trusting Your Children with Responsibility

Memory Verse: "Start children off on the way they should go, and even when they are old, they will not turn from it." - **Proverbs 22:6**

Bible Reading: Exodus 2:1-10

Read & Learn:

In Luke 15:11-32, we find the parable of the prodigal son. Although this story is often focused on the wayward son, it also highlights the father's trust in his children. When the younger son asks for his share of the inheritance and leaves, the father doesn't stop him. He trusts his son with the responsibility of managing his portion. Even when the son squanders it and returns in repentance, the father trusts him once more, celebrating his return. This story illustrates the importance of trusting your children with responsibility, allowing them to learn and grow through their choices, while being there to guide and support them.

Trusting your children with responsibility is a crucial aspect of parenting. Proverbs 22:6 encourages parents to start their children on the right path, implying that teaching them responsibility is part of that journey. Giving children age-appropriate responsibilities fosters their development, instils a sense of accountability, and builds their confidence. It shows that you trust them to make decisions and choices, teaching them important life skills. While trust comes with guidance and boundaries, it empowers children to learn from their actions and build character. Trusting your children with responsibility also reflects God's trust in us, giving us free will while providing guidance and forgiveness when we falter.

Prayer Point:

Father, grant us the wisdom to trust our children with appropriate responsibilities. Help us guide and support them as they learn and grow. Let our parenting reflect Your trust in us, providing love, guidance, and forgiveness.

Saturday February 24

Topic: The Importance of Compassion in Parenting

Memory Verse: "Be kind and compassionate to one another, forgiving each other, just as in Christ God forgave you." - **Ephesians 4:32**

Bible Reading: Luke 15:20-24

Read & Learn:

The story of the prodigal son in Luke 15:20-24 portrays the importance of compassion in parenting. When the prodigal son returns home after squandering his inheritance, his father's response is filled with compassion. Instead of scolding or rejecting him, the father runs to embrace his wayward child, forgives him, and celebrates his return. This powerful illustration demonstrates that compassion is a vital aspect of parenting. It can mend broken relationships, offer forgiveness, and provide a safe space for children to make amends and grow. Compassionate parenting reflects God's love and forgiveness toward us, and it has the potential to restore and transform lives.

Compassion in parenting means extending kindness, understanding, and love toward our children, even in their moments of mistakes or rebellion. Ephesians 4:32 encourages us to be compassionate, just as God has forgiven us through Christ. Compassion doesn't mean condoning wrong behaviour, but it means responding with love and grace, helping children learn from their mistakes, and providing a supportive environment for growth and change. As parents, our compassionate actions can have a lasting impact on our children's lives, teaching them about God's love and forgiveness. It also creates an atmosphere where children feel safe to communicate openly and seek guidance.

Prayer Point:
Father, help us as parents to emulate Your compassion in our relationships with our children. Grant us the wisdom to guide our children with kindness and understanding.

Sunday February 25

Topic: Filling Your Mind with Biblical Truth

Memory Verse: "I have hidden your word in my heart that I might not sin against you." - **Psalm 119:11**

Bible Reading: Psalm 1:1-3

Read & Learn:

The story of King David's encounter with Goliath in 1 Samuel 17 illustrates the power of filling your mind with biblical truth. Young David faced a giant warrior named Goliath. While others trembled in fear, David, armed with faith and truth from God's Word, confidently stepped forward. He declared, "You come against me with sword and spear, but I come against you in the name of the Lord Almighty" (1 Samuel 17:45, NIV). David's unwavering trust in God's promises and the knowledge of God's faithfulness enabled him to defeat the giant. By filling his mind with biblical truth, David overcame fear and achieved victory. This story reminds us of the importance of knowing and applying God's Word in our lives.

Filling your mind with biblical truth means saturating your thoughts with the teachings and promises found in God's Word. Psalm 1:1-3 highlights the benefits of delighting in God's law and meditating on it day and night. When we immerse ourselves in Scripture, it becomes a source of guidance, wisdom, and strength. Just as David faced Goliath with faith grounded in God's promises, we can overcome the challenges and giants in our lives by relying on the truth of God's Word. Scripture helps us discern right from wrong, empowers us to make godly choices, and keeps us from falling into sin. By consistently filling our minds with biblical truth, we grow spiritually, bear fruit, and experience prosperity in our walk with God.

Prayer Point:

Father, thank You for the gift of Your Word. Help us to delight in it and meditate on it day and night.

Monday February 26

Topic: The Power of Availability in God's Hands

Memory Verse:) - "Then I heard the voice of the Lord saying, 'Whom shall I send? And who will go for us?' And I said, 'Here am I. Send me!'"

— **Isaiah 6:8**

Bible Reading: Exodus 3:1-12

Read & Learn:

The encounter between Moses and the burning bush in Exodus 3:1-12 demonstrates the power of availability in God's hands. Moses, a humble shepherd, was approached by God through a miraculous burning bush. When God called him, Moses simply responded with, "Here I am." Despite his doubts and feelings of inadequacy, Moses made himself available to God's divine purpose. God assured Moses that He would be with him every step of the way. Moses' availability led to the liberation of the Israelites from Egypt, showcasing the transformative power of surrendering oneself to God's calling.

Availability in God's hands means being willing and open to God's call and purpose for your life, regardless of your perceived limitations. The memory verse from Isaiah 6:8 reflects a similar attitude of readiness to serve God. Just as Moses made himself available and said, "Here I am," we should also be prepared to respond when God calls. When we make ourselves available to God, He can use us in incredible ways, just as He did with Moses. It's about trusting that God equips us for His work and relying on His presence and strength as we step out in faith.

Prayer Point:

Father, help us to be willing to say, "Here I am" when You call. Remove our doubts and insecurities, and fill us with faith to step into Your purpose. Use our availability to accomplish Your divine plans and bring glory to Your name.

Tuesday February 27

Topic: Giving God the Credit and Pointing People to Him

Memory Verse: "So whether you eat or drink or whatever you do, do it all for the glory of God." - **1 Corinthians 10:31**

Bible Reading: Matthew 5:14-16

Read & Learn:

The story of John the Baptist in the New Testament serves as a powerful example of giving God the credit and pointing people to Him. John, despite his popularity, consistently redirected the attention to Jesus. When asked about his identity and purpose, John replied, "I am not the Messiah but am sent ahead of him" (John 3:28, NIV). He understood that his role was to prepare the way for Jesus, and he humbly embraced it. John's life and ministry teach us the importance of humility, acknowledging God's sovereignty, and directing others to the Saviour.

As Christians, it is crucial to recognise that everything we do should ultimately bring glory to God. This includes our actions, words, and attitudes. In Matthew 5:14-16, Jesus compares believers to the light of the world, emphasising that our lives should shine with good deeds that lead others to glorify our Father in heaven. It's not about seeking personal recognition but rather pointing people to God. Giving God the credit means acknowledging His role in our accomplishments, blessings, and daily lives. When we do this, we reflect Christ's humility and invite others to discover the source of our hope and joy.

Prayer Point:

Father, help us to always point people to Jesus. Teach us humility and remind us that all we have is from You. Let our lives reflect Your light, drawing others to glorify You.

Wednesday February 28

Topic: The Importance of Integrity in Christian Living

Memory Verse: "Whoever walks in integrity walks securely, but whoever takes crooked paths will be found out." - **Proverbs 10:9**

Bible Reading: Psalm 15

Read & Learn:

The life of Joseph in the Old Testament exemplifies the importance of integrity in Christian living. Despite facing numerous trials and temptations, Joseph consistently upheld his integrity. When Potiphar's wife attempted to seduce him, he refused, saying, "How then could I do such a wicked thing and sin against God?" (Genesis 39:9, NIV). This unwavering commitment to moral principles led to Joseph's rise from being a slave to becoming a ruler in Egypt. His life demonstrates that maintaining integrity, even in the face of adversity, not only honours God but also leads to blessings and favour.

Integrity is a foundational virtue in Christian living. It involves consistently living a life of honesty, truthfulness, and moral uprightness, both in private and public. Psalm 15 outlines several aspects of integrity, including speaking the truth, refraining from slander, doing no wrong to others, and keeping one's promises. These qualities reflect a heart that seeks to honour God in all areas of life. Proverbs 10:9 emphasises that a life of integrity leads to security and stability. As Christians, we are called to walk in integrity, knowing that it not only pleases God but also establishes a firm foundation for our faith.

Prayer Point:

Father, help us to walk in integrity, honouring You in all we do. Grant us the strength to resist temptation and uphold moral principles, even when it is difficult. Let our lives be a testimony to the importance of integrity in Christian living.

Thursday February 29

Topic: Overcoming Discouragement

Memory Verse: "The LORD is close to the broken-hearted and saves those who are crushed in spirit." - **Psalm 34:18**

Bible Reading: 1 Samuel 30:1-8

Read & Learn:

The story of Elijah from the Old Testament offers valuable insights into understanding and overcoming discouragement. After his great victory on Mount Carmel, Elijah faced intense opposition and threats from Queen Jezebel. Overwhelmed by fear and despair, he fled to the wilderness, sat under a broom tree, and prayed for death. In his moment of discouragement, God provided nourishment and guidance, showing His compassion. Through gentle reassurance, God restored Elijah's strength and purpose, leading him out of despair to continue his ministry. This story teaches us that even in our darkest moments of discouragement, God is near, ready to provide comfort, strength, and a renewed sense of purpose.

Discouragement is a common experience in the Christian journey. It often arises from various sources, including difficult circumstances, personal failures, or prolonged challenges. However, as Christians, we are not left to face discouragement alone. The Bible reminds us that God is close to the broken-hearted and offers salvation to those crushed in spirit. 2 Corinthians 4:7-9 reminds us that though we may be hard-pressed, perplexed, persecuted, or struck down, we are not defeated because God's power sustains us. To overcome discouragement, we must turn to God in prayer, seek His guidance, and remember that His strength is made perfect in our weakness. Through faith and trust in Him, we can rise above discouragement and find renewed hope.

Prayer Point:

Father, help us to trust in Your power to sustain us through life's challenges. Let us find comfort and renewed purpose in Your presence, even in times of despair.

Friday March 01

Topic: Walk by Faith, Not by Sight

Memory Verse: "For we live by faith, not by sight." - **2 Corinthians 5:7**

Bible Reading: Hebrews 11:1, 6

Read & Learn:

The story of Abraham and Sarah from the book of Genesis exemplifies walking by faith, not by sight. Despite their old age and the seemingly impossible promise of having a child, God assured them of descendants as numerous as the stars. Abraham and Sarah believed in God's promise, and their faith was credited to them as righteousness. Even when circumstances appeared bleak, they trusted in God's faithfulness. Eventually, God fulfilled His promise, and Sarah gave birth to Isaac. This story reminds us that faith in God's promises, even when they seem impossible, pleases Him and leads to His blessings.

Walking by faith, not by sight, is a core principle of the Christian journey. It means trusting in God's promises and guidance even when our physical senses or circumstances suggest otherwise. The Bible defines faith as confidence in what we hope for and assurance about what we do not see. Faith requires believing in God's existence, His goodness, and His ability to fulfil His promises. It is through faith that we please God. When we rely solely on our senses and visible evidence, we limit our understanding of God's plans and power. To walk by faith is to trust that God is working behind the scenes, even in the midst of challenges and uncertainties.

Prayer Point:

Father, thank You for being faithful and trustworthy. Help us to walk by faith, not by sight, in every aspect of our lives. Grant us the grace to trust in Your promises, especially when circumstances seem impossible.

Saturday March 02

Topic: Trusting God's Wisdom Over Our Feelings

Memory Verse: "Trust in the Lord with all your heart and lean not on your own understanding; in all your ways submit to him, and he will make your paths straight." - **Proverbs 3:5-6**

Bible Reading: 1 Kings 3:16-28

Read & Learn:

In a world that often tells us to "follow our hearts," it's easy to rely on our feelings as a compass. However, our emotions can be fickle and misleading. Proverbs 3:5-6 advises us to place our full trust in God rather than our own understanding. It assures us that when we submit to God's wisdom, He will guide us in the right direction.

In the Bible, King Solomon was offered anything he wanted by God. Instead of asking for wealth or power, he asked for wisdom. His choice pleased God, and Solomon became renowned for his wisdom. When two women came to him, each claiming to be the mother of a baby, Solomon used divine wisdom to resolve the dispute.

Our feelings can be influenced by a myriad of factors - our environment, our physical state, and even our past experiences. While feelings are a part of the human experience, they are not always rooted in truth. The Bible warns us against the deceitfulness of the heart (Jeremiah 17:9). On the other hand, God's wisdom is unchanging and reliable.

By choosing to trust God's wisdom over our feelings, we gain a more stable, reliable foundation for decision-making and problem-solving. We also grow in our relationship with God, who desires the best for us and guides us in the way we should go (Psalm 32:8).

Prayer Point:
Father, help me to trust Your wisdom over my fluctuating feelings. Guide me by Your truth and wisdom in the decisions I face. Renew my mind and help me to discern Your will in every situation.

Sunday March 03

Topic: Trusting God in Seasons of Waiting

Memory Verse: "But those who hope in the Lord will renew their strength. They will soar on wings like eagles; they will run and not grow weary, they will walk and not be faint." - **Isaiah 40:31**

Bible Reading: Genesis 17:15-22, Genesis 21:1-7

Read & Learn:

Waiting is a part of life that most of us dislike. Whether it's waiting for an answer to prayer, a change in circumstances, or a dream to be fulfilled, the process can be frustrating.

In the Bible, Abraham and Sarah had to wait many years for the fulfilment of God's promise - a son. Despite their old age and moments of doubt, they held onto God's promise. When Isaac was finally born, their joy was immeasurable, and their faith was strengthened. Their story teaches us that God's promises are worth the wait, and He is faithful to fulfil them in His perfect timing (Genesis 21:1-7).

Waiting is more than just the passage of time; it's a spiritual discipline that deepens our relationship with God. Waiting is an act of faith, acknowledging that God's timing is perfect, even when it doesn't align with ours.

In seasons of waiting, we are invited to renew our strength by hoping in the Lord, as Isaiah 40:31 tells us. This hope is not wishful thinking but a confident expectation that God will do what He has promised. So, in your season of waiting, lean into God, and allow Him to renew your strength.

Prayer Point:
Father, in my season of waiting, help me to place my hope in You and not in my own timing. Help me to trust that Your timing is perfect. Give me the patience to wait on Your promises. Amen.

Monday March 04

Topic: Turning Hopeless Ends into Endless Hope through Jesus

Memory Verse: "May the God of hope fill you with all joy and peace as you trust in him, so that you may overflow with hope by the power of the Holy Spirit." - **Romans 15:13**

Bible Reading: Exodus 14:15 -29

Read & Learn:

Life often presents us with situations that seem hopeless. Whether it's a failing relationship, a dire medical diagnosis, or a crumbling career, it's easy to lose hope..

In the Bible, the story of Lazarus showcases Jesus' power to turn a hopeless end into endless hope. Lazarus had died, and his sisters, Mary and Martha, were in despair. But when Jesus arrived, He did the unimaginable: He raised Lazarus from the dead. This miracle not only restored Lazarus but also filled everyone with awe and hope, proving that even in the face of death, Jesus offers endless hope (John 11:1-44).

When we face seemingly hopeless situations, it's natural to feel overwhelmed and defeated. However, the Bible repeatedly shows us that God specialises in turning hopeless ends into endless hope. Consider the story of Joseph, who went from being sold into slavery to becoming the second-in-command in Egypt (Genesis 41:41). Or think about the Apostle Paul, who transformed from a persecutor of Christians to one of the most influential apostles (Acts 9:1-19).

The key to experiencing this transformation lies in trusting God. Trusting God means surrendering control and believing that He can work all things for good (Romans 8:28).

Prayer Point:
Father, empower me to face hopeless situations with the assurance that You can turn them into opportunities for endless hope. Fill me with Your joy and peace as I navigate through challenging and hopeless seasons of life.

Tuesday March 05

Topic: Facing the Facts with Faith

Memory Verse: "Now faith is confidence in what we hope for and assurance about what we do not see." - **Hebrews 11:1**

Bible Reading: 1 Samuel 17:38 - 51

Read & Learn:

Life often confronts us with harsh realities - illness, financial struggles, broken relationships, and more. While it's crucial to acknowledge these facts, it's equally important to face them with faith. Hebrews 11:1 defines faith as having confidence in our hopes and assurance in the unseen. It's not about denying reality but about trusting God's promises despite what current circumstances indicate.

In the Bible, David faced the towering giant Goliath. The facts were against him: he was young, inexperienced, and unarmed compared to the seasoned warrior. Yet, David faced these facts with faith in God. Armed only with a sling and stones, he defeated Goliath, proving that faith can triumph over seemingly insurmountable facts (1 Samuel 17).

Facing the facts doesn't mean we have to accept defeat. The Bible is filled with stories of individuals who faced grim realities but emerged victorious through faith. Think of Moses leading the Israelites out of Egypt (Exodus 14) or Daniel in the lion's den (Daniel 6). These were dire situations, yet faith made a way where there seemed to be none. Hebrews 11:1 reminds us that faith is not about ignoring the facts but about seeing beyond them. Faith allows us to view our circumstances through the lens of God's promises. When we align our perspective with God's, we can face any fact, no matter how daunting, with a spirit of victory.

Prayer Point:

Father, help me to face the facts of my life with unwavering faith in Your promises. Grant me the courage to confront challenges, knowing that with faith, all things are surmountable.

Wednesday March 06

Topic: Reviving Hope in Hopeless Situations

Memory Verse: "May the God of hope fill you with all joy and peace as you trust in him, so that you may overflow with hope by the power of the Holy Spirit." - **Romans 15:13**

Bible Reading: Romans 4:13 - 21

Read & Learn:

There are moments in life when hope seems to vanish, leaving us in despair and confusion. Romans 15:13 encourages us to trust in God, the source of all hope. As we trust Him, we are filled with joy and peace, which leads to an overflow of hope through the Holy Spirit's power.

In the Bible, the story of Lazarus showcases the revival of hope in a hopeless situation. This story illustrates that even when all hope seems lost, God can still intervene miraculously.

When we face hopeless situations, it's easy to forget that we serve a God who specialises in the impossible. The story of Lazarus is a powerful reminder that God's timing and methods often defy our understanding. Just as Jesus revived Lazarus, He can revive our hope.

The key is to trust in God, as Romans 15:13 suggests. Trusting God doesn't mean ignoring the facts; it means looking beyond them to God's promises. When we trust Him, we invite His joy and peace into our lives, which in turn fuels our hope. Remember, hope is not a feeling but a choice. It's a decision to trust God regardless of the circumstances. So, when you find yourself in a hopeless situation, choose to trust God. Allow Him to fill you with joy, peace, and an overflow of hope.

Prayer Point:
Father, in my moments of despair, help me to trust You as the source of all hope. Fill me with joy and peace as I choose to trust You, so that my life may overflow with hope.

Thursday March 07

Topic: Finding Deliverance at Life's Dead Ends

Memory Verse: "The righteous cry out, and the Lord hears them; he delivers them from all their troubles." **- Psalm 34:17**

Bible Reading: Exodus 14:5 - 13

Read & Learn:

Life often presents us with situations that feel like dead ends - moments where we see no way out. It's easy to lose hope and feel trapped. Psalm 34:17 assures us that when we cry out to God in righteousness, He hears us and delivers us from our troubles. It's a promise of divine intervention when we feel stuck and see no way out.

In the Bible, the Israelites found themselves at a literal dead end at the Red Sea with Pharaoh's army closing in (Exodus 14). They were trapped and terrified. But Moses told them to stand still and see the deliverance of the Lord. Miraculously, God parted the Red Sea, providing a way out where there seemed to be none.

Dead ends in life can manifest in various forms—financial crises, health issues, broken relationships, or even spiritual dryness. The Israelites' experience at the Red Sea is a vivid illustration that God can make a way where there seems to be no way. The key is to cry out to God, as Psalm 34:17 encourages us to do. When we do, we invite God's intervention into our situation.

God's deliverance may not always come in the form we expect. For the Israelites, it was a miraculous parting of the sea. For you, it might be an unexpected job offer, a sudden improvement in health, or a restored relationship. The form may vary, but the Deliverer remains the same.

Prayer Point:
Father, thank you for being my Deliverer. Help me to always turn to You in times of trouble. Help me to trust that You can make a way where there seems to be no way

Friday March 08

Topic: Inner Transformation in Difficult Times

Memory Verse: "Not only so, but we also glory in our sufferings, because we know that suffering produces perseverance; perseverance, character; and character, hope." - **Romans 5:3-4**

Bible Reading: James 1:2 -5

Read & Learn:

Difficult times are inevitable, but how we respond to them can make all the difference. Romans 5:3-4 tells us that suffering isn't pointless; it has a purpose. It helps to develop perseverance, which in turn builds character, and ultimately, gives us hope. This verse assures us that God can use our difficulties for our spiritual growth.

Life's challenges can either make us bitter or better; the choice is ours. The Apostle Paul, in Romans 5:3-4, encourages us to see the silver lining in our sufferings. When we go through hardships, we are given the opportunity to grow in perseverance, character, and hope. Joseph's story is a prime example of this. Despite the injustices he faced, he chose to remain faithful to God and was ultimately used for a greater purpose. His internal transformation was even more significant than his external circumstances.

Similarly, when we focus on our inner growth during difficult times, we allow God to work in us and through us. We become more resilient, compassionate, and hopeful, qualities that not only enrich our own lives but also make us a blessing to others.

Prayer Point:

Father, thank you for the hope that comes from a relationship with You. Grant me the strength to persevere through challenges. Help me to focus on my inner growth during difficult times and trust that You are working for my good.

Saturday March 09

Topic: Learning Through Life's Storms

Memory Verse: "Consider it pure joy, my brothers and sisters, whenever you face trials of many kinds, because you know that the testing of your faith produces perseverance." - **James 1:2-3**

Bible Reading: Act 27: 27-34

Read & Learn:

Life's storms are inevitable, but they also serve as classrooms where we can learn valuable lessons. James 1:2-3 encourages us to view trials as opportunities for growth. The verse tells us that facing difficulties is a way to test and strengthen our faith, ultimately leading to perseverance.

In the Bible, the Apostle Paul faced a literal storm while sailing to Rome. Despite the terrifying circumstances, Paul remained calm and assured the crew that they would be saved. He had faith that God would deliver them, and indeed they were all saved. This storm served as a 'school,' teaching Paul and the crew about God's deliverance and faithfulness.

When we face our own 'storms,' whether they are health issues, financial troubles, or relationship conflicts, we have a choice. We can either let these trials overwhelm us, or we can see them as teachers, helping us to grow stronger in our faith and understanding of God's word.

Prayer Point:

Father, thank you for being my refuge in the storm. Help me to trust in your faithfulness in all circumstances. Give me the strength to persevere in the midst of trials and to focus on the growth and character you are building in me.

Sunday March 10

Topic: The Importance of Grieving Life's Losses

Memory Verse: "Blessed are those who mourn, for they will be comforted." - **Matthew 5:4**

Bible Reading: John 11:32 - 37

Read & Learn:

Grieving is often seen as a sign of vulnerability, but the Bible teaches us that it's a necessary part of the human experience. Loss is an inevitable part of life, and grieving is a necessary process for healing. Matthew 5:4 assures us that mourning is not a sign of weakness but a natural human response to loss. It also tells us that those who mourn will be comforted, highlighting the importance of grieving as a pathway to healing and comfort from God. Jesus promises that those who allow themselves to grieve will find comfort, emphasising God's compassion and understanding.

In the Bible, King David experienced profound grief when his son Absalom died, despite Absalom's rebellion against him (2 Samuel 18:33). David's grief was a natural, human response to loss. Despite being a strong leader, he didn't shy away from expressing his grief over the loss of his son. His mourning was not a sign of weakness but a testament to his humanity and his faith in God's ultimate comfort. This shows that even great leaders need time to mourn.

The Bible is filled with instances where God comforts those in sorrow. In Psalm 34:18, it says, "The Lord is close to the broken-hearted and saves those who are crushed in spirit." By allowing ourselves to grieve, we open the door for God's comfort and healing to enter our lives.

Prayer Point:

Father, thank you for being close to the broken-hearted. In my season of grief, help me to surrender my sorrow to You and trust You for comfort and healing.

Monday March 11

Topic: Finding Financial Security in God

Memory Verse: "Those who trust in their riches will fall, but the righteous will thrive like a green leaf." **- Proverbs 11:28**

Bible Reading: Mark 10:17-22

Read & Learn:

The story of the rich young ruler (Mark 10:17-22) serves as a cautionary tale. Despite his wealth, the young man felt empty and sought eternal life. Jesus told him to sell all he had and follow Him. Unable to part with his riches, the man walked away sorrowful. His wealth became his stumbling block, preventing him from finding true security in Christ.

In a world obsessed with financial stability, it's easy to forget where our true security lies. Proverbs 11:28 warns against placing trust in material wealth, which is fleeting and unreliable. Instead, it encourages us to be righteous, implying that our true security comes from a life aligned with God's principles. Financial security is a concern for many, but the Bible teaches that our ultimate security should be in God, not in our bank accounts. Proverbs 11:28 makes it clear that relying on material wealth is a shaky foundation.

The young ruler had abundant wealth but lacked spiritual richness. When faced with the choice between material security and eternal security, he chose the former and missed out on the latter. Matthew 6:19-21 also advises us not to store up treasures on earth but in heaven. This doesn't mean we shouldn't be financially responsible; rather, it means our priorities should be aligned with God's kingdom. When we seek first His kingdom (Matthew 6:33), all other things, including financial security, will be added unto us.

Prayer Point:
Father, thank you for providing for my needs. Help me to trust in You as my ultimate source of security, rather than my finances.

Tuesday March 12

Topic: Staying Hungry for God

Memory Verse: "Blessed are those who hunger and thirst for righteousness, for they will be filled." - **Matthew 5:6**

Bible Reading: Luke 10:38-42

Read & Learn:

In a world full of distractions, it's easy to lose our spiritual appetite. Matthew 5:6 promises a blessing for those who deeply desire righteousness. This hunger and thirst are not for physical sustenance but for a fulfilling relationship with God, which is the only thing that can truly satisfy us.

In the Bible, the story of Mary and Martha (Luke 10:38-42) illustrates the concept of spiritual hunger. Martha was busy with household chores, while Mary sat at Jesus' feet, listening to His teachings. When Martha complained, Jesus said that Mary had chosen the better part. Mary's hunger for spiritual nourishment took precedence over worldly concerns. The story of Mary and Martha serves as a reminder that it's easy to get caught up in the busyness of life and neglect our spiritual needs. Mary chose to prioritise her spiritual hunger, and Jesus affirmed that she had made the right choice

Spiritual hunger is a vital aspect of our relationship with God. Just as our bodies need food and water, our souls need the nourishment that comes from a close relationship with our Creator. Matthew 5:6 assures us that when we hunger for righteousness, we will be filled. This is not a temporary satisfaction but a deep, lasting fulfilment that only God can provide.

Prayer Point:

Father, thank You for the promise that when I hunger for You I will be filled. In the busyness of life, help me to prioritise my relationship with You.

Wednesday March 13

Topic: Overcoming Fear with Faith

Memory Verse: Isaiah 41:10 - "So do not fear, for I am with you; do not be dismayed, for I am your God. I will strengthen you and help you; I will uphold you with my righteous right hand."

Bible Reading: Psalm 27:1-14

Read & Learn:

In the early 18th century, John Newton, a former slave trader, experienced a profound spiritual transformation. Caught in a terrifying storm at sea, Newton's fear was overwhelming. He cried out to God for mercy, and in that moment of desperation, his heart began to change. This experience led him to abandon the slave trade and eventually become an Anglican clergyman. He wrote the hymn "Amazing Grace," reflecting his journey from fear to faith, illustrating how faith in God can transform the most fearful situations into opportunities for spiritual growth and change.

Fear is a common human experience, but it doesn't have to control us. David, in Psalm 27, declares his confidence in God even when evildoers come against him. This Psalm teaches us that focusing on God and seeking His presence are key to overcoming fear. Faith in God doesn't mean that we won't experience fear, but it gives us the strength to face our fears with courage and peace.

Prayer Point:

Father, Father, guide me to seek Your presence as my refuge and fortress in times of fear. Help me to trust in Your strength and not be overwhelmed by fear. Grant me the courage to face my fears with faith, knowing You are with me.

Thursday March 14

Topic: The Power of Prayer

Memory Verse: "The prayer of a righteous person is powerful and effective." - **James 5:16**

Bible Reading: Matthew 6:5-15

Read & Learn:

George Müller, a Christian evangelist and the director of the Ashley Down orphanage in Bristol, England, was known for his deep faith and commitment to prayer. In one famous incident, there was no food in the orphanage to feed the children breakfast, but Müller asked everyone to sit at the table and give thanks anyway. As they prayed, a baker knocked on the door, providing enough bread to feed everyone. Shortly after, a milkman offered them milk, as his cart had broken down right in front of the orphanage. This story demonstrates the remarkable power of prayer and Müller's unwavering faith in God's provision.

Prayer is a fundamental aspect of the Christian faith, serving as a direct line of communication with God. It's not just about asking for things; it's about building a relationship with our Creator. In Matthew 6, Jesus teaches the Lord's Prayer, emphasising the importance of sincerity and humility in prayer. He contrasts this with the hypocritical prayers of those who seek attention. This passage teaches us that prayer is not a public spectacle but a private communion with God. Through prayer, we align our will with God's, seek His guidance, express our gratitude, and find comfort in His presence. The power of prayer lies not in the words we say but in our faith and trust in God's sovereignty.

Prayer Point:

Father, guide me to trust in Your provision and care through my prayers. Help me to always remember the power of sincere prayer in my daily life.

Friday March 15

Topic: Understanding God's Love

Memory Verse: "And so we know and rely on the love God has for us. God is love. Whoever lives in love lives in God, and God in them."
- 1 John 4:16

Bible Reading: Romans 8:35-39

Read & Learn:

God's love is a central theme in Christianity, characterised by its unconditional and sacrificial nature. Romans 8:35-39 emphasises that nothing can separate us from the love of God in Christ Jesus. This passage reassures believers that, regardless of life's challenges or our own failings, God's love remains steadfast. Understanding God's love involves recognising its unmerited nature; we cannot earn it through deeds or lose it through failures. It's a love that embraces us in our imperfections and transforms us. This love is not just an abstract concept but is demonstrated profoundly in the life, death, and resurrection of Jesus Christ, offering redemption and hope to all.

Fanny Crosby, a prolific hymn writer was blind from infancy. Despite her physical limitation, God's love helped her write the lyrics of over 8,000 hymns, including beloved ones like "Blessed Assurance." Crosby's deep faith and understanding of God's love were evident in her hymns, which often spoke of the spiritual sight and insight she gained through her relationship with God. Her life is a testament to the power of God's love to work through our weaknesses and challenges. Crosby's story teaches us that God's love is not hindered by our physical or circumstantial limitations but is made perfect in our weaknesses, offering us a unique perspective and depth in our spiritual journey.

Prayer Point:

Father, thank You for Your love that embraces me in my imperfections. Help me to deeply understand and accept Your unconditional love. Guide me to live in a way that reflects Your love to others.

Saturday March 16

Topic: Living Out the Fruit of the Spirit

Memory Verse: "But the fruit of the Spirit is love, joy, peace, forbearance, kindness, goodness, faithfulness, gentleness and self-control. Against such things, there is no law." **- Galatians 5:22-23**

Bible Reading: John 15:1-11

Read & Learn:

Reflect on the story of the Good Samaritan in Luke 10:25-37. The Samaritan exemplified the fruit of the Spirit by showing love, kindness, and compassion to a wounded stranger, transcending cultural and societal norms. His actions demonstrated the genuine outworking of love, illustrating what it means to live out the fruit of the Spirit in everyday encounters.

The Bible teaches that the Holy Spirit produces specific fruit in the lives of believers. Galatians 5:22-23 outlines these virtues, emphasizing their importance in Christian living. The story of the Good Samaritan aligns with these attributes, showcasing love, kindness, and compassion. Living out the fruit of the Spirit involves cultivating a Christ like character, allowing the Holy Spirit to shape our attitudes, behaviours, and relationships. John 15:1-11 underscores the significance of abiding in Christ, the true vine, to bear fruit. As believers abide in Christ, His life becomes evident in their actions, reflecting the transformative power of the Holy Spirit.

Prayer Point:

Father, help me bear the fruit of the Spirit. Guide me to abide in Christ daily, cultivating a Christ-like character through the power of the Holy Spirit. Empower me to express genuine love and compassion in my interactions, reflecting Your transformative work in my life.

Sunday March 17

Topic: The Importance of Forgiveness

Memory Verse: "Be kind and compassionate to one another, forgiving each other, just as in Christ God forgave you." **- Ephesians 4:32**

Bible Reading: Matthew 18:21-35

Read & Learn:

The biblical account of Joseph and his brothers is a profound example of forgiveness. Sold into slavery by his own brothers, Joseph endured years of hardship and injustice. Yet, when he rose to power in Egypt and his brothers came seeking aid, Joseph faced a pivotal choice. In Genesis 45, we witness a remarkable moment of reconciliation. Joseph reveals his identity to his brothers, who fear retribution. However, Joseph, moved by compassion and guided by his faith in God's plan, chooses forgiveness over revenge. This act of forgiveness not only reunites a family but also showcases the power of God's grace in transforming hearts and healing deep wounds. Joseph's story teaches us that forgiveness is not a sign of weakness but a courageous act of faith, love, and trust in God's greater plan.

In Matthew 18:21-35, Jesus emphasises the importance of forgiving from the heart. This parable teaches us that forgiveness is not optional but essential in our walk with God. It's a divine mandate that frees us from bitterness and resentment, allowing God's healing and restoration to work in our lives. Forgiveness is challenging, especially when the hurt is deep, but it's a journey worth taking. It leads to peace, reconciliation, and a deeper understanding of God's love and mercy.

Prayer Point:
Father, grant me the strength to forgive as You have forgiven me. Help me to let go of bitterness and embrace Your peace. Heal the wounds of my heart as I forgive those who have hurt me and fill me with Your love and compassion.

Monday March 18

Topic: Building Strong Christian Relationships

Memory Verse: "A new command I give you: Love one another. As I have loved you, so you must love one another." - **John 13:34**

Bible Reading: 1 Corinthians 13:1-13

Read & Learn:

In the early Christian community, as described in Acts 2:42-47, believers exemplified strong relationships. They devoted themselves to the apostles' teaching, fellowship, breaking of bread, and prayer. Their unity was so profound that they shared everything they had, ensuring no one was in need. This story illustrates the power of Christian fellowship. Their love and care for one another were a testimony to their faith, attracting more people to the faith. This account is a timeless reminder of how Christian relationships should be: rooted in love, selflessness, and a shared commitment to God's word.

Building strong Christian relationships is fundamental to our faith journey. These relationships, grounded in Christ's love, are characterised by mutual support, accountability, and encouragement. As seen in 1 Corinthians 13, love is the cornerstone of these relationships. It's patient, kind, and selfless. In Galatians 6:2, we're encouraged to "carry each other's burdens," highlighting the importance of empathy and support. Furthermore, Proverbs 27:17 compares a friend to iron sharpening iron, suggesting that Christian relationships should inspire personal and spiritual growth. By fostering these relationships, we create a supportive community that mirrors Christ's love and strengthens our collective faith.

Prayer Point:

Father, guide me to build relationships that reflect Your love and grace. Help me to be patient, kind, and supportive in my interactions with others. Strengthen the bonds within my Christian community that we may grow together in faith.

Tuesday March 19

Topic: Navigating Life's Challenges with Biblical Wisdom

Memory Verse: "If any of you lacks wisdom, you should ask God, who gives generously to all without finding fault, and it will be given to you."

— James 1:5

Bible Reading: Proverbs 3:5-6, 13-18

Read & Learn:

Consider the story of Joseph in Genesis 37-50. Sold into slavery by his brothers, falsely accused, and imprisoned, Joseph faced immense challenges. Yet, he consistently relied on God's wisdom to navigate these hardships. When interpreting Pharaoh's dreams, Joseph didn't take credit for his wisdom but acknowledged it as God's revelation. His reliance on divine wisdom not only led to his personal elevation but also saved many lives during a severe famine. Joseph's story teaches us that in our challenges, seeking and applying God's wisdom can lead to unexpected and far-reaching blessings.

Life's challenges often leave us feeling overwhelmed and uncertain. However, as Christians, we have access to an invaluable resource: biblical wisdom. This wisdom, rooted in a deep understanding of God's word and character, provides guidance and clarity in difficult times. Proverbs 3:5-6 encourages us to trust in the Lord rather than our understanding, assuring that He will make our paths straight. This trust involves seeking God's guidance in prayer, immersing ourselves in Scripture, and being attentive to the Holy Spirit's leading. By applying biblical wisdom, we can make decisions that align with God's will, bringing peace and direction amidst life's complexities.

Prayer Point:

Father, help me to trust in You and not lean on my understanding. Guide me through Your word and Spirit to make wise decisions in difficult times. Grant me the wisdom to navigate life's challenges according to Your will.

Wednesday March 20

Topic: Growing in Spiritual Maturity

Memory Verse: "But grow in the grace and knowledge of our Lord and Saviour Jesus Christ. To him be glory both now and forever! Amen."

- **2 Peter 3:18**

Bible Reading: Ephesians 4:11-16

Read & Learn:

Consider the transformation of the Apostle Peter. Initially impulsive and often misunderstanding Jesus' teachings, Peter's journey is a testament to spiritual growth. From denying Christ to boldly proclaiming the gospel after Pentecost, Peter's life reflects a deepening understanding and application of Jesus' teachings. His letters, especially 1 and 2 Peter, reveal a matured perspective, emphasising growth in faith, holiness, and love. Peter's life encourages us that spiritual maturity is a continual process, nurtured by experiences, reflections, and an ever-growing relationship with Christ.

Spiritual maturity isn't about age or knowledge; it's about how we apply our faith in daily life. It involves growing in grace and knowledge of Jesus Christ, as stated in 2 Peter 3:18. This growth is a lifelong journey, marked by increasing Christlikeness in character and actions. Ephesians 4:11-16 describes the church's role in this process, equipping believers for service and building up the body of Christ. As we engage with God's Word, participate in community, and practice spiritual disciplines, we develop attributes like love, patience, humility, and self-control. Spiritual maturity also involves discernment, understanding deeper truths of the faith, and applying them in complex life situations.

Prayer Point:

Father, guide me in growing more like Christ each day. Help me to deepen my understanding and application of Your teachings. Strengthen me in my journey of spiritual maturity, surrounded by Your grace.

Thursday March 21

Topic: The Role of the Church in a Believer's Life

Memory Verse: "And let us consider how we may spur one another on toward love and good deeds, not giving up meeting together, as some are in the habit of doing, but encouraging one another—and all the more as you see the Day approaching." - Hebrews 10:24-25

Bible Reading: 1 Corinthians 12:12-27

Read & Learn:

In the early church, as described in Acts 2:42-47, believers devoted themselves to the apostles' teaching, fellowship, breaking of bread, and prayer. They shared everything they had, sold property and possessions to give to anyone in need, and met together in the temple courts and homes. This story illustrates the church's role as a community of support, learning, worship, and service. The early Christians' commitment to one another and their collective mission provides a powerful example of how the church should function in a believer's life.

The church is not just a building or a weekly service; it's a community of believers united in Christ. According to 1 Corinthians 12:12-27, the church is like a body with many parts, each with a unique role but all essential. The church offers a place for spiritual growth through teaching, fellowship, and worship. It's where believers are equipped for service (Ephesians 4:11-12), held accountable, and encouraged in their faith journey. The church also serves as a beacon of God's love and truth in the world, engaging in outreach and missions. Involvement in a local church helps believers grow in their faith, discover and use their spiritual gifts, and experience the joy of community and shared purpose.

Prayer Point:

Father, help me to value and engage with my church community. Use the church to grow and strengthen my faith. Let Your love and truth shine through our church to the world.

Friday March 22

Topic: Finding Peace in God's Presence

Memory Verse: "You will keep in perfect peace those whose minds are steadfast, because they trust in you." - Isaiah 26:3

Bible Reading: Philippians 4:6-7

Read & Learn:

Consider the story of Mary and Martha in Luke 10:38-42. Martha was anxious and troubled about many things while preparing her home for Jesus. In contrast, her sister Mary chose to sit at Jesus' feet, listening to His teaching. Jesus commended Mary for choosing what was better. This story illustrates the peace found in prioritising God's presence over life's distractions and worries. Mary's choice to focus on Jesus brought her a sense of peace and fulfilment that Martha missed in her busyness.

Finding peace in God's presence is a profound aspect of the Christian faith. In a world filled with chaos and uncertainty, God offers a peace that transcends understanding (Philippians 4:7). This peace comes from trusting in God's sovereignty and goodness, spending time in prayer, and immersing oneself in His Word. It's not about the absence of trouble but about the presence of God amidst life's storms. As believers draw near to God, they experience His calming presence, which guards their hearts and minds. This peace is a gift from God, available to all who seek Him earnestly and prioritise their relationship with Him.

Prayer Point:

Father, help me to focus on You amidst life's distractions and anxieties. Guide me to trust in You for a peace that surpasses understanding.

Saturday March 23

Topic: Exploring Biblical Prophecy and End Times

Memory Verse: "Look, I am coming soon! Blessed is the one who keeps the words of the prophecy written in this scroll." - **Revelation 22:7**

Bible Reading: Matthew 24:3-14

Read & Learn:

Consider the life of Daniel, a prophet who lived in a time of great upheaval and change. In Daniel 9:24-27, he received a vision about the future, including the coming of the Messiah and the end times. Despite the challenges of living in exile and facing opposition, Daniel remained faithful to God, seeking understanding through prayer and scripture. His story reminds us that in all times, especially in periods of uncertainty and change, our focus should be on faithfulness to God, who holds the future.

Biblical prophecy and the study of end times, known as eschatology, offer both a challenge and an opportunity for believers. These prophecies, found in books like Daniel and Revelation, provide insights into God's plan for the world's future. While interpretations vary, the central theme is the return of Christ and the establishment of God's kingdom. Exploring these prophecies encourages believers to live with hope, vigilance, and a sense of urgency, knowing that Christ's return could be imminent. It also reminds us of the importance of sharing the Gospel, as the end times will be a period of both great turmoil and great opportunity for salvation.

Prayer Point:

Father, help me understand Your prophetic Word and live in readiness for Your return. Give me wisdom to discern the signs of the times and remain faithful. Use me to share the hope of Your coming kingdom with others.

Sunday March 24

Topic: Christian Stewardship and Generosity

Memory Verse: "Each of you should give what you have decided in your heart to give, not reluctantly or under compulsion, for God loves a cheerful giver." - **2 Corinthians 9:7**

Bible Reading: Luke 12:13-21

Read & Learn:

Reflect on the story of George Müller, a Christian evangelist and the director of the Ashley Down orphanage in Bristol, England, in the 19th century. Müller never made requests for financial support, nor did he go into debt, yet he managed to care for over 10,000 orphans during his lifetime. He relied solely on God's provision through prayer. His life exemplified extraordinary faith and generosity, showing how God faithfully provides for those who commit to stewardship and rely on Him for their needs.

Christian stewardship and generosity are fundamental aspects of the Christian life. Stewardship involves recognising that everything we have is a gift from God and should be used wisely for His glory. This includes our time, talents, and treasures. Generosity, as taught in the Bible, is not just about giving to the church or the needy, but it is an attitude of the heart. It reflects our trust in God's provision and our commitment to serving Him and others. By practicing stewardship and generosity, we become more like Christ, who gave everything for us, and we demonstrate the love of God to the world.

Prayer Point:

Father, help me to be a good steward of the resources You have entrusted to me. Cultivate in me a generous heart that reflects Your love and generosity. Guide me to use my time, talents, and treasures for Your glory and the benefit of others.

Monday March 25

Topic: Trusting God to Supply Your Needs

Memory Verse: "And my God will meet all your needs according to the riches of his glory in Christ Jesus." **- Philippians 4:19**

Bible Reading: Matthew 6:25-34

Read & Learn:

In the passage from Matthew, Jesus teaches His disciples not to worry about their basic needs such as food and clothing. He uses examples from nature, like the birds and the flowers, to illustrate God's care and provision. Just as God provides for the birds and adorns the flowers with beauty, He will also supply the needs of His children. This teaching highlights the importance of trusting in God's faithfulness and prioritising the pursuit of His kingdom and righteousness above earthly concerns. It's a reminder that God knows our needs and invites us to cast our anxieties upon Him.

Trusting God to supply our needs is a fundamental aspect of our faith journey. The Bible assures us that our Heavenly Father knows what we need even before we ask Him (Matthew 6:8). When we worry excessively about our material needs, we risk losing sight of God's sovereignty and provision. Jesus encourages us to shift our focus from worldly anxieties to seeking His kingdom and righteousness. As we prioritise our relationship with God and align our lives with His will, we can trust that He will faithfully provide for our needs, just as He cares for the birds and the flowers.

Prayer Point:

Father, thank You for being our loving and caring Heavenly Father. Help us to trust in Your faithful provision for our needs.

Tuesday March 26

Topic: The Significance of Jesus' Teachings

Memory Verse: "Heaven and earth will pass away, but my words will never pass away." **- Matthew 24:35**

Bible Reading: Matthew 5:1-12

Read & Learn:

Reflect on the story of Zacchaeus, the tax collector, as told in Luke 19:1-10. Zacchaeus, a wealthy man despised by many for his profession and corruption, sought to see Jesus out of curiosity. Despite his social status and the crowd's disapproval, Jesus called out to him, inviting Himself to Zacchaeus' home. This encounter with Jesus and His teachings led to a profound transformation in Zacchaeus. He promised to give half of his possessions to the poor and repay anyone he had cheated four times over. This story illustrates the transformative power of Jesus' teachings and His focus on repentance, forgiveness, and social justice.

Jesus' teachings, encapsulated in the Gospels, are foundational to Christian ethics and spirituality. They challenge believers to live out principles of love, mercy, and humility. The Beatitudes, for instance, overturn conventional wisdom, blessing the poor in spirit, the meek, and the peacemakers. Jesus' parables and sermons call for a radical reorientation of one's life towards God's kingdom values. Understanding and applying these teachings is vital for personal spiritual growth and for reflecting Christ's love in the world.

Prayer Point:

Father, help me to embrace and live out Your transformative words. Guide me to be humble and merciful as Jesus taught. Empower me to be a peacemaker and a light in the world, following Jesus' example.

Wednesday March 27

Topic: Learning from Biblical Heroes and Heroines

Memory Verse: "Now faith is confidence in what we hope for and assurance about what we do not see. This is what the ancients were commended for." **- Hebrews 11:1-2**

Bible Reading: Hebrews 11:1-12

Read & Learn:

Consider the story of Esther, a Jewish woman who became queen of Persia. Her bravery and faith are highlighted in the book of Esther. When a decree threatened the Jewish people, Esther, despite the risk to her own life, approached the king to plead for her people. Her courage and wisdom, underpinned by fasting and prayer, led to the deliverance of the Jews in Persia. Esther's story teaches us about the power of courage, faith, and strategic action in the face of adversity.

Biblical heroes and heroines, like Esther, demonstrate qualities that believers can aspire to emulate. Their stories, filled with faith, courage, and wisdom, offer practical lessons for our lives. For instance, David's trust in God against Goliath, Ruth's loyalty to Naomi, and Daniel's unwavering commitment to prayer in a hostile environment. These characters didn't rely on their strength but on their faith in God. Their stories encourage believers to trust in God's plan, remain steadfast in faith, and act with integrity and courage.

Prayer Point:

Father, inspire me with the courage and faith of Esther in challenging times. Help me to emulate Ruth's loyalty and kindness in my relationships. Grant me the boldness and trust of David in facing my giants.

Thursday March 28

Topic: The Power of Redemption and Grace

Memory Verse: "In him we have redemption through his blood, the forgiveness of sins, in accordance with the riches of God's grace."
                                          - Ephesians 1:7

Bible Reading: Ephesians 1:3-14

Read & Learn:

The story of the Prodigal Son in Luke 15:11-32 beautifully illustrates redemption and grace. A young man demands his inheritance, squanders it in reckless living, and finds himself in dire poverty. In his despair, he decides to return to his father, expecting to be treated as a servant. Instead, his father welcomes him with open arms, celebrating his return. This story mirrors our relationship with God. No matter how far we stray, God's grace is sufficient to redeem us, and His love is always waiting to embrace us when we return.

Redemption and grace are central themes in Christianity. Redemption refers to being freed from the bondage of sin through Jesus Christ's sacrifice. Grace is the unmerited favour we receive from God. Unlike earthly systems where we earn our way, God's grace is freely given, not because of our works but because of His love and mercy. This concept is transformative, offering hope and a new beginning to everyone, regardless of past mistakes. It encourages believers to live in the freedom of forgiveness and to extend the same grace to others.

Prayer Point:

Heavenly Father, thank You for Your grace and the redemption found in Jesus Christ. Help me to understand the depth of Your grace and to live in the freedom it brings. Guide me to extend Your grace and love to those around me.

Friday March 29

Topic: Reflecting on the Sacrifice of Good Friday

Memory Verse: "But he was pierced for our transgressions, he was crushed for our iniquities; the punishment that brought us peace was on him, and by his wounds we are healed." **- Isaiah 53:5**

Bible Reading: John 19:16-30

Read & Learn:

On Good Friday, we remember the crucifixion of Jesus Christ, a pivotal moment in Christian history. The story of Simon of Cyrene, who was compelled to carry Jesus' cross (Mark 15:21), invites reflection on the weight of what Christ endured for humanity. Simon's physical act of bearing the cross alongside Jesus symbolises the call for every believer to understand and share in the suffering of Christ. This act of sacrifice, where Jesus took upon Himself the sins of the world, demonstrates the depth of God's love and the extent of Jesus' obedience to the Father's will.

Good Friday is a solemn day of remembrance and gratitude for the ultimate sacrifice Jesus made on the cross. John 19:16-30 recounts the final moments of Jesus' life and His crucifixion, a fulfilment of prophecy and the cornerstone of Christian faith. Isaiah 53:5 prophesied this sacrifice, highlighting its purpose for our redemption. This day calls us to reflect on the gravity of our sin, the cost of our redemption, and the profound love and grace extended to us. It's a time to meditate on the meaning of sacrifice, forgiveness, and the hope that comes from Jesus' victory over sin and death.

Prayer Point:

Lord Jesus, on this Good Friday, I reflect on Your sacrifice on the cross. Thank You for bearing my sins and offering me forgiveness and new life. Help me to grasp the depth of Your love and the magnitude of Your sacrifice, that I may live in gratitude and obedience.

Saturday March 30

Topic: Between Crucifixion and Resurrection

Memory Verse: "Don't be alarmed,' he said. 'You are looking for Jesus the Nazarene, who was crucified. He has risen! He is not here. See the place where they laid him.'" **- Mark 16:6**

Bible Reading: Matthew 27:45-66

Read & Learn:

The period between Jesus' crucifixion and resurrection is marked by darkness, despair, and uncertainty. It was a time when Jesus' followers mourned His death, and His enemies sought to prevent any possible deception regarding His resurrection. The earth quaked, rocks split, and even the dead were raised to life at the moment of Jesus' death on the cross. Amid this turmoil, the women who had followed Jesus, including Mary Magdalene and Mary the mother of James and Joseph, watched from a distance. Joseph of Arimathea, a rich man who had become a disciple of Jesus, boldly asked for Jesus' body and placed it in his own tomb. The chief priests and Pharisees, fearing Jesus' prediction of His resurrection, secured the tomb and posted guards.

This period serves as a reminder of the dark moments in life when hope seems lost. Just as the earth shook and the curtain in the temple tore, our lives can be shaken by unexpected events and challenges. But this period also teaches us that God's power is not limited by darkness or despair. Just as Jesus rose from the dead, bringing hope and victory, we too can find hope in the midst of our darkest moments. The guarded tomb could not contain the resurrected Jesus, and the challenges we face cannot thwart God's plans for our lives.

Prayer Point:

Heavenly Father, thank You for the victory and hope we have in the resurrection of Jesus Christ. Help me trust in Your power to bring hope in my darkest moments. Grant me the strength and faith for victory when I face uncertainty and despair.

Sunday March 31

Topic: Celebrating the Resurrection on Easter Sunday

Memory Verse: "He is not here; he has risen, just as he said. Come and see the place where he lay." **- Matthew 28:6**

Bible Reading: Luke 24:1-12

Read & Learn:

On the first Easter Sunday, Mary Magdalene and other women went to Jesus' tomb, only to find it empty. An angel told them that Jesus had risen, as He had promised. This incredible news was initially met with disbelief by the disciples until Jesus Himself appeared to them, transforming their sorrow into joy and their doubt into faith. This pivotal event in Christian history is not just a historical account; it's a reminder of the hope and new life that Jesus' resurrection brings to all who believe in Him. It signifies the victory over sin and death and the promise of eternal life.

Easter Sunday is a day of joy and celebration for Christians worldwide, commemorating Jesus Christ's resurrection from the dead. This event, as described in Luke 24:1-12, is the cornerstone of Christian faith, affirming Jesus as the Son of God and the fulfilment of God's salvation plan for humanity. The resurrection is a testament to God's power and a source of eternal hope for believers. It assures us of our own resurrection and eternal life in Christ. As we celebrate Easter, we are reminded of the transformative power of the resurrection in our lives, offering us a fresh start and a living hope.

Prayer Point:

Risen Lord, on this Easter Sunday, I celebrate your victory over death and the new life you offer to all who believe in You. Father, thank You for the gift of Your Son and the hope His resurrection brings. Help me to live each day in the light of your victory and love.

Monday April 01

Topic: Lessons from the Walk on the Road to Emmaus

Memory Verse: "They asked each other, 'Were not our hearts burning within us while he talked with us on the road and opened the Scriptures to us?'" **- Luke 24:32**

Bible Reading: Luke 24:13-35

Read & Learn:

The encounter on the road to Emmaus is a profound story of revelation and transformation. Two of Jesus' disciples, Cleopas and another, were disheartened after His crucifixion. As they walked to Emmaus, Jesus Himself appeared to them, though they did not recognise Him. He inquired about their conversation, and they explained the recent events. Jesus then revealed how all these events were in fulfilment of the Scriptures, opening their eyes to the truth. When they reached their destination and sat down to eat, Jesus took bread, blessed it, and broke it. At that moment, their eyes were opened, and they recognised Him. This encounter transformed their despair into joy and propelled them back to Jerusalem to share the news of Jesus' resurrection.

The walk to Emmaus teaches us several lessons. First, it emphasises the importance of recognising Jesus in our lives. Often, He is with us, even when we do not perceive His presence. Second, it underscores the significance of understanding Scripture as a means of recognising God's plan and purpose. Jesus explained the Scriptures to Cleopas and the other disciple, revealing how they pointed to Him. Third, the breaking of bread during the meal mirrors the significance of the Communion in Christian worship, where Jesus is present among His followers. Lastly, this story reminds us that our encounters with Jesus can transform our lives, turning sorrow into joy and despair into hope.

Prayer Point:
Father, open my eyes to recognise Your presence in my life. Help me understand and apply the teachings of Scripture to my daily walk.

Tuesday April 02

Topic: Walking in Obedience to God's Word

Memory Verse: "But be doers of the word, and not hearers only, deceiving yourselves." - **James 1:22**

Bible Reading: Psalm 119:1-15

Read & Learn:

Consider the story of Jonah. God commanded Jonah to go to Nineveh, but Jonah fled in the opposite direction. His disobedience led to dire consequences, including being swallowed by a great fish. After three days, Jonah repented and obeyed God, leading to the salvation of Nineveh. This story illustrates the importance of obedience to God's Word. Disobedience can lead us away from God's best for our lives, but obedience, even after failure, can bring about God's redemptive plans.

Obedience to God's Word is a fundamental aspect of Christian living. It's not just about hearing or reading the Bible; it's about applying its teachings to our daily lives. Obedience demonstrates our faith and trust in God. It often requires courage and faith, especially when God's instructions seem challenging or counterintuitive. However, walking in obedience brings blessings, aligns us with God's will, and transforms our lives. It's a journey of continual learning and growth, where we increasingly align our will with God's.

Prayer Point:

Father, help me to be a doer of Your Word, not just a hearer. Guide me daily to align my actions and decisions with Your Word. Give me the strength to walk in obedience, even when it's difficult.

Wednesday April 03

Topic: Balancing Faith, Work, and Family

Memory Verse: "But seek first his kingdom and his righteousness, and all these things will be given to you as well." **- Matthew 6:33**

Bible Reading: Colossians 3:23-24; Ephesians 5:22-33; 6:1-4

Read & Learn:

The story of Martha and Mary in Luke 10:38-42 offers a profound lesson on balance. Martha was busy with the necessary task of serving, while Mary chose to sit at Jesus' feet, listening to his teaching. Jesus commended Mary for choosing what was better. This story teaches us about the importance of prioritising our relationship with God amidst our daily tasks and responsibilities. It reminds us that while work and family duties are important, they should not overshadow our spiritual growth and devotion to God.

Balancing faith, work, and family is a challenge faced by many Christians. It requires wisdom, discernment, and often, tough choices. Prioritising our relationship with God is crucial, as it is the foundation upon which other aspects of our lives should be built. Our work should be done as unto the Lord, with integrity and diligence. Family, a precious gift from God, should be nurtured with love and care. However, none of these should replace our personal time with God. Striking this balance is not about dividing our time equally but about integrating our faith into every aspect of our lives.

Prayer Point:

Father, Father, help me to prioritise my relationship with You above all else. Grant me wisdom to integrate my faith into every aspect of my daily life. Guide me to balance my faith, work, and family life in a way that honours You.

Thursday April 04

Topic: Engaging in Effective Evangelism

Memory Verse: "Go therefore and make disciples of all nations, baptising them in the name of the Father and of the Son and of the Holy Spirit." **- Matthew 28:19**

Bible Reading: Acts 8:26-40

Read & Learn:

The story of Philip and the Ethiopian eunuch in Acts 8:26-40 is a powerful example of effective evangelism. Philip, led by the Holy Spirit, approached the Ethiopian who was reading the prophet Isaiah. Philip asked if he understood the passage, which opened a conversation about Jesus. The Ethiopian's heart was open, and he accepted Christ, requesting baptism right away. This story highlights the importance of being sensitive to the Holy Spirit's leading, being prepared to share the Gospel, and the readiness to act when an opportunity arises.

Effective evangelism is not just about speaking; it's about listening to the Holy Spirit and the people we engage with. It requires a balance of boldness and sensitivity, knowing when to speak and when to listen. Evangelism is not a one-size-fits-all approach; it varies from person to person. It's about building relationships, understanding where people are in their spiritual journey, and gently guiding them towards the truth of the Gospel. It's also about living a life that reflects Christ, as our actions often speak louder than our words.

Prayer Point:
Father, let my life reflect Your love and truth, drawing others to You. Guide me to effectively share the Gospel with sensitivity and boldness. Lead me to those who are seeking, and give me the right words to say.

Friday April 05

Topic: Cultivating a Heart of Worship

Memory Verse: "God is spirit, and his worshipers must worship in the Spirit and in truth." - **John 4:24**

Bible Reading: Psalm 95:1-7

Read & Learn:

Consider the story of King David bringing the Ark of the Covenant to Jerusalem in 2 Samuel 6. David danced before the Lord with all his might, wearing a linen ephod. His wife Michal despised him for his undignified display. David's response was that it was before the Lord, who chose him over her father, and he would celebrate before the Lord. This story illustrates a heart of worship that is not concerned with human dignity or opinion but is focused on genuine, heartfelt praise and honour to God.

Cultivating a heart of worship involves more than just singing songs; it's about living a life that honours God in every aspect. Worship is an expression of our love and reverence for God, reflecting our gratitude and awe. It's a personal, intimate relationship with the Creator, where we acknowledge His sovereignty and goodness. True worship comes from a heart that seeks God above all else, desires to please Him, and is grateful for His blessings and grace. It's about surrendering our lives to God and living in a way that glorifies Him.

Prayer Point:

Father, create in me a heart that seeks to honour You in all aspects of my life. Let my daily actions be an expression of my worship and love for You.

Saturday April 06

Topic: Understanding God's Sovereignty and Plan

Memory Verse: "For I know the plans I have for you," declares the Lord, "plans to prosper you and not to harm you, plans to give you hope and a future." - **Jeremiah 29:11**

Bible Reading: Romans 8:28-39

Read & Learn:

Reflect on the story of Joseph in Genesis 37-50. Sold into slavery by his brothers, falsely accused, and imprisoned, Joseph faced tremendous hardship. Yet, he remained faithful to God. Eventually, he rose to become the second most powerful man in Egypt and saved many from famine, including his own family. Joseph's story is a powerful testament to God's sovereignty and plan. Despite the evil intentions of others, God used Joseph's circumstances for good, preserving a nation and demonstrating His faithfulness and sovereignty.

Understanding God's sovereignty and plan is to recognise that God is in control of all things and has a purpose for our lives. This belief doesn't mean that life will be free from hardship, but it does mean that even in difficult times, God is working for our good. His plans are not always immediately clear, and His ways are higher than ours. Trusting in God's sovereignty means having faith that He is working behind the scenes, orchestrating events for the ultimate benefit of His people and the glory of His name.

Prayer Point:

Lord, Father, guide me to find peace in Your purpose for my life. Strengthen my faith to see Your hand at work in all circumstances. Help me trust in Your sovereignty and plan, even when I don't understand.

Sunday April 07

Topic: The Role of Discipleship in Christian Growth

Memory Verse: "Therefore go and make disciples of all nations, baptising them in the name of the Father and of the Son and of the Holy Spirit." **- Matthew 28:19**

Bible Reading: 2 Timothy 2:1-2, 15

Read & Learn:

Consider the relationship between Paul and Timothy in the New Testament. Timothy, a young believer, was mentored by Paul, an experienced apostle. Paul's letters to Timothy are filled with guidance, encouragement, and instruction in faith and ministry. This mentorship illustrates the essence of discipleship – experienced believers guiding newer ones, fostering spiritual growth and maturity. Through Paul's discipleship, Timothy grew into a capable leader in the early church, demonstrating the transformative power of discipleship in Christian growth.

Discipleship is a vital aspect of Christian growth. It involves a more mature believer guiding a less experienced one, much like a mentorship. This relationship is rooted in learning and living out the teachings of Jesus Christ. Discipleship is not just about acquiring knowledge but about transformation – changing how we live, think, and interact with others. It's a journey of becoming more like Christ. Through discipleship, believers are equipped to face life's challenges, grow in their faith, and learn to disciple others, creating a multiplying effect in the Christian community.

Prayer Point:

Father, help me to grow in wisdom and understanding through discipleship. Use me to mentor others in their faith journey, just as You have guided me.

Monday April 08

Topic: Confronting Social and Ethical Issues with a Biblical Perspective

Memory Verse: "Do not conform to the pattern of this world, but be transformed by the renewing of your mind. Then you will be able to test and approve what God's will is - his good, pleasing and perfect will."

- Romans 12:2

Bible Reading: Micah 6:8, James 1:27, Matthew 5:13-16

Read & Learn:

In the early church, as recorded in Acts 6:1-7, a significant social issue arose: a group of widows was being overlooked in the daily distribution of food. The apostles responded not by ignoring the problem but by addressing it head-on. They appointed seven men of good repute to ensure equitable distribution. This story illustrates how the early church confronted a social issue with fairness and integrity, guided by biblical principles. It's a powerful example of how Christians can and should actively engage in resolving social and ethical issues in their communities.

As Christians, we are called to confront social and ethical issues not with the world's wisdom but through a biblical lens. This means seeking God's perspective on justice, mercy, and humility, as outlined in Micah 6:8. It involves being 'salt and light' in the world, as Jesus taught in Matthew 5:13-16. By doing so, we can offer solutions that reflect God's heart for justice and compassion. This approach requires discernment, prayer, and a deep understanding of Scripture, as well as a willingness to act justly, love mercy, and walk humbly with our God.

Prayer Point:

Father, grant me wisdom and courage to confront social and ethical issues with Your truth and love. Help me to be salt and light in this world, reflecting Your justice and mercy.

Tuesday April 09

Topic: The Importance of Biblical Knowledge and Study

Memory Verse: "All Scripture is God-breathed and is useful for teaching, rebuking, correcting and training in righteousness." - **2 Timothy 3:16**

Bible Reading: Psalm 119:9-18

Read & Learn:

The Bereans, mentioned in Acts 17:10-12, set an exemplary standard in biblical study. When Paul and Silas preached to them, they received the message with great eagerness but also examined the Scriptures daily to see if what was said was true. This diligence in studying God's Word not only affirmed the truth of the Gospel but also strengthened their faith. Their approach demonstrates the importance of not just accepting teachings at face value but diligently studying the Bible to understand and apply God's truth in our lives.

Biblical knowledge and study are crucial for every believer. It's through the study of God's Word that we gain insight into His character, understand His will, and learn how to live righteously. Psalm 119 highlights the value of meditating on God's laws and decrees. Studying the Bible isn't just an intellectual exercise; it's a spiritual discipline that shapes our thoughts, attitudes, and actions. It equips us to discern truth from falsehood and to grow in spiritual maturity. As we immerse ourselves in Scripture, we are transformed by the renewing of our minds, becoming more like Christ in our thoughts and deeds.

Prayer Point:

Father, give me a heart that seeks wisdom and knowledge in the Scriptures. Help me to apply Your teachings in my daily life, that I may grow in understanding and wisdom and maturity

Wednesday April 10

Topic: Experiencing God in Everyday Life

Memory Verse: "Be still, and know that I am God." - **Psalm 46:10**

Bible Reading: James 4:7-10

Read & Learn:

Consider the story of Brother Lawrence, a 17th-century monk known for his practice of the presence of God. In his simple life as a kitchen helper, he found deep communion with God amidst mundane tasks. He didn't reserve his spiritual life for church or prayer times alone; instead, he cultivated a continuous conversation with God, finding His presence in every moment and task. This humble approach transformed ordinary activities into acts of worship and fellowship with God, demonstrating that experiencing God isn't confined to religious settings but is accessible in the simplicity of everyday life.

Experiencing God in everyday life is about recognising His presence in all aspects of our lives. It's not just about feeling His presence during worship or prayer but also about acknowledging Him in our daily routines. James 4 encourages us to draw near to God, and He will draw near to us. This promise implies an ongoing relationship that permeates our everyday activities. Whether we're at work, with family, or doing chores, we can practice the presence of God. By being mindful of His love, guidance, and sovereignty in every situation, we can experience a deeper, more intimate relationship with Him.

Prayer Point:

Father, guide me to be still and know You more deeply in my everyday life. Help me to recognise Your presence in every moment of my day. Teach me to find You in the ordinary and to turn my daily tasks into worship.

Thursday April 11

Topic: My Lot Is Secured

Memory Verse: "Lord, you alone are my portion and my cup; you make my lot secure. The boundary lines have fallen for me in pleasant places; surely I have a delightful inheritance." - **Psalm 16:5-6**

Bible Reading: Psalm 16:1-11

Read & Learn:

The story of Joseph in the book of Genesis is a powerful illustration of how God secures the lot of His children. Despite facing numerous challenges, including betrayal and imprisonment, Joseph held onto his faith in God. Ultimately, God elevated Joseph to a position of great authority in Egypt, where he played a crucial role in saving his family and many others from famine. Joseph's story reminds us that even in the most challenging circumstances, God is at work securing our lot and guiding us toward His divine purpose. Our trust in Him is the key to finding security and purpose in our lives.

The psalmist in Psalm 16 expresses confidence and security in God as the source of their portion and inheritance. This assurance is rooted in the understanding that God is the ultimate provider and protector. As Christians, we can take comfort in knowing that our lot is secured by the Lord. Our inheritance is not just in this world, but it extends into eternity. We are encouraged to keep our eyes on the Lord, seek His counsel, and trust in His guidance. In doing so, we find security, joy, and purpose in Him, even in the face of life's challenges.

Prayer Point:

Father, thank you for being my security and my portion in life. Help me to trust in Your guidance and promises, knowing that my lot is secured by Your grace. Let my hearts find rest and joy in Your presence, recognising that my inheritance is in You.

Friday April 12

Topic: Embracing Humility and Servanthood

Memory Verse: "Do nothing out of selfish ambition or vain conceit. Rather, in humility value others above yourselves." - **Philippians 2:3**

Bible Reading: John 13:1-17

Read & Learn:

Consider the story of Mary, the sister of Lazarus, in John 12:1-8. Mary, in an act of profound humility and devotion, anoints Jesus' feet with expensive perfume and wipes them with her hair. This act, performed in a room full of guests, displayed her willingness to humble herself and honour Christ without regard for her own dignity or the cost of the perfume. Her actions were criticised by Judas, yet Jesus defended her, acknowledging her deep love and humility. Mary's story teaches us the essence of true servanthood and humility - to honour Christ selflessly and wholeheartedly.

Embracing humility and servanthood is a fundamental aspect of the Christian faith. It involves putting others' needs above our own and serving without expecting anything in return. Jesus exemplified this in John 13 when He washed His disciples' feet, a task reserved for servants. This act was not just about physical cleanliness but a demonstration of humility and love. As Christians, we're called to follow Jesus' example, serving others humbly and selflessly. This means being willing to perform even the most menial tasks and putting others' welfare above our pride or status.

Prayer Point:

Father, grant me a heart of humility to value and serve others as Jesus did. Teach me to embrace and demonstrate selfless service in my daily life, reflecting Your love.

Saturday April 13

Topic: The Impact of Faith on Mental Health

Memory Verse: "Do not be anxious about anything, but in every situation, by prayer and petition, with thanksgiving, present your requests to God." **- Philippians 4:6**

Bible Reading: Psalm 34:4-18

Read & Learn:

In the Bible, the story of Elijah in 1 Kings 19:4-15 offers a profound insight into mental health and faith. Elijah, after a significant victory, finds himself in despair and isolation, wishing for death. Yet, in this moment of vulnerability, God meets Elijah not in dramatic displays of power, but in a gentle whisper. This encounter illustrates how faith can provide solace and strength in times of mental anguish. It shows that God is attentive to our struggles and can bring peace and direction even when we feel most alone and overwhelmed.

Faith can play a crucial role in mental health by offering hope, purpose, and a sense of belonging. The Bible acknowledges the reality of mental struggles, as seen in the Psalms, where expressions of despair coexist with affirmations of God's presence and help. Prayer, meditation on Scripture, and involvement in a faith community can foster resilience and provide coping mechanisms. However, it's important to recognise that faith complements but does not replace professional mental health care. Seeking help from counsellors or therapists, alongside spiritual practices, can lead to a holistic approach to mental well-being.

Prayer Point:

Father, thank You for being my refuge and comfort in times of mental distress. In my anxious moments, help me to find peace and strength in You. Guide me to seek help when overwhelmed, both spiritually and professionally.

Sunday April 14

Topic: The Power of Christian Hope

Memory Verse: "May the God of hope fill you with all joy and peace as you trust in him, so that you may overflow with hope by the power of the Holy Spirit." - **Romans 15:13**

Bible Reading: Hebrews 11:1-12

Read & Learn:

The story of Abraham in Genesis is a powerful testament to the strength of Christian hope. Despite his advanced age, Abraham held onto God's promise that he would father a nation. His hope was not based on the visible or the probable, but on God's word. Even when everything seemed impossible, Abraham's faith did not waver. His story teaches us that Christian hope is not mere wishful thinking, but a confident expectation rooted in God's promises, and it can sustain us through the most challenging circumstances.

Christian hope is a fundamental aspect of the believer's life. It is not a passive waiting but an active and confident expectation in God's promises. This hope is grounded in the character of God and the truth of His word, not in our circumstances. It brings joy and peace, as stated in Romans 15:13, and empowers believers to endure trials and tribulations. Christian hope looks forward to the fulfilment of God's promises, the return of Christ, and the realisation of eternal life. It changes how we live, infusing our daily actions with purpose and direction, as we align ourselves with God's will.

Prayer Point:

Father, fill my heart with the joy and peace of Your hope. Let Your hope guide my actions and decisions, aligning them with Your will. Strengthen my faith to trust in Your promises, even when circumstances challenge my hope.

Monday April 15

Topic: Living a Life of Integrity and Honesty

Memory Verse: "The integrity of the upright guides them, but the unfaithful are destroyed by their duplicity." **- Proverbs 11:3**

Bible Reading: Psalm 15:1-5

Read & Learn:

The story of Daniel in the Bible exemplifies a life of integrity and honesty. Despite being in a foreign land and under immense pressure to conform to the ways of the Babylonian empire, Daniel remained steadfast in his commitment to God. He refused to compromise his beliefs, even when it meant facing the lion's den. His unwavering integrity not only preserved his life but also brought glory to God. Daniel's story teaches us that living a life of integrity may not be the easiest path, but it is always the most rewarding and honourable one.

Integrity and honesty are foundational Christian virtues that reflect the character of God. Living a life of integrity means aligning our actions with our beliefs and values, even when it's challenging. It involves being truthful, keeping our promises, and living consistently, both in public and in private. Honesty is not just about telling the truth but also about living truthfully. This lifestyle earns us respect, builds trust in our relationships, and provides a clear conscience before God. As Christians, our integrity and honesty are powerful testimonies of our faith and can influence others towards righteousness.

Prayer Point:

Father, guide me in Your ways, that my life may be a reflection of Your righteousness. Help me to live a life of integrity, aligning my actions with Your truth. Grant me the courage to be honest in all my dealings and relationships.

Tuesday April 16

Topic: Understanding the Holy Spirit's Role

Memory Verse: "But the Helper, the Holy Spirit, whom the Father will send in my name, he will teach you all things and bring to your remembrance all that I have said to you." - **John 14:26**

Bible Reading: Romans 8:26-27; Galatians 5:22-25

Read & Learn:

In the book of Acts, the story of the early church vividly illustrates the Holy Spirit's transformative role. On the day of Pentecost, the disciples, once fearful and uncertain, were filled with the Holy Spirit. This divine empowerment led them to preach boldly, perform miracles, and spread the Gospel fearlessly across nations. The Holy Spirit's presence brought unity, wisdom, and spiritual gifts to the early believers, enabling them to establish a thriving, dynamic Christian community. This account reminds us that the Holy Spirit is not just a distant force but an active, guiding presence in the life of every believer.

The Holy Spirit plays a crucial role in the Christian life. As our Helper, He guides us into all truth, providing wisdom and understanding of God's Word. He convicts us of sin, leads us in righteousness, and empowers us for service. The Holy Spirit also intercedes for us, praying in ways we cannot express. He produces the fruit of the Spirit in our lives, such as love, joy, peace, patience, kindness, goodness, faithfulness, gentleness, and self-control, transforming us to reflect Christ's character. Understanding and cooperating with the Holy Spirit's work is essential for spiritual growth and effective Christian living.

Prayer Point:

Father, thank You for the gift of the Holy Spirit, my Helper and Guide. let the Holy Spirit guide me in truth and wisdom to produce in me the fruits of righteousness and love.

Wednesday April 17

Topic: The Blessings of Obedience to God

Memory Verse: "Blessed are all who fear the Lord, who walk in obedience to him." **- Psalm 128:1**

Bible Reading: Deuteronomy 28:1-14

Read & Learn:

The biblical account of Daniel showcases the blessings of obedience. Despite being in exile and under a foreign king's rule, Daniel remained steadfast in his obedience to God. He refused to compromise his faith, even when faced with the lion's den. His unwavering obedience not only protected him miraculously but also led to the glorification of God among the Babylonians. Daniel's life exemplifies how obedience to God can lead to divine protection, favour, and the opportunity to be a powerful witness for God's glory, even in challenging circumstances.

Obedience to God is not merely about following rules; it's about aligning our lives with His will and purpose. It brings numerous blessings, including peace, joy, and spiritual prosperity. When we obey God, we open ourselves to His guidance and provision. Obedience also leads to spiritual growth, as we learn to trust God more deeply. It fosters a closer relationship with Him, as we align our hearts and actions with His desires. Furthermore, obedience serves as a testimony to others, demonstrating the transformative power of a life surrendered to God.

Prayer Point:

Father, give me the strength to walk in obedience to Your word, even in challenging situations. Thank You for the peace and joy that come from living in obedience to Your will.

Thursday April 18

Topic: Exploring the Parables of Jesus

Memory Verse: "He who has ears to hear, let him hear."
                                        - Matthew 11:15

Bible Reading: Luke 15:1-7

Read & Learn:

One of the most profound parables Jesus told is the Parable of the Prodigal Son in Luke 15:11-32. This story illustrates God's unconditional love and forgiveness. A young man demands his inheritance, squanders it, and returns home in shame, expecting punishment. Instead, his father welcomes him with open arms, celebrating his return. This parable beautifully depicts how God receives us when we repent, regardless of our past. It's a story of grace, redemption, and the joy in heaven over one sinner who repents.

Jesus' parables are rich in meaning and spiritual insight. They use everyday scenarios to convey deep spiritual truths, making them accessible and relatable. Parables like the Lost Sheep, the Good Samaritan, and the Mustard Seed teach about God's kingdom, love, and faith. They challenge us to reflect on our values and actions, encouraging a deeper understanding of God's nature and our relationship with Him. These stories invite us to ponder, question, and grow in our faith, revealing new layers of wisdom with each reading.

Prayer Point:

Father, thank You for revealing Your love and wisdom through parables. Help me to open my ears and heart to hear, learn, understand and apply the lessons from the parables in my life.

Friday April 19

Topic: Cultivating Patience and Perseverance

Memory Verse: "But if we hope for what we do not see, we wait for it with patience." - **Romans 8:25**

Bible Reading: James 1:2-4, 12

Read & Learn:

The Bible story of Joseph, found in Genesis 37-50, is a powerful example of patience and perseverance. Sold into slavery by his brothers, falsely accused, and imprisoned, Joseph faced tremendous trials. Yet, he remained faithful to God, interpreting dreams in prison, which eventually led to his rise to power in Egypt. His patience and trust in God's plan were rewarded when he was reunited with his family and able to save them from famine. Joseph's story teaches us that even in our darkest moments, patience and faith can lead to incredible outcomes.

Patience and perseverance are vital Christian virtues, often developed through trials and tribulations. They are not passive resignation but active trust in God's timing and faithfulness. As James 1:2-4 teaches, trials test our faith, producing steadfastness. This steadfastness leads to spiritual maturity and completeness. Patience is not simply waiting; it's maintaining faith and hope in God's promises, even when the fulfilment of those promises isn't immediately visible. Perseverance is the courage to continue, despite difficulties, trusting that God is working for our good in all things.

Prayer Point:

Father, strengthen my faith, so I may patiently endure, trust Your timing and persevere through life's challenges. Help me to see trials as opportunities to grow in steadfastness and maturity.

Saturday April 20

Topic: The Importance of Rest and Sabbath

Memory Verse: "Remember the Sabbath day, to keep it holy."

- Exodus 20:8

Bible Reading: Genesis 2:2-3; Exodus 20:8-11

Read & Learn:

In 1 Kings 19, we find the prophet Elijah exhausted and fearful, fleeing from Queen Jezebel's threats. He reaches a point of utter despair, yet it is in this moment of vulnerability that God meets him. Instead of immediate action, God first provides Elijah with rest and sustenance. This story illustrates the importance of rest in our spiritual and physical lives. It shows that even in times of crisis, taking time to rest is not only necessary but divinely endorsed.

The concept of Sabbath and rest is deeply rooted in the Bible, emphasising the need for physical, mental, and spiritual rejuvenation. In Genesis, God rested on the seventh day, setting a precedent for humanity. The Sabbath is a time to step back from work and daily concerns, to refocus on God and spiritual matters. It's a reminder of God's sovereignty and our need to depend on Him. In Mark 2:27, Jesus emphasises that the Sabbath was made for man's benefit, not as a burden. Observing the Sabbath and finding time for rest is crucial for a balanced, God-centred life.

Prayer Point:

Father, teach me to balance my life with periods of work and rest, as You designed. In my busiest moments, remind me of the importance of rest for my body and soul. Help me to find true find rest in You

Sunday April 21

Topic: Dealing with Doubt and Unbelief

Memory Verse: "Immediately the boy's father exclaimed, 'I do believe; help me overcome my unbelief!'" **- Mark 9:24**

Bible Reading: Mark 9:17-29; James 1:5-8; Jude 1:22

Read & Learn:

The story of Thomas, often called "Doubting Thomas," in John 20:24-29, is a powerful example of dealing with doubt. After Jesus' resurrection, Thomas refused to believe without physical proof. When Jesus appeared and invited Thomas to touch His wounds, Thomas' doubt turned to faith, and he exclaimed, "My Lord and my God!" This story teaches us that it's normal to experience doubt, but it also highlights the importance of seeking truth and allowing Jesus to reveal Himself to us in our doubts.

Doubt and unbelief are common experiences in the Christian journey. They can stem from personal struggles, intellectual questions, or emotional turmoil. The Bible doesn't condemn doubt but encourages believers to seek answers and strengthen their faith. In James 1:5-8, we are reminded to ask God for wisdom when we face doubts. God is patient and understanding, willing to guide us through our uncertainties. Jude 1:22 encourages us to show mercy to those who doubt, reminding us that doubt can be a pathway to deeper faith and understanding. Embracing our doubts and seeking God's guidance can lead to a more robust and authentic faith.

Prayer Point:

Father, strengthen my faith and help me overcome my unbelief. In moments of doubt, help me to seek Your truth and wisdom. Guide me to be understanding and supportive of others who face doubts.

Monday April 22

Topic: The Joy of Salvation

Memory Verse: "Restore to me the joy of your salvation and grant me a willing spirit, to sustain me." - **Psalm 51:12**

Bible Reading: Romans 5:1-11

Read & Learn:

Consider the story of Zacchaeus in Luke 19:1-10. Zacchaeus, a wealthy tax collector, was despised by many. Yet, his encounter with Jesus transformed him. Overwhelmed by Jesus' acceptance and love, Zacchaeus joyfully repented and promised to make amends for his wrongs. This story illustrates the profound joy and transformation that comes with salvation. It's a joy that changes hearts and lives, leading to a new way of living that reflects the love and grace received.

The joy of salvation is a deep, abiding sense of peace and happiness that comes from knowing we are saved by grace through faith in Jesus Christ. This joy transcends circumstances and is rooted in the assurance of God's love and forgiveness. Psalm 51 shows us David's earnest plea for restoration of this joy following his own failings. Romans 5:1-11 speaks of the peace and joy we have in our relationship with God through Jesus Christ. 1 Peter 1:8-9 describes this joy as "inexpressible and glorious," a result of believing in and loving Jesus, even though we have not seen Him. This joy is a gift from God, sustaining believers through trials and renewing their spirit.

Prayer Point:

Father, thank You for the joy of salvation. Let the joy of Your salvation be evident in my life, transforming me from the inside out and help me to spread this joy to others.

Tuesday April 23

Topic: Biblical Perspectives on Money and Wealth

Memory Verse: "For the love of money is a root of all kinds of evil. Some people, eager for money, have wandered from the faith and pierced themselves with many griefs." - **1 Timothy 6:10**

Bible Reading: Matthew 6:19-24

Read & Learn:

The story of the rich young ruler in Mark 10:17-27 offers a profound lesson on money and wealth. This young man, who had great wealth, approached Jesus to ask about eternal life. Jesus, knowing his heart, challenged him to sell all he had and give to the poor. The young man went away sad, unable to part with his possessions. This story illustrates the danger of allowing wealth to become an idol, overshadowing our relationship with God and our willingness to follow Him fully.

The Bible offers balanced perspectives on money and wealth. It neither condemns wealth nor glorifies poverty but warns against the love of money (1 Timothy 6:10). Proverbs 11:28 teaches that those who trust in their wealth will fall, but the righteous will thrive like a green leaf, emphasising the importance of placing our trust in God, not in material wealth. Matthew 6:19-24 reminds us that we cannot serve both God and money, urging us to store up treasures in heaven. Finally, 1 Timothy 6:17-19 instructs the wealthy to be generous and willing to share, laying up treasures as a firm foundation for the coming age. These passages teach us that our attitude towards money should be one of stewardship, generosity, and a focus on eternal values.

Prayer Point:

Father, help me to use the resources you have given me wisely and generously. Guard my heart against the love of money and help me to seek your kingdom first. Grant me the wisdom to steward my wealth in a way that honours you.

Wednesday April 24

Topic: Fostering a Grateful Heart

Memory Verse: "Give thanks in all circumstances; for this is God's will for you in Christ Jesus." - **1 Thessalonians 5:18**

Bible Reading: Psalm 100:1-5

Read & Learn:

Consider the story of King David in 2 Samuel 6:12-15. When the Ark of the Covenant was brought to Jerusalem, David, the king of Israel, danced before the Lord with all his might, wearing a linen ephod. Despite his high status, David showed profound gratitude and humility before God. His actions were a public display of thanksgiving, celebrating God's presence and blessings. This story teaches us that gratitude is not dependent on our circumstances but is a heartfelt response to God's goodness and faithfulness.

Gratitude is a fundamental aspect of the Christian life. Psalm 100 encourages us to enter God's gates with thanksgiving and his courts with praise. This attitude of gratitude acknowledges God as the Creator and sustainer of all things. Colossians 3:15-17 teaches us to let the peace of Christ rule in our hearts and to be thankful. Gratitude should permeate our words and actions, as we do everything in the name of the Lord Jesus, giving thanks to God the Father. Philippians 4:6-7 reminds us to present our requests to God with thanksgiving, which leads to the peace of God guarding our hearts and minds. Cultivating a grateful heart helps us recognise God's hand in our lives, deepens our trust in Him, and enhances our witness to others.

Prayer Point:

Father, thank You for Your endless blessings. Teach me to express my thankfulness in all circumstances, as a witness of Your love and grace. In times of challenge and abundance, let my heart overflow with gratitude for Your faithfulness.

Thursday April 25

Topic: Confronting Temptation and Sin

Memory Verse: "No temptation has overtaken you except what is common to mankind. And God is faithful; he will not let you be tempted beyond what you can bear. But when you are tempted, he will also provide a way out so that you can endure it." **- 1 Corinthians 10:13**

Bible Reading: James 1:12-15; 1 Corinthians 10:12-13

Read & Learn:

Reflect on the temptation of Jesus in the wilderness (Matthew 4:1-11). After fasting for 40 days and nights, Jesus was hungry and vulnerable. Satan tempted Him three times, each time challenging His identity and mission. Jesus responded not with His own strength but with Scripture, demonstrating the power of God's Word in resisting temptation. This account teaches us that temptation is a part of the human experience, but through reliance on God's Word and truth, we can overcome it.

Temptation and sin are realities that every believer faces. James 1:12-15 explains that temptation comes from our own desires, which entice and drag us away. These desires, when acted upon, lead to sin, and sin, when it is fully grown, leads to death. However, 1 Corinthians 10:13 offers hope, reminding us that God is faithful and will not let us be tempted beyond what we can bear. He provides a way out so that we can endure. The story of Jesus' temptation shows us the importance of knowing and relying on God's Word to confront and overcome temptation. As believers, we are called to be vigilant, prayerful, and grounded in Scripture to resist sin and live righteously.

Prayer Point:

Father, thank You for providing a way out in every tempting situation. Guide me to recognise and resist the enticements of sin. In times of temptation, strengthen me to stand firm in Your truth.

Friday April 26

Topic: The Value of Christian Fellowship

Memory Verse: "And let us consider how we may spur one another on toward love and good deeds, not giving up meeting together, as some are in the habit of doing, but encouraging one another - and all the more as you see the Day approaching." - **Hebrews 10:24-25**

Bible Reading: Acts 2:42-47

Read & Learn:

Consider the early church described in Acts 2:42-47. The believers devoted themselves to the apostles' teaching, fellowship, breaking of bread, and prayer. They shared everything they had, sold property and possessions to give to anyone in need, and met together in the temple courts and homes. This fellowship was marked by awe, joy, and the favour of all people. Their unity and love for one another were profound expressions of their faith, leading to the Lord adding to their number daily those who were being saved. This story exemplifies the transformative power of Christian fellowship.

This kind of fellowship is essential for spiritual growth and encouragement. It provides a support system for believers to spur one another on toward love and good deeds (Hebrews 10:24-25). In fellowship, we find accountability, encouragement, and a place to exercise our spiritual gifts. It's in these relationships that we can confess our sins to one another and pray for each other, as instructed in James 5:16. Christian fellowship is a reflection of our unity in Christ and a testimony to the world of His love.

Prayer Point:

Father, thank You for the gift of Christian community. Help us to value and nurture the fellowship we have in You. Guide us to build each other up in love and good deeds and to honour You in our relationships.

Saturday April 27

Topic: Discovering God's Will and Purpose

Memory Verse: "For I know the plans I have for you," declares the Lord, "plans to prosper you and not to harm you, plans to give you hope and a future." - **Jeremiah 29:11**

Bible Reading: Romans 12:1-2

Read & Learn:

Consider the life of Esther in the Bible. A young Jewish woman, Esther, found herself in a position of influence as queen of Persia, not by her own design but as part of a greater plan orchestrated by God. When a decree threatened her people, Esther had to discern God's will. It was her uncle Mordecai who reminded her that perhaps she was in her royal position "for such a time as this" (Esther 4:14). Esther's story shows that discovering God's will often involves understanding how our unique position and circumstances can serve a greater purpose, especially in challenging times.

Discovering God's will and purpose in our lives is a journey of faith and trust. It involves seeking God through prayer, scripture, and the counsel of wise believers. Romans 12:1-2 encourages us to offer ourselves as living sacrifices and be transformed by the renewing of our minds, which helps in discerning God's good, pleasing, and perfect will. Proverbs 3:5-6 teaches us to trust in the Lord with all our heart and lean not on our own understanding, acknowledging Him in all our ways. Ephesians 2:10 reminds us that we are God's handiwork, created in Christ Jesus to do good works, which God prepared in advance for us to do. Understanding God's will is not about a one-time revelation but a continuous journey of obedience, trust, and stepping out in faith.

Prayer Point:

Father, guide me in understanding Your will and purpose for my life. Grant me the wisdom and courage to follow the path You have set for me. Help me to trust in Your plan, even when the way is not clear.

Sunday April 28

Topic: The Power of Christian Testimony

Memory Verse: "They triumphed over him by the blood of the Lamb and by the word of their testimony..." - **Revelation 12:11**

Bible Reading: Acts 22:1-15

Read & Learn:

Consider the Apostle Paul's transformation from Saul, a persecutor of Christians, to a devoted follower of Christ. In Acts 22, Paul recounts his dramatic encounter with Jesus on the road to Damascus. This experience radically changed his life, leading him to become one of the most influential figures in spreading the Gospel. Paul's testimony is powerful because it demonstrates a profound change of heart and life, showing that no one is beyond the reach of God's grace and redemption. His story continues to inspire and encourage believers worldwide, reminding us of the transformative power of a personal encounter with Christ.

Christian testimony is a powerful tool in sharing the Gospel and encouraging fellow believers. It's a personal account of how God has worked in an individual's life, showcasing His love, mercy, and transformative power. Testimonies can vary greatly, from dramatic conversions like Paul's to gradual journeys of faith. They serve as living evidence of God's presence and activity in the world. Sharing our testimonies helps to strengthen our faith and the faith of others, offering hope and encouragement. It's a way of glorifying God and acknowledging His work in our lives, as seen in Acts 22, where Paul's testimony becomes a pivotal moment in his ministry.

Prayer Point:

Father, thank You for the work You have done in my life, making my testimonies a powerful witness of Your love. Use my story to bring hope and encouragement to others. Help me to boldly share my testimonies to glorify Your name.

Monday April 29

Topic: The Significance of Baptism and Communion

Memory Verse: "Therefore go and make disciples of all nations, baptising them in the name of the Father and of the Son and of the Holy Spirit." - **Matthew 28:19**

Bible Reading: 1 Corinthians 11:23-26

Read & Learn:

In the early church, as described in Acts 2:41-42, new believers were baptised and devoted themselves to the apostles' teaching, fellowship, breaking of bread, and prayer. This practice demonstrated their commitment to Christ and the community of believers. Baptism symbolised their new life in Christ, while communion, the breaking of bread, was a continual reminder of Jesus' sacrifice and a testament to their unity in faith. These acts were not mere rituals but deeply spiritual practices that connected them with the death, burial, and resurrection of Jesus, and with each other as members of one body.

Baptism and Communion are two foundational sacraments in Christianity, each with profound spiritual significance. Baptism represents a believer's identification with Christ's death, burial, and resurrection, signifying the washing away of sins and the start of a new life in Christ. It's an outward expression of an inward faith, a public declaration of commitment to Jesus. Communion, or the Lord's Supper, is a commemoration of Jesus' sacrifice on the cross. It's a time for believers to remember Christ's body broken and blood shed for the forgiveness of sins. Both practices are not only individual acts of faith but also communal, strengthening the bond within the body of Christ.

Prayer Point:

Father, help us to understand and cherish the profound meanings of Baptism and Communion. As we partake in Communion, let us remember Your sacrifice with gratitude and reverence.

30. Tuesday April 30

Topic: The Role of Prophecy in the Church

Memory Verse: "Follow the way of love and eagerly desire gifts of the Spirit, especially prophecy." - **1 Corinthians 14:1**

Bible Reading: 1 Corinthians 14:1-5

Read & Learn:

In the early church, as recorded in Acts 11:27-30, prophets from Jerusalem visited the church in Antioch. One of them, Agabus, stood up and through the Spirit predicted a severe famine that would spread over the entire Roman world. This prophecy moved the disciples to provide help to the brothers and sisters living in Judea, demonstrating the practical and edifying role of prophecy in the church. It wasn't just about foretelling future events but also about encouraging and strengthening the faith of believers, guiding them in their actions and decisions in accordance with God's will.

Prophecy in the church serves as a vital spiritual gift, intended for edification, encouragement, and consolation of the congregation. It's not about predicting the future in a general sense but about conveying God's message to His people in a specific context. Prophecy can reveal the heart of God, offer guidance, and bring correction or comfort. It's a means through which the Holy Spirit speaks to the church, fostering unity, growth, and spiritual maturity. While prophecy is important, it must always align with Scripture and be approached with discernment and humility, ensuring that it uplifts and edifies the body of Christ.

Prayer Point:

Father, grant us discernment to understand and embrace the true purpose of prophecy in Your church. Guide Your church to approach prophecy with a heart aligned with Your Word and Your love.

Wednesday May 01

Topic: Finding Strength in Weakness

Memory Verse: "But he said to me, 'My grace is sufficient for you, for my power is made perfect in weakness.' Therefore I will boast all the more gladly about my weaknesses, so that Christ's power may rest on me." - **2 Corinthians 12:9**

Bible Reading: 2 Corinthians 12:7-10

Read & Learn:

The Bible tells the story of Gideon in Judges 6-7. Gideon perceived himself as weak, coming from the least clan in Manasseh and being the least in his family. Yet, God chose him to save Israel from the Midianites. With an intentionally reduced army, Gideon's weakness was highlighted, but it was through this weakness that God's strength was magnificently displayed. The victory was clearly not by human might or numbers but by God's power. Gideon's story teaches us that God often uses our weaknesses as a canvas to display His strength and glory.

The concept of finding strength in weakness is counterintuitive in a world that often values power and self-reliance. However, in the Christian faith, acknowledging our weaknesses is vital for spiritual growth. It is in our moments of vulnerability and insufficiency that we lean more into God's grace and power. When we are weak, we are more likely to depend on God, allowing His strength to work through us. This principle encourages believers not to despair in their limitations but to see them as opportunities for God to work powerfully in and through their lives, transforming weaknesses into platforms for His grace and power.

Prayer Point:

Father, help me to embrace my limitations as opportunities for Your power to shine through. Teach me to rely on Your strength in every area of my life where I feel weak. In my weaknesses, let Your strength be revealed and glorified.

Thursday May 02

Topic: Celebrating God's Creation and Stewardship

Memory Verse: "The earth is the Lord's, and everything in it, the world, and all who live in it." - **Psalm 24:1**

Bible Reading: Psalm 8:1-9

Read & Learn:

The story of Noah in Genesis 6-9 is a powerful testament to God's creation and the responsibility of stewardship. When the earth was filled with corruption, God chose Noah, a righteous man, to build an ark and save a remnant of His creation. Noah's task was not just to build an ark but to care for and preserve the various species of animals. This story illustrates the importance of respecting and protecting God's creation. It shows that humans are entrusted by God to be stewards of the earth, caring for and preserving it for future generations.

Celebrating God's creation involves recognising the beauty and intricacy of the world He has made. It is an acknowledgment of God's sovereignty over the earth and everything in it. As Christians, stewardship of the earth is a sacred responsibility. It means caring for the environment, using resources wisely, and preserving the natural world for future generations. This stewardship reflects our reverence for the Creator and our understanding of the interconnectedness of all life. By engaging in practices that honour and protect God's creation, believers demonstrate their gratitude for His gifts and their commitment to His command to "tend and keep" the garden of the world.

Prayer Point:

Father, thank you for the wonder of your creation. Help me to appreciate the beauty of Your creation and to care for it responsibly. Guide me to be a good steward of the earth and its resources.

Friday May 03

Topic: Understanding Biblical Justice and Mercy

Memory Verse: "He has shown you, O mortal, what is good. And what does the Lord require of you? To act justly and to love mercy and to walk humbly with your God." - **Micah 6:8**

Bible Reading: Micah 6:6-8; Matthew 23:23

Read & Learn:

The parable of the Good Samaritan in Luke 10:25-37 beautifully illustrates biblical justice and mercy. A man, beaten and left for dead, is ignored by those who should have helped. Yet, a Samaritan, viewed as an outsider and enemy, shows compassion and care. He goes beyond societal norms, offering not just immediate aid but also ensuring the man's continued care. This story challenges us to look beyond our prejudices and societal boundaries, embodying God's justice and mercy in our actions, especially towards those marginalised or in need.

Biblical justice and mercy are deeply intertwined concepts that reflect God's character. Justice in the Bible is about right relationships and ensuring everyone, especially the marginalised and oppressed, is treated fairly and with dignity. Mercy is compassion and kindness shown to someone whom it's within one's power to punish or harm. It's not merely feeling pity but actively working to alleviate suffering. As Christians, understanding and practicing these principles means advocating for the oppressed, forgiving others, and showing compassion. It's about creating a community where love, fairness, and kindness prevail, mirroring the kingdom of God.

Prayer Point:

Father, thank You for Your justice and mercy; guide me to reflect these in my daily life. Give me the courage to stand for justice, show mercy and walk humbly with You every day.

Saturday May 04

Topic: The Challenge of Christian Leadership

Memory Verse: "Do nothing out of selfish ambition or vain conceit. Rather, in humility value others above yourselves." **- Philippians 2:3**

Bible Reading: Philippians 2:1-11

Read & Learn:

In the early church, Stephen stands out as a remarkable leader. Chosen as one of the first deacons, he was full of faith and the Holy Spirit. His story, detailed in Acts 6-7, is a powerful example of leadership marked by humility, courage, and unwavering faith. Despite facing fierce opposition and false accusations, Stephen remained steadfast, using his position not for personal gain but to serve others and boldly proclaim the truth. His ultimate sacrifice, becoming the first Christian martyr, exemplifies the cost of true Christian leadership – a willingness to lay down one's life for the sake of Christ and His church.

Christian leadership is fundamentally different from worldly leadership. It's not about power or prestige but serving others and glorifying God. Philippians 2:1-11 encourages leaders to have the same mindset as Christ, who, despite being God, humbled Himself and served others to the point of death. Christian leaders are called to be servant leaders, prioritising the needs of others, leading with humility and love, and being examples of Christ-like character. This kind of leadership can be challenging, as it goes against the grain of worldly values, but it's essential for the growth and health of the Christian community.

Prayer Point:

Grant me the courage to lead with faith, integrity, humility and love, always putting others first. Teach me to follow Jesus' example in my leadership, serving selflessly.

Sunday May 05

Topic: Nurturing Faith in Family Life

Memory Verse: "Train up a child in the way he should go; even when he is old he will not depart from it." **- Proverbs 22:6**

Bible Reading: Deuteronomy 6:4-9

Read & Learn:

The story of Timothy in the New Testament is a beautiful example of faith nurtured within a family. Timothy was a young man with a sincere faith, which first lived in his grandmother Lois and his mother Eunice (2 Timothy 1:5). This legacy of faith, passed down through generations, highlights the impact of a family's spiritual influence. Timothy's knowledge of the Scriptures from an early age (2 Timothy 3:15) equipped him for a life of service and leadership in the early church. His story encourages families to prioritise faith and Scripture in their daily lives, shaping the next generation's spiritual journey.

Nurturing faith in family life is crucial for spiritual growth and continuity. Deuteronomy 6:4-9 emphasises the importance of teaching children about God's commands and discussing them in everyday life. This involves more than just formal instruction; it's about integrating faith into every aspect of family life – from mealtime conversations to bedtime prayers. It's about modelling a genuine relationship with God, showing grace, forgiveness, and love in action. Families play a vital role in laying a foundation of faith that can guide children throughout their lives, helping them to navigate life's challenges with biblical wisdom and strength.

Prayer Point:

Father, guide our family in Your ways and help us to nurture faith in our home. Bless our efforts to teach our children about Your love and Your Word. Strengthen our family bond through shared faith and love for You.

Monday May 06

Topic: Embracing Change with God's Guidance

Memory Verse: "Trust in the Lord with all your heart, and do not lean on your own understanding. In all your ways acknowledge him, and he will make straight your paths." **- Proverbs 3:5-6**

Bible Reading: Isaiah 43:18-19

Read & Learn:

Consider the story of Abraham in Genesis 12. God called Abraham to leave his homeland and go to a place he would later receive as an inheritance. Without knowing the destination, Abraham embraced this significant change, trusting in God's guidance. His journey was filled with uncertainty, yet his faith in God's promise remained steadfast. Abraham's story teaches us about the courage to embrace change, trusting that God's plans, though sometimes unknown, are always for our good and His glory.

Embracing change with God's guidance is a fundamental aspect of the Christian journey. Isaiah 43:18-19 encourages us to not dwell on the past but to look forward to the new things God is doing. Change, whether in our personal lives, careers, or spiritual walk, can be daunting. However, trusting in God's wisdom and guidance, as Proverbs 3:5-6 advises, provides us with the assurance that our paths will be directed rightly. God's guidance in times of change is not always about immediate clarity but often about learning to walk in faith, trusting in His character and promises.

Prayer Point:

Father, help me to acknowledge You in all my ways, knowing You will direct my paths. Give me the courage to step into the new paths You are leading me to. Help me to embrace change with faith, trusting in Your guidance.

Tuesday May 07

Topic: Understanding Christian Marriage Principles

Memory Verse: "Therefore a man shall leave his father and his mother and hold fast to his wife, and they shall become one flesh." **- Genesis 2:24**

Bible Reading: Ephesians 5:21-33

Read & Learn:

The story of Ruth and Boaz in the Book of Ruth offers profound insights into Christian marriage principles. Ruth, a Moabite widow, shows loyalty and devotion to her mother-in-law, Naomi, and later to Boaz, her kinsman redeemer. Boaz, in turn, displays integrity, respect, and protection towards Ruth. Their story is not just about romantic love but also about mutual respect, kindness, and fulfilling God's law. Their union, blessed by God, becomes part of the lineage of Jesus Christ. This story teaches us about the importance of faith, loyalty, and God's providence in Christian marriage.

Christian marriage is a sacred covenant that reflects Christ's relationship with the church. Ephesians 5:21-33 emphasises mutual submission, love, and respect. The husband is called to love his wife as Christ loved the church, sacrificially and unconditionally, while the wife is encouraged to respect and support her husband. This mutual submission is not about power but about serving each other in love, just as Jesus served. Christian marriage principles are grounded in selflessness, commitment, and a deep understanding that marriage is not just a social contract but a spiritual covenant that mirrors God's unwavering love for His people.

Prayer Point:

Father, guide us to understand and live out Your principles in our marriages. Bless our unions with love, respect, and a deep commitment to each other. May our marriages reflect the love of Christ for the church, growing stronger each day.

Wednesday May 08

Topic: The Art of Biblical Meditation

Memory Verse: "This Book of the Law shall not depart from your mouth, but you shall meditate on it day and night, so that you may be careful to do according to all that is written in it. For then you will make your way prosperous, and then you will have good success." - **Joshua 1:8**

Bible Reading: Psalm 1:1-3

Read & Learn:

Consider the life of Daniel, a man of devout faith and commitment to God. In Daniel 6, despite the decree against prayer, Daniel continued his practice of praying and meditating on God's Word three times a day. His dedication to meditation and prayer, even in the face of potential death, demonstrates the power and importance of connecting with God through His Word. Daniel's unwavering commitment to biblical meditation not only sustained him in the lions' den but also made him a trusted advisor to kings. His story teaches us the transformative power of meditating on God's Word in all circumstances.

Biblical meditation is a spiritual discipline that involves pondering, studying, and applying God's Word in a reflective and contemplative manner. Unlike Eastern meditation, which often focuses on emptying the mind, biblical meditation is about filling the mind with Scripture and allowing the Holy Spirit to illuminate its truths. It's a process of deeply engaging with the Bible, not just reading it for information but for transformation. Psalm 1:1-3 highlights the blessings of delighting in and meditating on God's law. Through meditation, believers gain wisdom, strength, and guidance, leading to a fruitful and prosperous life in accordance with God's will.

Prayer Point:

Father, grant me the discipline and desire to continually meditate on Your Word, growing closer to You, finding wisdom and guidance. Let the truth of Your word sink deep into my heart as I reflect on Your teachings.

Thursday May 09

Topic: Witnessing to Non-Believers

Memory Verse: "But in your hearts honour Christ the Lord as holy, always being prepared to make a defence to anyone who asks you for a reason for the hope that is in you; yet do it with gentleness and respect."
- 1 Peter 3:15

Bible Reading: Acts 17:22-34

Read & Learn:

In Acts 17, Paul's approach to witnessing in Athens provides a powerful example. He observed their culture and beliefs, finding a point of connection through an altar inscribed "To an unknown god." Paul used this as a starting point to introduce the Athenians to the true God. He didn't dismiss their beliefs but respectfully built a bridge from their understanding to the truth of the Gospel. This story illustrates the importance of understanding and respecting the beliefs of others while confidently sharing the message of Christ.

Witnessing to non-believers is a vital aspect of the Christian faith. It involves sharing the Gospel message with those who do not yet know Christ. This task requires sensitivity, understanding, and a deep knowledge of the Bible. As seen in Acts 17, Paul's approach was to understand the cultural context of his audience and find common ground. Witnessing is not about winning arguments but about showing the love and truth of Christ. It requires patience, prayer, and a reliance on the Holy Spirit to guide our words and actions. Effective witnessing is grounded in a life that reflects Christ's love and grace.

Prayer Point:

Father, guide me to be an effective witness, living a life that reflects Your grace and love. Help me to understand and connect with those who do not know You, sharing Your love and truth.

Friday May 10

Topic: Lessons from Old Testament Prophets

Memory Verse: "For whatever was written in former days was written for our instruction, that through endurance and through the encouragement of the Scriptures we might have hope." - **Romans 15:4**

Bible Reading: Isaiah 40:28-31

Read & Learn:

The life of the prophet Elijah, as narrated in 1 Kings 17-19, offers profound lessons. Elijah, a man of great faith, experienced God's miraculous provision during a drought and triumphed over the prophets of Baal. Yet, he also faced moments of fear and despair, fleeing from Jezebel's threats. In a moment of vulnerability, God met Elijah not in dramatic displays, but in a gentle whisper. This story teaches us that even the mightiest of God's servants can experience fear and doubt, and God's presence and guidance are often found in quiet, unexpected ways.

The Old Testament prophets, like Elijah, Isaiah, and Jeremiah, provide valuable lessons for believers today. They were ordinary people called by God to deliver extraordinary messages. Their lives remind us that faithfulness to God can involve challenges and opposition, but God's presence and strength are always available. These prophets also demonstrate the importance of obedience, the power of prayer, and the necessity of trusting God even in difficult circumstances. Their messages, often calling for repentance and a return to God, are as relevant today as they were then, reminding us of God's unchanging nature and His desire for a relationship with His people.

Prayer Point:

Father, help me to learn from the faith and courage of the Old Testament prophets. Strengthen me to face challenges with trust in Your guidance and provision. Teach me to seek Your presence in both the extraordinary and the ordinary moments of life.

Saturday May 11

Topic: Faith in the Workplace

Memory Verse: "Whatever you do, work heartily, as for the Lord and not for men." - **Colossians 3:23**

Bible Reading: Proverbs 16:3-9

Read & Learn:

Daniel, in the Book of Daniel, chapters 1-6, exemplifies living out faith in the workplace. Taken into Babylonian captivity, Daniel was placed in a high government position because of his exceptional qualities. Despite the pressures and challenges in a pagan society, he remained steadfast in his faith, praying to God even when it was outlawed. His integrity and trust in God led to miraculous deliverance from the lions' den and influenced the king to acknowledge God's sovereignty. Daniel's story teaches us that maintaining our faith and integrity in the workplace can have a profound impact, even in environments that seem hostile to our beliefs.

Integrating faith into our professional lives can be challenging, yet it's essential for living a holistic Christian life. Our workplaces are mission fields where we can demonstrate Christ-like attitudes and ethics. This includes integrity, excellence in our work, kindness, and respect towards colleagues, and ethical decision-making. It's not about preaching at every opportunity, but rather letting our actions reflect our faith. Challenges will arise, but like Daniel, our consistent faith can influence those around us and bring glory to God. Balancing professional responsibilities with our Christian values is a powerful testimony to the transformative power of our faith.

Prayer Point:

Father, guide me to reflect Your love and integrity in my workplace. Help me to be a light, showing Your grace and truth through my actions. Strengthen me to face workplace challenges with faith and wisdom, honouring You in all I do.

Sunday May 12

Topic: The Role of Prayer in Personal Growth

Memory Verse: "But grow in the grace and knowledge of our Lord and Saviour Jesus Christ. To him be glory both now and forever! Amen." - 2 Peter 3:18

Bible Reading: Philippians 4:6-7

Read & Learn:

The story of Hannah in 1 Samuel 1-2 illustrates the transformative power of prayer in personal growth. Hannah, deeply distressed by her childlessness and the provocation of her rival, turned to God in fervent prayer. Her prayers were not just requests for a child, but a journey of emotional and spiritual growth. She poured out her soul before the Lord, exemplifying vulnerability and trust in God. Her prayer journey led to the birth of Samuel, whom she dedicated to God's service. Hannah's story teaches us that prayer is not just about presenting our requests to God, but a process that shapes us, refines our desires, and aligns us more closely with God's will.

Prayer is a vital tool in personal growth for a believer. It's a dialogue with God where we express our innermost thoughts, fears, and desires, and in return, gain wisdom, strength, and guidance. Through prayer, we develop a deeper relationship with God, understanding His character and His will for our lives. It's in these moments of prayer that we often find clarity and peace, even amidst life's challenges. Prayer also changes us, helping us to grow in patience, humility, and faith. As we consistently engage in prayer, we become more attuned to God's voice and leading, which is essential for our spiritual growth and maturity.

Prayer Point:

Father, teach me to pray with a heart open to Your guidance and wisdom. Help me to grow through my prayer life, deepening my trust in You. Make my prayer life to be a journey of personal transformation, aligning me more with Your will for my life.

Monday May 13

Topic: Handling Life's Disappointments God's Way

Memory Verse: "And we know that in all things God works for the good of those who love him, who have been called according to his purpose."
— **Romans 8:28**

Bible Reading: Psalm 34:17-19

Read & Learn:

The story of Joseph, found in Genesis 37-50, is a powerful example of handling life's disappointments with faith and trust in God. Betrayed by his brothers, sold into slavery, falsely accused, and imprisoned, Joseph faced numerous disappointments. Yet, he did not become bitter or lose faith. Instead, he trusted God's plan, which eventually led him to a position of power in Egypt, enabling him to save many lives during a famine, including those of his family. Joseph's story teaches us that even in our deepest disappointments, God is at work, weaving our struggles into His greater plan for good.

Disappointments are an inevitable part of life, but as Christians, we are called to handle them differently. Instead of succumbing to despair or bitterness, we are encouraged to trust in God's sovereignty and goodness. This trust doesn't mean denying our pain or pretending everything is fine; it means believing that God can use even our disappointments for our growth and His glory. It's about seeing beyond the immediate pain to the bigger picture of God's plan. Prayer, scripture, and the support of a faith community are essential tools in navigating disappointments. They provide comfort, perspective, and guidance, helping us to grow in resilience, faith, and character.

Prayer Point:

Father, grant me the strength to face disappointments with faith and hope. In my disappointments, help me to trust in Your loving plan. Use my disappointments to mould me into a stronger, more compassionate believer.

Tuesday May 14

Topic: Biblical Insights on Raising Children

Memory Verse: "Train up a child in the way he should go; even when he is old he will not depart from it." **- Proverbs 22:6**

Bible Reading: Ephesians 6:1-4

Read & Learn:

In the book of 1 Samuel, the story of Hannah and her son Samuel offers profound insights into raising children. Hannah, deeply longing for a child, promised to dedicate her son to the Lord's service. When Samuel was born, she kept her promise and entrusted him to Eli, the priest. Samuel grew up in the temple, learning to serve and follow God. This story highlights the importance of dedicating our children to God and nurturing their relationship with Him from a young age. It also shows the power of a parent's faith and prayer in shaping a child's life.

Raising children is one of the most significant tasks God entrusts to parents. The Bible provides guidance for this responsibility, emphasising the importance of teaching children about God and His ways. This includes modelling godly behaviour, instructing them in Scripture, and nurturing their faith. Discipline, when done in love and fairness, helps children learn right from wrong and understand the consequences of their actions. Importantly, Christian parenting is not just about rules and discipline; it's about demonstrating the love, grace, and forgiveness of Christ. Encouraging children to develop a personal relationship with God and involving them in a faith community are also crucial aspects of spiritual nurturing.

Prayer Point:

Father, help me to model Your love and grace in my parenting. Guide me in teaching my children Your ways with love and wisdom. Bless my children with a deep and lasting relationship with You.

Wednesday May 15

Topic: Spiritual Warfare and the Believer

Memory Verse: "For we do not wrestle against flesh and blood, but against the rulers, against the authorities, against the cosmic powers over this present darkness, against the spiritual forces of evil in the heavenly places." - **Ephesians 6:12**

Bible Reading: Ephesians 6:10-18

Read & Learn:

The story of Job is a powerful example of spiritual warfare in a believer's life. Job, a righteous man, faced severe trials as Satan challenged his faithfulness to God. Despite losing his wealth, children, and health, Job remained steadfast in his faith. This story teaches us that spiritual warfare is not just a physical struggle but a test of faith and trust in God.

Spiritual warfare is a reality for every believer. It involves battles against unseen spiritual forces that seek to hinder our relationship with God and our effectiveness in His kingdom. The Bible teaches us to be aware of these spiritual battles and equips us with the armour of God to stand firm. This includes truth, righteousness, the gospel of peace, faith, salvation, and the Word of God. Prayer is also a crucial weapon in spiritual warfare, enabling us to seek God's strength and guidance. Understanding our identity in Christ and relying on the Holy Spirit are key to overcoming these spiritual challenges. As believers, we are called to be vigilant, prayerful, and grounded in Scripture to successfully navigate spiritual warfare.

Prayer Point:

Father, guide me in prayer and reliance on Your Word in times of spiritual warfare. Strengthen my faith and trust in You during trials and temptations. Equip me with Your armour to stand firm against spiritual battles

Thursday May 16

Topic: The Concept of Christian Freedom

Memory Verse: "For freedom Christ has set us free; stand firm therefore, and do not submit again to a yoke of slavery." **- Galatians 5:1**

Bible Reading: Galatians 5:1-15

Read & Learn:

Consider the story of the Apostle Paul in Acts 16. Paul and Silas, imprisoned for preaching the Gospel, were miraculously freed from their physical chains. However, the greater demonstration of freedom was in their spirits; they sang praises to God even in captivity. Their example shows that Christian freedom is not about physical circumstances but a spiritual state. When the jailer, witnessing their faith, asked how to be saved, they shared the Gospel, leading to his and his family's salvation. This story illustrates that true freedom in Christ enables us to live above our circumstances and be a witness to others, regardless of our situation.

Christian freedom is a profound concept that goes beyond the absence of physical constraints. It's about being liberated from the bondage of sin and the law, through faith in Jesus Christ. This freedom is a gift of grace, not something we earn. It empowers us to live a life pleasing to God, not as a means of salvation, but as a response to the salvation we've received. However, this freedom is not a license to indulge in sinful desires; rather, it's an opportunity to serve one another in love, as Paul emphasises in Galatians. Understanding Christian freedom involves recognising that our liberty is meant for serving others and glorifying God, not for selfish gain.

Prayer Point:

Father, thank You for the freedom You've given me from sin and death. Guide me to live in the true freedom that glorifies God in all I do. Help me to use my freedom to serve others in love and not for selfish desires.

Friday May 17

Topic: Living a Purpose-Driven Life

Memory Verse: "For I know the plans I have for you, declares the Lord, plans for welfare and not for evil, to give you a future and a hope." - **Jeremiah 29:11**

Bible Reading: Ephesians 2:8-10

Read & Learn:

The life of Esther in the Bible is a remarkable example of living a purpose-driven life. Esther, an ordinary Jewish girl, became a queen and used her position to save her people from annihilation. Despite the risk to her own life, Esther embraced her divine purpose and intervened with courage and wisdom. Her story teaches us that God places us in specific situations for a reason. It's not about our comfort or safety, but about fulfilling God's plan and serving others. Esther's life exemplifies how understanding and embracing God's purpose can lead to impactful and meaningful actions.

Living a purpose-driven life means understanding that we are created by God for specific reasons. As Ephesians 2:10 says, we are God's workmanship, created in Christ Jesus for good works, which God prepared beforehand. This purpose is not just about what we do, but also about who we become in Christ. It involves growing in faith, character, and love, and using our unique gifts and opportunities to serve others and glorify God. A purpose-driven life is not necessarily a life of comfort or ease, but it is a life of fulfilment, knowing that we are participating in God's grand design.

Prayer Point:

Father, guide me to understand and embrace the purpose You have for my life. Grant me the courage and faith to fulfil Your plans, even in the face of challenges. Help me to use my gifts and opportunities to serve You and others, living a life that reflects Your love and grace.

Saturday May 18

Topic: The Relevance of the Beatitudes Today

Memory Verse: "Blessed are the peacemakers, for they shall be called sons of God." - **Matthew 5:9**

Bible Reading: Matthew 5:1-12

Read & Learn:

Consider the story of Martin Luther King Jr., a modern example of living the Beatitudes. King, a Baptist minister and civil rights leader, embodied the principles of the Beatitudes in his nonviolent approach to social change. His life exemplified the teachings of Jesus in the Beatitudes, particularly "Blessed are the peacemakers." King faced persecution, yet he responded with love and a commitment to peace, demonstrating the transformative power of living out the Beatitudes in contemporary society. His legacy shows how these ancient blessings continue to be relevant and powerful in addressing today's challenges.

The Beatitudes, part of Jesus' Sermon on the Mount, are not just ancient sayings but timeless principles that are profoundly relevant today. They describe the values of God's kingdom, contrasting worldly attitudes. Each Beatitude starts with "Blessed," indicating a state of happiness or fulfilment. They teach us about humility, mercy, purity of heart, and seeking peace. In a world often driven by power, wealth, and self-promotion, the Beatitudes call us to a different way of living - one that values gentleness, compassion, righteousness, and peace-making. Embracing these principles can transform our lives and impact the world around us.

Prayer Point:

Father, comfort me in times of mourning and persecution, reminding me of the blessings you promised in the beatitudes. Help me to embody the beatitudes in my daily life, showing humility, mercy, and a pure heart.

Sunday May 19

Topic: Understanding Biblical Forgiveness

Memory Verse: "Be kind to one another, tender-hearted, forgiving one another, as God in Christ forgave you." - **Ephesians 4:32**

Bible Reading: Matthew 18:21-35

Read & Learn:

The story of Joseph and his brothers in Genesis 45:1-15 is a powerful example of biblical forgiveness. Betrayed and sold into slavery by his brothers, Joseph endured years of hardship. Yet, when he rose to power in Egypt and his brothers came seeking help, Joseph chose forgiveness over revenge. He revealed his identity and embraced them, providing for their needs. Joseph's forgiveness reflected an understanding of God's sovereignty and a heart aligned with God's grace. His story teaches us that true forgiveness is not just a one-time act but a continuous attitude that mirrors God's forgiveness towards us.

Biblical forgiveness is a central theme in Christianity, reflecting the very nature of God's grace. It's not just about letting go of grudges or absolving someone from their mistakes; it's a profound expression of love and mercy, mirroring the forgiveness we receive from God through Christ. Forgiveness in the Bible involves recognising the wrong done, yet choosing to release resentment and seek reconciliation. It's a decision to not hold sins against someone, as God does not hold our sins against us. This kind of forgiveness can be challenging, especially when the hurt is deep, but it's essential for healing, peace, and spiritual growth.

Prayer Point:

Father, help me to understand the depth of Your forgiveness and to extend it to those around me. Grant me the strength to forgive others as You have forgiven me, releasing any bitterness and resentment. Guide me in reconciling with those I have wronged or who have wronged me, reflecting Your love and mercy.

Monday May 20

Topic: The Church's Role in Community Service

Memory Verse: "As each has received a gift, use it to serve one another, as good stewards of God's varied grace." **- 1 Peter 4:10**

Bible Reading: James 2:14-26

Read & Learn:

In the early church, as described in Acts 4:32-37, believers were deeply committed to serving their community. They shared their possessions and ensured that no one among them was in need. Barnabas, in particular, sold a field he owned and brought the money to the apostles' feet, which was then used to support those in need. This act of generosity and community service was a hallmark of the early church, demonstrating how Christian faith is expressed through practical, loving actions towards others. It's a powerful reminder of how the church can be a force for good in the community, meeting physical needs while also sharing the love of Christ.

The church's role in community service is an essential aspect of its mission. It's not only about spiritual nourishment but also about being the hands and feet of Jesus in the world. Community service by the church can take many forms, from feeding the hungry and clothing the needy to providing shelter for the homeless and care for the sick. These acts of service are expressions of God's love and grace. They are a practical demonstration of faith in action, as James emphasises that faith without works is dead. By serving the community, the church becomes a living testimony of God's compassion and mercy, drawing people not just to physical aid but also to the spiritual hope found in Christ.

Prayer Point:

Father, help our church to be a beacon of Your love through active community service. Guide us to use our gifts and resources to meet the needs of those around us. Let our service in the community draw others to Your grace and mercy.

Tuesday May 21

Topic: Developing a Christ-like Attitude

Memory Verse: "Have this mind among yourselves, which is yours in Christ Jesus." **- Philippians 2:5**

Bible Reading: Philippians 2:1-11

Read & Learn:

Consider the story of the Good Samaritan in Luke 10:25-37. A man was robbed and left for dead. A priest and a Levite, both respected in society, passed by without helping. But a Samaritan, viewed as an outsider and enemy by the Jews, stopped to help. He treated the man's wounds and paid for his care. This story, told by Jesus, illustrates a Christ-like attitude - one of compassion, mercy, and action, transcending social boundaries and prejudices. It challenges us to embody the same attitude in our daily lives, looking beyond our comfort and convenience to care for others.

Developing a Christ-like attitude involves cultivating qualities such as humility, selflessness, love, and compassion. It means considering others' interests above our own, as Jesus did. This attitude is not just about feeling compassionate but also about taking action, as demonstrated by the Good Samaritan. It involves daily choices to forgive, to serve, and to love, even when it's challenging. This attitude is a reflection of the transformation that occurs within us through the Holy Spirit. As we grow in our relationship with Christ, our thoughts and actions increasingly align with His. This transformation impacts not only our personal lives but also how we interact with others, influencing our families, workplaces, and communities.

Prayer Point:

Father, help me to develop an attitude that reflects Your love and compassion. Work in me, transforming my mind and heart to be more like Jesus. Guide me to put others' needs before my own, following Christ's example.

Wednesday May 22

Topic: The Influence of Christian Values in Society

Memory Verse: "Let your light shine before others, that they may see your good deeds and glorify your Father in heaven." **- Matthew 5:16**

Bible Reading: Matthew 5:13-16

Read & Learn:

In the early 19th century, William Wilberforce, a devout Christian and British politician, played a pivotal role in the abolition of the slave trade. His faith deeply influenced his values and actions. Despite facing immense opposition and challenges, Wilberforce remained steadfast in his conviction that slavery was morally wrong. His persistent efforts, driven by his Christian beliefs, eventually led to the passing of the Slave Trade Act in 1807, marking a significant step towards the abolition of slavery. Wilberforce's life exemplifies how Christian values, when lived out, can profoundly impact society and bring about transformative change.

Christian values such as love, justice, compassion, and integrity have a profound influence on society. When individuals embody these values, they become agents of positive change. These values prompt actions that uphold the dignity and rights of others, foster community, and promote ethical standards. For instance, the principle of loving one's neighbour can lead to social initiatives that address poverty, inequality, and injustice. The pursuit of justice, as demonstrated by figures like Wilberforce, can bring about significant legislative and societal changes. Moreover, Christian values influence personal and professional ethics, contributing to a more honest and compassionate society. Ultimately, these values reflect the character of God.

Prayer Point:
Father, use me as a light in my community. Grant me the courage to stand for justice and love. Help me to live out Christian values in a way that positively influences society.

Thursday May 23

Topic: Personal Revival and Renewal

Memory Verse: "Create in me a clean heart, O God, and renew a right spirit within me." **- Psalm 51:10**

Bible Reading: Isaiah 40:28-31

Read & Learn:

The story of John Newton, the author of the hymn "Amazing Grace," is a powerful example of personal revival and renewal. Newton, once a slave trader, experienced a profound spiritual awakening during a storm at sea. This turning point led him to renounce his former life and dedicate himself to God's service. His transformation was so complete that he became an Anglican clergyman and an influential supporter of the abolition movement. Newton's life demonstrates how an encounter with God can lead to a complete personal renewal and a life dedicated to righteousness and justice.

Personal revival and renewal are about a transformative encounter with God that leads to a renewed commitment to living a life aligned with His will. It involves a deep, introspective look at one's life, acknowledging areas that need God's touch, and seeking His presence for change. This process often includes repentance, a renewed focus on prayer and the study of Scripture, and a rekindling of one's first love for God. Isaiah 40:28-31 reminds us that God gives strength to the weary and increases the power of the weak. In moments of personal revival, believers find new strength and hope in God, leading to a refreshed and vibrant faith that impacts every aspect of their lives.

Prayer Point:

Father, renew my heart and spirit, that I may walk closely with You. Guide me in paths of renewal, that I may serve You faithfully.

Friday May 24

Topic: The Journey of Spiritual Healing

Memory Verse: "He heals the broken-hearted and binds up their wounds." - **Psalm 147:3**

Bible Reading: Psalm 34:17-22

Read & Learn:

Consider the biblical account of the woman with the issue of blood (Luke 8:43-48). For twelve years, she suffered with a condition that left her physically and socially debilitated. Despite her circumstances, she believed that touching Jesus' garment would bring healing. Her faith was rewarded, and Jesus acknowledged her, saying, "Daughter, your faith has healed you. Go in peace." This story illustrates the profound impact of faith in the journey of spiritual healing. It shows that healing often begins with a step of faith, even in the midst of long-standing struggles.

Spiritual healing is a process where individuals experience restoration and wholeness through God's divine intervention. It often involves healing of the mind, emotions, and spirit, sometimes even extending to physical healing. This journey requires faith, patience, and trust in God's timing and methods. Psalm 34:17-22 reassures us that the Lord is close to the broken-hearted and saves those who are crushed in spirit. Spiritual healing is not just about the cessation of pain or suffering, but about a deeper reconciliation with God, leading to inner peace and renewed strength. It's about laying down our burdens and allowing God to work in and through our lives.

Prayer Point:

Heavenly Father, God of all comfort, bind up my wounds and bring peace to my soul. Heal my broken heart and renew my spirit in Your love. In my journey of healing, let my faith in You grow stronger.

Saturday May 25

Topic: Biblical Perspectives on Environmental Stewardship

Memory Verse: "The earth is the Lord's, and everything in it, the world, and all who live in it." **- Psalm 24:1**

Bible Reading: Genesis 2:15; Psalm 8:3-9

Read & Learn:

Consider the story of Noah (Genesis 6-9). God chose Noah to save the diversity of life from a catastrophic flood. Noah's task was not just to save his family but to preserve various animal species. This story highlights the responsibility entrusted to humans to care for God's creation. It shows that every species has a role in God's plan and that humans are appointed as stewards of the earth. Noah's obedience in building the ark and caring for the animals exemplifies the stewardship God desires from all of us.

Environmental stewardship is a fundamental aspect of Christian responsibility, rooted in the understanding that the earth is God's creation. Genesis 2:15 emphasises that humans are to "work and take care" of the earth, indicating a balance between utilising resources and preserving them. Psalm 8:3-9 reflects on the majesty of God's creation and the role of humans as caretakers. This stewardship involves respecting the natural world, using resources wisely, and ensuring the sustainability of the environment for future generations. It's a reflection of our reverence for the Creator, acknowledging that we are part of a larger, divinely orchestrated ecosystem.

Prayer Point:

Father, Grant me wisdom to use Your resources wisely and sustainably. Help me to be a responsible steward of Your creation. Teach me to care for the earth as a reflection of my love for You.

Sunday May 26

Topic: Navigating Christian Dating and Relationships

Memory Verse: "Love is patient, love is kind. It does not envy, it does not boast, it is not proud..." **- 1 Corinthians 13:4-7**

Bible Reading: Ephesians 5:21-33

Read & Learn:

In the early church, there was a young couple, Aquila and Priscilla, who worked closely with the Apostle Paul. Their relationship was not just romantic but also a partnership in ministry. They were tentmakers by trade, which they used to support their ministry. Their story, though briefly mentioned in the Bible, shows a model of a Christian couple who balanced their relationship, work, and ministry effectively. They were known for their hospitality, teaching Apollos more accurately about the way of God. Their story exemplifies a Christian relationship grounded in mutual respect, shared faith, and service to God.

Navigating Christian dating and relationships requires understanding and applying biblical principles of love, respect, and selflessness. The memory verse from 1 Corinthians 13:4-7 describes the attributes of love that should be present in any Christian relationship. These scriptures guide us to form relationships that honour God, where both individuals grow in faith and love. In a world where relationships are often based on selfish desires, Christian dating should be a journey of getting to know each other in a way that is pleasing to God, focusing on building a foundation of friendship, respect, and shared faith.

Prayer Point:
Father, grant me discernment and strength to honour You in all my relationships. Guide me in my relationships to reflect Your love and patience.

Monday May 27

Topic: The Importance of Scripture Memorisation

Memory Verse: "I have hidden your word in my heart that I might not sin against you." - **Psalm 119:11**

Bible Reading: Joshua 1:8; Psalm 119:9-16

Read & Learn:

During the Reformation, William Tyndale dedicated his life to translating the Bible into English, believing that everyone should have access to Scripture. Despite facing immense opposition, he memorised large portions of the Bible, which sustained him in his mission and during his imprisonment. His commitment to Scripture memorisation was not just for personal edification but also a tool for sharing God's Word with others. Tyndale's story is a powerful testament to the transformative and sustaining power of God's Word, especially in times of trial and adversity.

Psalm 119:11 highlights the protective power of memorising Scripture, helping us resist temptation and sin. Joshua 1:8 emphasises the importance of meditating on God's law day and night for success and prosperity in life. Memorising Scripture allows for constant meditation and application, leading to a deeper understanding of God's will and character. It equips believers for evangelism and apologetics, strengthens faith during trials, and enhances prayer life. As seen in the life of William Tyndale, Scripture memorisation can be a source of courage and guidance, especially in challenging circumstances.

Prayer Point:

Father, grant me the discipline to memorise Scripture and apply it in my life. Help me to treasure Your Word in my heart and live by it daily.

Tuesday May 28

Topic: Exploring the Miracles of Jesus

Memory Verse: "Very truly I tell you, whoever believes in me will do the works I have been doing, and they will do even greater things than these, because I am going to the Father." - **John 14:12**

Bible Reading: John 6:1-14

Read & Learn:

In the early 4th century, Saint Nicholas, who later became known as Santa Claus, was renowned for his faith and miracles that echoed those of Jesus. One of the most famous stories is when he provided dowries for three impoverished sisters, which were mysteriously delivered as bags of gold, appearing as if by divine intervention. This act of miraculous generosity not only saved the sisters from destitution but also inspired countless others to acts of kindness and faith.

The miracles of Jesus are not just historical events; they are powerful demonstrations of God's love and power. In John 6:1-14, the feeding of the five thousand shows Jesus' compassion and ability to provide abundantly. This miracle, like others performed by Jesus, signifies the breaking in of God's kingdom, where physical and spiritual needs are met beyond human expectations. Miracles are signs pointing to Jesus' divine nature and His authority over creation. They invite us to deeper faith and participation in God's work. As believers, we are called to trust in Jesus' power and be conduits of His miraculous work in our world, as exemplified by Saint Nicholas and many others.

Prayer Point:
Lord Jesus, help me to see Your power and love in the miracles You performed. Increase my faith to believe in and witness Your miraculous works in my life. Use me as a vessel to extend Your miraculous love and compassion to others.

Wednesday May 29

Topic: The Power of Confession and Repentance

Memory Verse: "If we confess our sins, He is faithful and just and will forgive us our sins and purify us from all unrighteousness."

— 1 John 1:9

Bible Reading: Psalm 51:1-10

Read & Learn:

The story of the Prodigal Son in Luke 15:11-32 beautifully illustrates the power of confession and repentance. The younger son, after squandering his inheritance, finds himself in dire straits. In his desperation, he decides to return to his father, confessing his sins and acknowledging his unworthiness. His father, instead of condemnation, welcomes him with open arms, celebrating his return. This parable vividly demonstrates God's readiness to forgive and restore us when we turn back to Him with a contrite heart.

Confession and repentance are foundational to the Christian faith. They are not merely about acknowledging wrongdoing; they are about turning away from sin and turning towards God. Psalm 51, written by King David after his sin with Bathsheba, is a profound expression of repentance and reliance on God's mercy.. Confession brings our sins into the light, allowing God's grace to heal and restore us. It's an act of humility and trust in God's justice and mercy. As believers, embracing confession and repentance leads to spiritual renewal and deeper intimacy with God.

Prayer Point:

Heavenly Father, thank You for Your mercy and love that welcomes me back each time I stray. I confess my sins to You, trusting in Your forgiveness and grace. Grant me a heart of repentance and guide me in Your path of righteousness.

Thursday May 30

Topic: Balancing Grace and Truth

Memory Verse: "The Word became flesh and made his dwelling among us. We have seen his glory, the glory of the one and only Son, who came from the Father, full of grace and truth." **- John 1:14**

Bible Reading: John 8:1-11

Read & Learn:

Consider the account of Jesus and the woman caught in adultery (John 8:1-11). The Pharisees brought a woman caught in adultery before Jesus, testing Him to see if He would condemn her according to the Law of Moses. Jesus, embodying both grace and truth, responded not with immediate judgment but with wisdom, saying, "Let any one of you who is without sin be the first to throw a stone at her." One by one, they left, and Jesus, left alone with the woman, offered her grace, saying, "Neither do I condemn you," and truth, "Go now and leave your life of sin."

Balancing grace and truth is a delicate yet essential aspect of the Christian life. Jesus exemplified this balance perfectly. He never compromised the truth of God's Word, yet He extended grace and compassion to those who were lost and hurting. In Ephesians 4:15, Paul encourages believers to speak the truth in love, which is the essence of balancing grace and truth. This balance is not about being permissive of sin or compromising on biblical principles; it's about approaching each situation with a heart that reflects Jesus' love and righteousness. As Christians, we are called to uphold the truth of God's Word while also demonstrating His grace and love to others.

Prayer Point:
Father, thank You for showing me perfect grace and truth through Jesus Christ. Help me to embody Your grace and truth in all my interactions. Give me wisdom and courage to speak the truth in love.

Friday May 31

Topic: The Significance of Christian Unity

Memory Verse: "Make every effort to keep the unity of the Spirit through the bond of peace." **- Ephesians 4:3**

Bible Reading: 1 Corinthians 12:12-27

Read & Learn:

The early church, as described in Acts 2:42-47, is a powerful example of Christian unity. These believers devoted themselves to the apostles' teaching, fellowship, breaking of bread, and prayer. They shared everything they had, sold property and possessions to give to anyone in need, and met together in the temple courts and homes. Their unity was so profound that the Lord added to their number daily those who were being saved. This story illustrates how unity in the body of Christ not only strengthens the church internally but also serves as a compelling witness to the world.

Christian unity is not merely a nice idea but a fundamental aspect of our faith. In 1 Corinthians 12:12-27, Paul uses the metaphor of the body to describe how each believer, though different, is part of one body in Christ. This unity is not based on uniformity in personality, gifts, or opinions but on our shared faith in Jesus Christ. Unity in the church reflects the unity of the Father, Son, and Holy Spirit and is essential for the church's health and mission. It fosters a supportive community, enhances our witness to the world, and allows us to effectively work together for God's kingdom.

Prayer Point:
Heavenly Father, Father, guide us to value and respect each member of Your body, recognising our interconnectedness in Christ. Help us to foster and actively work to maintain unity in our church community, reflecting Your love and peace.

Saturday June 01

Topic: Understanding God's Timing

Memory Verse: "He has made everything beautiful in its time. He has also set eternity in the human heart; yet no one can fathom what God has done from beginning to end." **- Ecclesiastes 3:11**

Bible Reading: Habakkuk 2:1-3

Read & Learn:

The story of Abraham and Sarah in Genesis is a profound illustration of understanding God's timing. God promised them a son, but years passed without the fulfilment of this promise. In their old age, when it seemed impossible, Sarah gave birth to Isaac. This long period of waiting tested their faith, but ultimately, they witnessed God's promise fulfilled at the perfect time. Their story teaches us that God's timing often doesn't align with ours, but His promises are sure and He is faithful to fulfil them.

Understanding God's timing is a vital aspect of faith. It requires trust in God's plan and patience in waiting for His perfect timing. Ecclesiastes 3:11 reminds us that God makes everything beautiful in its time, suggesting that His timing is purposeful and precise. Habakkuk 2:1-3 encourages believers to wait for the vision, as it will surely come and not delay. This passage teaches us that God's timing may not align with our expectations, but it is always perfect. Trusting in God's timing means believing that He knows what is best for us and that His plans are to prosper us, not to harm us.

Prayer Point:
Heavenly Father, grant me the patience to trust in Your perfect timing in all things. Help me to rest in the assurance that Your plans are always for my good. Strengthen my faith as I wait for Your timing, knowing that You make everything beautiful in its time.

Sunday June 02

Topic: The Virtue of Self-Control

Memory Verse: "Like a city whose walls are broken through is a person who lacks self-control." **- Proverbs 25:28**

Bible Reading: Galatians 5:22-23

Read & Learn:

In 1 Samuel 24, we find a compelling example of self-control in the life of David. King Saul, consumed by jealousy, was pursuing David to kill him. David and his men were hiding in a cave when Saul entered it alone, unaware of David's presence. David's men saw this as an opportunity to kill Saul, but David restrained himself. He only cut off a corner of Saul's robe, later feeling remorse even for this act. David's self-control, respect for Saul as God's anointed, and refusal to harm Saul, despite having the opportunity, demonstrate the strength and virtue of self-control in the face of intense personal challenge.

Self-control is a crucial aspect of Christian character, listed as a fruit of the Spirit in Galatians 5:22-23. It involves the ability to control impulses, emotions, and desires, aligning them with God's will. Proverbs 25:28 compares a person without self-control to a city with broken walls, vulnerable to attack. This metaphor highlights the protective nature of self-control in our spiritual and moral lives. Self-control is not about suppressing emotions or desires but managing them in a way that honours God. It requires reliance on the Holy Spirit, prayer, and practice. As seen in David's life, self-control can lead to wise decisions, preserve integrity, and maintain peace.

Prayer Point:

Father, grant me the virtue of self-control in my thoughts, words, and actions. Help me to rely on Your strength and wisdom to manage my impulses and desires. Cultivate in me the fruit of self-control, that I may live a life that honours You.

Monday June 03

Topic: Reflecting Christ in Everyday Life

Memory Verse: "In the same way, let your light shine before others, that they may see your good deeds and glorify your Father in heaven." **- Matthew 5:16**

Bible Reading: Colossians 3:12-17

Read & Learn:

In the book of Daniel, particularly in Daniel 6, we find Daniel as an exemplary figure for reflecting Christ in everyday life. Despite being in a pagan land and under a government that did not honour God, Daniel consistently displayed integrity, devotion, and faithfulness. His commitment to prayer and to following God's laws, even when it led to being thrown into the lion's den, showed his unwavering faith. Daniel's life was a testament to his deep relationship with God, influencing those around him, including King Darius, who eventually acknowledged the power of Daniel's God.

Reflecting Christ in everyday life means embodying the values, attitudes, and behaviours that Jesus Christ exemplified. Colossians 3:12-17 encourages believers to clothe themselves with compassion, kindness, humility, gentleness, and patience, and to let the peace of Christ rule in their hearts. Reflecting Christ is not limited to religious settings; it extends to our daily activities, relationships, and how we respond to challenges. It involves showing love, grace, and forgiveness, being a light in the darkness, and making choices that honour God.

Prayer Point:
Father, help and guide me to reflect Your love and light in every aspect of my life. Let my life be a testament to Your grace, virtues of compassion, kindness, and humility, drawing others closer to You.

Tuesday June 04

Topic: God's Guidance in Decision Making

Memory Verse: "Trust in the Lord with all your heart and lean not on your own understanding; in all your ways submit to him, and he will make your paths straight." - **Proverbs 3:5-6**

Bible Reading: James 1:5-8

Read & Learn:

The story of Solomon asking for wisdom in 1 Kings 3:5-14 is a profound example of seeking God's guidance in decision-making. When God appeared to Solomon in a dream and asked what he wanted, Solomon could have asked for wealth, power, or the death of his enemies. Instead, he asked for wisdom to govern God's people rightly. Pleased with Solomon's request, God granted him unparalleled wisdom, which Solomon used to lead Israel with discernment and fairness. This story illustrates the importance of prioritising Godly wisdom over personal gain when making decisions.

Seeking God's guidance in decision-making is a crucial aspect of a faithful Christian life. Proverbs 3:5-6 encourages us to trust in the Lord rather than our own understanding and to acknowledge Him in all our decisions. James 1:5-8 reminds us that if we lack wisdom, we should ask God, who gives generously to all without finding fault. This process involves prayer, seeking counsel from God's Word, and sometimes godly advice from others. It's about aligning our desires with God's will and being open to His leading, even when it contradicts our initial plans.

Prayer Point:
Father, help me to trust in You with all my heart and not lean on my own understanding. Guide me in my decisions and grant me wisdom to discern Your will. In every choice I face, let Your Word light my path and direct my steps.

Wednesday June 05

Topic: The Role of Worship in Spiritual Growth

Memory Verse: "God is spirit, and his worshipers must worship in the Spirit and in truth." - **John 4:24**

Bible Reading: Psalm 95:1-7

Read & Learn:

In 2 Chronicles 20:15-24, King Jehoshaphat faced a vast army. Instead of relying solely on military might, he sought the Lord and proclaimed a fast throughout Judah. The people came together to seek help from the Lord. God's response through the prophet Jahaziel was to not be afraid or discouraged, for the battle was not theirs, but God's. Jehoshaphat appointed men to sing to the Lord and to praise Him for the splendour of His holiness as they went out at the head of the army. As they began to sing and praise, the Lord set ambushes against the enemy, leading to their defeat. This story powerfully illustrates how worship can be a catalyst for spiritual breakthrough and victory.

Worship plays a crucial role in spiritual growth. It's not just a Sunday activity but a lifestyle of recognising and responding to God's holiness, goodness, and sovereignty. John 4:24 reminds us that true worship is in spirit and truth, going beyond mere formality to a heartfelt connection with God. Worship shifts our focus from our circumstances to God, aligning our hearts with His. It's in worship that we often find strength, perspective, and renewal. As we worship, we grow in our understanding of God's nature and His will for our lives, leading to deeper faith, obedience, and victory.

Prayer Point:
Father, help me to worship You in spirit and truth, growing closer to You each day. Through worship, strengthen my faith and align my life more closely with Your will.

Thursday June 06

Topic: Developing a Lifestyle of Evangelism

Memory Verse: "He said to them, 'Go into all the world and preach the gospel to all creation.'" **- Mark 16:15**

Bible Reading: Acts 8:26-40

Read & Learn:

In Acts 8:26-40, we encounter Philip, an early Christian, who provides a model for a lifestyle of evangelism. Led by the Holy Spirit, Philip meets an Ethiopian eunuch who is reading the prophet Isaiah but does not understand the passage. Philip uses this opportunity to explain the Scriptures and share the good news about Jesus. This encounter results in the eunuch's conversion and baptism. Philip's readiness to share his faith, guided by the Spirit, and his ability to use the current situation to speak about Christ, exemplifies how believers can incorporate evangelism into their daily lives.

Developing a lifestyle of evangelism means integrating the sharing of the gospel into our everyday interactions and activities. It's about being alert to opportunities presented by the Holy Spirit to witness to others, as seen in Philip's encounter with the Ethiopian eunuch. Mark 16:15's command to preach the gospel to all creation is not just for missionaries or pastors; it's a call for every believer. This doesn't necessarily mean standing on street corners preaching; it can be as simple as sharing how Jesus has changed your life with a friend, colleague, or neighbour. It involves living out the gospel through acts of kindness, integrity, and love.

Prayer Point:
Father, open doors for me to witness to others about Your love and salvation. Empower me to share Your gospel boldly and lovingly in my everyday life. Help me to live a life that reflects Your grace and truth, drawing others to You.

Friday June 07

Topic: Overcoming Spiritual Dryness

Memory Verse: "As the deer pants for streams of water, so my soul pants for you, my God. My soul thirsts for God, for the living God. When can I go and meet with God?" - **Psalm 42:1-2**

Bible Reading: Isaiah 44:3-4

Read & Learn:

After a significant victory at Mount Carmel, Elijah finds himself fleeing from Jezebel's threats and feeling alone and despondent in the wilderness. In his moment of spiritual dryness and despair, God meets Elijah not in the wind, earthquake, or fire, but in a gentle whisper. This encounter reminds Elijah (and us) that God's presence is not always in the dramatic but often in the quiet, gentle moments of life. It's a powerful lesson on seeking and finding God in the stillness, especially during times of spiritual dryness.

Spiritual dryness is a common experience in the Christian journey, characterised by a sense of distance from God, lack of joy in spiritual activities, and a feeling of emptiness. Overcoming this dryness involves actively seeking God, as the Psalmist expresses a deep thirst for God. Isaiah 44:3-4 promises that God will pour out His Spirit on the thirsty land. This passage encourages us to seek God's presence and the refreshing of His Spirit. Overcoming spiritual dryness often requires intentional steps: spending time in prayer and Scripture, engaging in worship, seeking fellowship with other believers, and sometimes just sitting in silence before God.

Prayer Point:
Heavenly Father, in times of spiritual dryness, renew my thirst for You and fill me with Your living water. Whenever You seem distant, help me to find You in the stillness and quiet of my heart and draw closer to Your refreshing presence.

Saturday June 08

Topic: The Power of a Thankful Heart

Memory Verse: "Give thanks in all circumstances; for this is God's will for you in Christ Jesus." - **1 Thessalonians 5:18**

Bible Reading: Psalm 100

Read & Learn:

In Luke 17:11-19, we find the story of the ten lepers who were healed by Jesus. These ten men stood at a distance and called out to Jesus for mercy. Healed as they went to show themselves to the priests, only one of them, a Samaritan, returned to thank Jesus. This man's act of gratitude not only demonstrated his faith but also his recognition of Jesus' power and mercy. His thankfulness set him apart and earned Jesus' commendation. This story highlights the importance of a thankful heart, not just for what we receive but for who God is and His work in our lives.

A thankful heart is a powerful aspect of the Christian faith. It's not just about expressing gratitude when things go well but maintaining a posture of thankfulness in all circumstances, as instructed in 1 Thessalonians 5:18. Psalm 100 encourages us to enter God's gates with thanksgiving and His courts with praise. Thankfulness shifts our focus from our problems and challenges to God's goodness and faithfulness. It fosters a positive outlook, strengthens our faith, and deepens our relationship with God. A thankful heart can also impact those around us, serving as a witness to God's love and grace. In practicing gratitude, we align ourselves with God's will and open our lives to His joy and peace.

Prayer Point:
Lord, cultivate in me a thankful heart that recognises and appreciates Your goodness in all circumstances.

Sunday June 09

Topic: Biblical Views on Social Justice

Memory Verse: "He has shown you, O mortal, what is good. And what does the Lord require of you? To act justly and to love mercy and to walk humbly with your God." **- Micah 6:8**

Bible Reading: Luke 10:25-37, Isaiah 1:16-17

Read & Learn:

The story of the Good Samaritan in Luke 10:25-37 exemplifies the biblical view of social justice. A man traveling from Jerusalem to Jericho is robbed, beaten, and left for dead. A priest and a Levite pass by without helping, but a Samaritan, considered an outsider and enemy to the Jews, stops to help. He treats the man's wounds and ensures his care, demonstrating compassion and justice transcending cultural and ethnic boundaries. This parable, told by Jesus, challenges us to see social justice as an integral part of living out our faith.

The Bible presents a clear and compelling message about social justice, emphasising the need to care for the vulnerable, fight for the oppressed, and uphold justice and mercy. Micah 6:8 highlights that justice is a fundamental aspect of God's character and, therefore, should be reflected in His followers. Isaiah 1:16-17 urges us to seek justice, encourage the oppressed, defend the cause of the fatherless, and plead the case of the widow. Biblical social justice is about more than charity; it's about systemic change and advocating for policies and practices that promote fairness and equality.

Prayer Point:
Heavenly Father, inspire me to act justly, love mercy, and walk humbly with You in all areas of life. Give me the courage to stand up for the oppressed and be a voice for the voiceless. Help me to reflect Your love and justice in my actions and advocacy for social change.

Monday June 10

Topic: The Role of Fasting in Spiritual Life

Memory Verse: "But when you fast, anoint your head and wash your face, so that it will not be obvious to others that you are fasting, but only to your Father, who is unseen; and your Father, who sees what is done in secret, will reward you." **- Matthew 6:17-18**

Bible Reading: Isaiah 58:6-11

Read & Learn:

When faced with the threat of her people's annihilation, Queen Esther, along with all the Jews in Susa, engaged in a three-day fast before she approached King Xerxes to plead for their lives. This fast was not merely an act of self-denial but a collective turning to God in a time of desperation. Esther's fast demonstrated her dependence on God's guidance and strength. The successful outcome - the king's favour and the deliverance of the Jews - highlights the power of fasting combined with prayer in seeking God's intervention.

Fasting, a voluntary abstinence from food for spiritual purposes, has been a practice in the spiritual life of believers across generations. Isaiah 58:6-11 reveals the true purpose of fasting: to lose the chains of injustice, set the oppressed free, share food with the hungry, provide shelter for the homeless, and clothe the naked. Fasting is more than a physical discipline; it's a spiritual act that aligns our hearts with God's heart, especially concerning matters of justice and compassion. It's a time of seeking God's will, humbling oneself, and focusing on prayer and spiritual growth.

Prayer Point:
Father, guide me in my fasting, that it may be a time of spiritual renewal and alignment with Your will. Let my fasting be a true act of worship, drawing me closer to Your heart and purposes.

Tuesday June 11

Topic: Dealing with Life Transitions

Memory Verse: "Have I not commanded you? Be strong and courageous. Do not be afraid; do not be discouraged, for the Lord your God will be with you wherever you go." **- Joshua 1:9**

Bible Reading: Ecclesiastes 3:1-8

Read & Learn:

The transition of leadership from Moses to Joshua in the Bible (Deuteronomy 31:1-8) is a powerful example of dealing with life transitions. Moses, who had led Israel for decades, was at the end of his journey. Joshua was appointed to lead the people into the Promised Land. This transition was challenging for Joshua, stepping into the shoes of a great leader, and facing the enormous task ahead. However, God's assurance to Joshua to be strong and courageous, for He would be with him, is a timeless reminder that in every transition in life, God's presence and guidance are our constant source of strength and direction.

Ecclesiastes 3:1-8 reminds us that there is a time for every activity under heaven, indicating that change is a natural and inevitable part of life. In dealing with transitions, it is crucial to seek God's guidance, as Joshua did. The assurance in Joshua 1:9 to be strong and courageous is not just about personal strength but about relying on God's presence and promises. It's also important to seek support from others and maintain a positive outlook, trusting that God is working through these changes for our growth and His purposes.

Prayer Point:
Heavenly Father, Father, guide me through the changes in life, and help me to embrace them with faith and hope. In times of transition, grant me the strength and courage to trust in Your plan.

Wednesday June 12

Topic: The Christian Approach to Grief and Loss

Memory Verse: "Praise be to the God and Father of our Lord Jesus Christ, the Father of compassion and the God of all comfort, who comforts us in all our troubles, so that we can comfort those in any trouble with the comfort we ourselves receive from God."

                                               - 2 Corinthians 1:3-4

Bible Reading: John 11:17-36

Read & Learn:

The story of Mary and Martha in John 11:17-36 provides a vivid example of the Christian approach to grief and loss. When their brother Lazarus dies, both sisters express their sorrow to Jesus. Mary falls at Jesus' feet, weeping, and the people who come to mourn with her also weep. Jesus is deeply moved and weeps with them. This account shows Jesus' empathy and compassion in the face of grief. He doesn't dismiss their feelings but shares in their sorrow, demonstrating that grief is a natural, human response to loss and that God is present in our deepest moments of pain.

The Christian approach to grief and loss acknowledges that sorrow and mourning are natural and valid responses to loss. Psalm 34:18 reminds us that the Lord is close to the broken-hearted and saves those who are crushed in spirit. Grieving is not a sign of weak faith but a heartfelt response to loss. The comfort God offers does not necessarily remove the pain but provides strength and hope in the midst of it.

Prayer Point:
Father, thank You for being close to the broken-hearted and for Your promise of hope and healing. In my season grief, wrap me in Your comfort and peace. Grant me the wisdom and empathy to be a source of Your comfort to others in their times of loss.

Thursday June 13

Topic: Cultivating Godly Relationships

Memory Verse: "As iron sharpens iron, so one person sharpens another." - **Proverbs 27:17**

Bible Reading: Colossians 3:12-14

Read & Learn:

The relationship between David and Jonathan in 1 Samuel 18:1-4 provides a beautiful example of a godly friendship. Their bond was marked by selflessness, loyalty, and a deep commitment to each other's well-being. Jonathan, King Saul's son, recognised God's hand on David and chose to support him, even when it meant sacrificing his own claim to the throne. Their friendship was rooted in their shared faith in God, which guided their actions and decisions. This story illustrates the essence of godly relationships: putting the other's needs above one's own, being loyal, and encouraging each other in faith.

Cultivating godly relationships involves more than just common interests or mutual benefit; it's about building connections that encourage spiritual growth and reflect Christ's love. Colossians 3:12-14 encourages believers to clothe themselves with compassion, kindness, humility, gentleness, and patience, bearing with each other and forgiving one another. These qualities are essential in developing healthy, godly relationships. Such relationships are characterised by mutual edification, accountability, and a shared commitment to following Christ. They provide a source of strength, encouragement, and wisdom, helping us to grow in our faith and walk with God.

Prayer Point:

Heavenly Father, help me to cultivate godly relationships that honour You and encourage spiritual growth. Grant me the wisdom to be a friend who sharpens others in their faith journey.

Friday June 14

Topic: The Role of the Holy Spirit in Sanctification

Memory Verse: "But we ought always to thank God for you, brothers and sisters loved by the Lord, because God chose you as first fruits to be saved through the sanctifying work of the Spirit and through belief in the truth." **- 2 Thessalonians 2:13**

Bible Reading: Romans 8:12-17

Read & Learn:

The transformation of the disciples at Pentecost (Acts 2:1-4) vividly illustrates the role of the Holy Spirit in sanctification. Before the Holy Spirit's descent, the disciples were often uncertain, fearful, and lacking understanding. However, when they received the Holy Spirit, there was a marked change in their boldness, understanding, and commitment to God's mission. This event signifies the Holy Spirit's power to transform believers, guiding them into deeper truth, empowering them for service, and sanctifying them in their walk with God.

Sanctification is the process of being made holy, set apart for God's purposes, and it is a vital role of the Holy Spirit in a believer's life. As stated in 2 Thessalonians 2:13, it is through the Spirit's work that we are sanctified. The Holy Spirit convicts us of sin, guides us into truth, and empowers us to live in a way that reflects Christ's character. Sanctification is a lifelong journey, involving daily surrender to the Spirit's leading, allowing Him to mould and shape our character to be more like Jesus.

Prayer Point:
Father, thank You for the gift of the Holy Spirit, who guides, convicts, and empowers me in my spiritual journey. Help me to be sensitive to Your Spirit's leading each day, surrendering to Your transformative work in my life.

Saturday June 15

Topic: Christian Ethics in a Modern World

Memory Verse: "So that you may become blameless and pure, 'children of God without fault in a warped and crooked generation.' Then you will shine among them like stars in the sky."
- Philippians 2:15

Bible Reading: Matthew 5:13-16

Read & Learn:

Daniel's life in Babylon (Daniel 1:8-20) is a compelling example of maintaining Christian ethics in a challenging environment. Despite being in a foreign land with different customs and pressures, Daniel resolved not to defile himself with the royal food and wine. Their commitment to their beliefs, even in a setting that encouraged assimilation, demonstrated integrity and faithfulness. God honoured their steadfastness, granting them favour and wisdom. Daniel's story teaches us the importance of holding onto our ethical convictions, even when they go against the cultural norm.

Christian ethics in a modern world involves navigating complex and often morally ambiguous situations while maintaining a commitment to biblical principles. Matthew 5:13-16 calls Christians to be the salt and light of the world, influencing society positively while upholding Christ's teachings. In a world that often values relativism and self-interest, Christian ethics stand as a testament to the transformative power of living a life rooted in Christ's love and truth.

Prayer Point:
Father, help me to be salt and light by living a life that reflects Your love, justice, and truth in every situation I face. Grant me the wisdom and strength to positively influence the complex world around me while staying true to Your principles.

Sunday June 16

Topic: Understanding God's Promises

Memory Verse: "Through these he has given us his very great and precious promises, so that through them you may participate in the divine nature, having escaped the corruption in the world caused by evil desires." **- 2 Peter 1:4**

Bible Reading: Hebrews 11:1-12

Read & Learn:

The story of Abraham, particularly in Genesis 12:1-7 and 15:1-6, is a powerful illustration of understanding and trusting in God's promises. God promised Abraham that he would be the father of many nations, despite his old age and Sarah's barrenness. This promise seemed impossible in human terms, but Abraham chose to believe God. His faith was credited to him as righteousness. Despite years of waiting and moments of doubt, Abraham held onto God's promise, which was ultimately fulfilled through the birth of Isaac. Abraham's journey teaches us about patience, faith, and the certainty of God's promises, even when they seem delayed or impossible.

Understanding God's promises involves recognising that His assurances are rooted in His character - faithful, true, and unchanging. Hebrews 11:1-12, often known as the "faith chapter," recounts the faith of various individuals who trusted in God's promises, even when they did not see them fulfilled in their lifetimes. These stories teach us that God's promises often require faith and patience.

Prayer Point:
Heavenly Father, thank You for Your great and precious promises that give me hope and a future. Strengthen my faith in Your promises, trusting that You are faithful to fulfil them. Help me to patiently wait on Your timing, knowing that Your plans are perfect.

Monday June 17

Topic: The Importance of Church History

Memory Verse: "Remember your leaders, who spoke the word of God to you. Consider the outcome of their way of life and imitate their faith. Jesus Christ is the same yesterday and today and forever."
— **Hebrews 13:7-8**

Bible Reading: Acts 2:42-47

Read & Learn:

The early Christians devoted themselves to the apostles' teaching, fellowship, breaking of bread, and prayer. Their communal life, marked by generosity, worship, and mutual care, led to growth and favour in the wider community. This account is not just historical; it's instructional, showing how the principles and practices established in the early church can guide modern Christian communities. Understanding this history helps us appreciate the roots of our faith and the journey of the church through the ages, including times of persecution, reformation, and revival.

The study of church history is crucial for understanding how the Christian faith has been lived out, defended, and developed over the centuries. It provides context for our beliefs and practices, showing how they have been shaped by different cultural, political, and theological challenges. Hebrews 13:7-8 encourages us to remember and learn from the faith of past leaders, understanding that while times change, Jesus Christ remains constant.

Prayer Point:
Father, inspire me with the stories of those who faithfully followed You through the ages and help me to learn from them to live out my faith more effectively today.

Tuesday June 18

Topic: Faith and Politics in Christian Life

Memory Verse: "Jesus said, 'Render to Caesar the things that are Caesar's, and to God the things that are God's.'" - **Matthew 22:21**

Bible Reading: Romans 13:1-7

Read & Learn:

The account of Joseph in Genesis 41:37-57 provides a profound example of faith intersecting with politics. Joseph, a Hebrew in Egypt, rises to a position of political power because of his faith in God and his ability to interpret Pharaoh's dreams. In his role, Joseph implements policies to save Egypt and surrounding nations from famine. His story shows that it is possible to engage in political life while maintaining integrity and faith. Joseph used his political position to serve God's purposes, demonstrating that faith can guide political actions to achieve justice and mercy.

Matthew 22:21 and Romans 13:1-7 provide guidance on this issue. Christians are called to respect and pray for those in authority and to be law-abiding citizens. However, this does not mean blind allegiance. Our ultimate allegiance is to God, and our political engagement should reflect His values of justice, mercy, and love. Christians can and should participate in the political process, but this participation should be characterised by the fruits of the Spirit, rather than the divisive rhetoric often associated with politics. The goal is to be salt and light in the political arena, influencing society for the better while upholding Christian principles.

Prayer Point:
Father, grant me discernment to balance my civic responsibilities with my ultimate allegiance to You. Help me to be a positive influence in the political sphere and guide me to engage in politics with wisdom, integrity, and a focus on Your values.

Wednesday June 19

Topic: The Art of Christian Listening

Memory Verse: "My dear brothers and sisters, take note of this: Everyone should be quick to listen, slow to speak and slow to become angry." - **James 1:19**

Bible Reading: Proverbs 18:13, 15

Read & Learn:

The account of Jesus with Mary and Martha in Luke 10:38-42 highlights the importance of listening in the Christian life. While Martha was busy with the duties of hosting, Mary chose to sit at Jesus' feet, listening to His teaching. Jesus commended Mary for choosing what was better. This story contrasts the busyness that often distracts us from truly listening to God and others, with the focused attention that Mary showed. It teaches the value of being present and attentive, demonstrating that listening is a form of love and respect, and a way to gain wisdom and understanding.

Christian listening goes beyond just hearing words; it involves active, empathetic engagement with the speaker, whether it's God through His Word, or others in conversation. James 1:19 emphasises the need to be quick to listen and slow to speak, suggesting that listening is a skill that requires patience and self-control. Proverbs 18:13, 15 highlights that understanding comes from listening well. Christian listening is about seeking to understand before being understood, showing compassion, and providing a space where others feel heard and valued. It's a way of mirroring God's attentiveness to us, fostering deeper relationships, and growing in wisdom.

Prayer Point:

Lord, help me to cultivate the art of Christian listening, being present and attentive to You and those around me. Use my listening ears to be a source of comfort and wisdom, reflecting Your love and care.

Thursday June 20

Topic: Living Out the Great Commission

Memory Verse: "Therefore go and make disciples of all nations, baptising them in the name of the Father and of the Son and of the Holy Spirit, and teaching them to obey everything I have commanded you. And surely I am with you always, to the very end of the age."
                                                                 - Matthew 28:19-20

Bible Reading: Acts 1:8

Read & Learn:

Paul's commitment to spreading the Gospel across diverse cultures and regions, often facing persecution and hardship, shows his dedication to Christ's command. His approach was not just about converting individuals but about establishing and nurturing churches, teaching new believers, and appointing leaders. Paul's life demonstrates that living out the Great Commission involves perseverance, adaptability, and a deep reliance on the Holy Spirit.

The Great Commission is not just a call to evangelism but to discipleship - teaching and nurturing believers in their faith journey. Matthew 28:19-20 emphasises making disciples of all nations, indicating that this mission transcends cultural and geographical boundaries. Acts 1:8 highlights the role of the Holy Spirit in empowering believers for this task. Living out the Great Commission involves sharing the Gospel through our words and actions, engaging in cross-cultural missions, and contributing to the spiritual growth of others.

Prayer Point:
Lord, empower me through Your Spirit to live out the Great Commission, sharing Your love and truth with all.

Friday June 21

Topic: The Power of Christian Community

Memory Verse: "And let us consider how we may spur one another on toward love and good deeds, not giving up meeting together, as some are in the habit of doing, but encouraging one another - and all the more as you see the Day approaching." **- Hebrews 10:24-25**

Bible Reading: Acts 2:42-47

Read & Learn:

The believers devoted themselves to the apostles' teaching, fellowship, breaking of bread, and prayer. They shared their possessions, met each other's needs, and worshipped together with glad and sincere hearts. This unity and generosity resulted in favour with all the people and the Lord added to their number daily.

The power of Christian community lies in its ability to foster spiritual growth, provide support and accountability, and extend Christ's love to others. Hebrews 10:24-25 emphasises the importance of meeting together to encourage one another in faith and good works. Christian community is where we can learn, grow, and be challenged in our faith. It's a place of refuge and strength, especially in difficult times. In a Christian community, we experience the tangible presence of Christ as we live out the "one another" commands of the New Testament - loving, serving, forgiving, and bearing each other's burdens. It's in this context that we grow more effectively than in isolation, becoming more like Christ and impacting the world around us.

Prayer Point:
Father, help me to actively participate in and contribute to the spiritual growth and support of my fellow believers. Use our Church community to be a light in the world, drawing others to Your love and grace.

Saturday June 22

Topic: Causes and Impact of Division

Memory Verse: "I appeal to you, brothers and sisters, in the name of our Lord Jesus Christ, that all of you agree with one another in what you say and that there be no divisions among you, but that you be perfectly united in mind and thought." **- 1 Corinthians 1:10**

Bible Reading: 1 Corinthians 1:1-17

Read & Learn:

The Apostle Paul addressed the issue of divisions among the church in Corinth due to allegiance to different leaders (1 Corinthians 1:12-13). This division was not just a disagreement but a fundamental breakdown in unity, affecting the church's witness and fellowship. Paul's response was not to take sides but to point them back to Christ, the true foundation of the church. This situation in Corinth serves as a cautionary tale about the dangers of division, especially when it shifts focus from Christ to human leaders or ideologies.

According to James 3:16 the causes of division often stem from pride, envy, and placing personal or group interests above the collective good. Such divisions can lead to a weakened community, hindered spiritual growth, and a compromised witness to the world. Unity, on the other hand, is not about uniformity in all opinions but about harmony in purpose and love.

Prayer Point:
Father, help us to recognise and address the causes of division, fostering unity in our community through love and mutual respect. Guide us to be peacemakers, seeking harmony in our relationships. and focusing on our shared faith in You. Heal the divisions within Your church and help us to be a united witness of Your grace and truth in a divided world.

Sunday June 23

Topic: Facing Persecution with Faith

Memory Verse: "Indeed, all who desire to live a godly life in Christ Jesus will be persecuted." **- 2 Timothy 3:12**

Bible Reading: Matthew 5:10-12

Read & Learn:

The story of Shadrach, Meshach, and Abednego in Daniel 3 is a profound example of facing persecution with faith. These three young men, living in exile in Babylon, refused to bow down to King Nebuchadnezzar's golden statue. Their refusal, grounded in their unwavering faith in God, led to their being thrown into a fiery furnace. Remarkably, they emerged unscathed, without even the smell of fire on them. Their faith under fire literally and their miraculous deliverance became a powerful testimony to God's protection and sovereignty, even in the face of intense persecution.

Facing persecution with faith is a challenging yet integral part of the Christian journey. Matthew 5:10-12 reminds us that those who are persecuted for righteousness are blessed, for theirs is the kingdom of heaven. This beatitude, along with 2 Timothy 3:12, underscores that persecution is often a reality for those living out their faith. It requires a steadfast trust in God, a willingness to endure hardship for the sake of Christ, and a perspective that values eternal rewards over temporal comfort. Persecution, while difficult, can deepen our faith, strengthen our character, and serve as a powerful witness to the truth and power of the Gospel.

Prayer Point:

Lord, in times of persecution, strengthen my faith and help me to trust in Your sovereign protection. Give me the courage to stand firm in my beliefs, even when faced with opposition.

Monday June 24

Topic: Biblical Wisdom for Financial Management

Memory Verse: "Honour the Lord with your wealth, with the first fruits of all your crops; then your barns will be filled to overflowing, and your vats will brim over with new wine." **- Proverbs 3:9-10**

Bible Reading: Luke 16:10-13

Read & Learn:

The parable of the talents in Matthew 25:14-30 offers profound insights into financial management from a biblical perspective. In this parable, a man going on a journey entrusts his property to his servants according to their abilities. Upon his return, he assesses how each servant managed his resources. The servants who diligently invested and multiplied their talents were commended and rewarded, while the servant who fearfully hid his talent was reprimanded. This story teaches the importance of responsible stewardship, wise investment, and the understanding that all we have is entrusted to us by God and should be used for His glory.

Proverbs 3:9-10 emphasises honouring God with our wealth, which includes responsible management and giving. Luke 16:10-13 teaches the importance of being faithful in small things, including our finances, and warns against the idolatry of money. Managing finances biblically isn't just about personal prosperity but about using our resources in a way that reflects our values and priorities as followers of Christ. It involves budgeting, avoiding debt and saving for the future.

Prayer Point:
Father, guide me in managing my finances with wisdom, stewardship, and generosity, honouring You in all that I do. Help me to be a faithful steward of the resources You have entrusted to me, using them for Your glory and purpose.

Tuesday June 25

Topic: The Importance of Christian Education

Memory Verse: "Start children off on the way they should go, and even when they are old they will not turn from it." **- Proverbs 22:6**

Bible Reading: Deuteronomy 6:6-7

Read & Learn:

Timothy's upbringing, as referenced in 2 Timothy 1:5 and 3:14-17, is an excellent example of the impact of Christian education. Timothy was taught the Scriptures from an early age by his mother Eunice and grandmother Lois. This foundation in the faith prepared him for a life of ministry alongside Paul. Their influence on Timothy underscores the vital role of Christian education in nurturing faith, developing a biblical worldview, and preparing individuals for a life of service and witness.

Christian education, whether formal or informal, plays a crucial role in shaping beliefs, values, and character. It's not just about academic knowledge but about instilling a deep understanding and love for God's Word, as seen in Deuteronomy 6:6-7. This passage emphasises the importance of diligently teaching children God's commands, integrating them into every aspect of daily life. Christian education helps individuals to discern truth, make wise decisions, and engage with the world from a Christ-centred perspective. It equips believers to navigate life's challenges with biblical wisdom and to effectively contribute to their communities and the Kingdom of God.

Prayer Point:

Father, bless our efforts in Christian education, that we may raise up a generation grounded in Your truth and love. Guide educators and parents in teaching Your Word, that it may deeply root in the hearts of learners. Use Christian education to equip us for effective service and witness in Your Kingdom and the world.

Wednesday June 26

Topic: The Role of Mentoring in Spiritual Growth

Memory Verse: "In everything set them an example by doing what is good. In your teaching show integrity, seriousness and soundness of speech that cannot be condemned, so that those who oppose you may be ashamed because they have nothing bad to say about us."
- Titus 2:7-8

Bible Reading: 2 Timothy 2:1-2

Read & Learn:

The relationship between Paul and Timothy, as depicted in the New Testament, exemplifies the role of mentoring in spiritual growth. Paul, an experienced apostle, took young Timothy under his wing, guiding him in his faith and ministry. Through letters, personal visits, and shared missionary journeys, Paul imparted wisdom, encouragement, and practical advice to Timothy. This mentorship not only helped Timothy grow in his faith and leadership skills but also ensured the continuation of sound teaching and strong leadership in the early church.

Mentoring in a Christian context is a relational process where a more mature believer guides and supports a less experienced believer in their spiritual journey. 2 Timothy 2:1-2 highlights the importance of passing on what has been learned to faithful individuals who can teach others. This process of discipleship is essential for spiritual growth, as it provides personal guidance, accountability, and encouragement. It's about investing in others, just as Christ invested in His disciples, fostering a legacy of faith that multiplies and extends beyond individual lives.

Prayer Point:
Father, guide me to be both a mentor and a mentee, learning from others and passing on Your wisdom.

Thursday June 27

Topic: Exploring the Psalms of Praise and Lament

Memory Verse: "Let everything that has breath praise the Lord. Praise the Lord." **- Psalm 150:6**

Bible Reading: Psalm 22:1-5; Psalm 150

Read & Learn:

The life of King David, the author of many Psalms, embodies the full spectrum of human emotion expressed in the Psalms of praise and lament. David's life was marked by both high victories and deep valleys of despair. In times of triumph, such as the defeat of Goliath, David's response was one of exuberant praise (1 Samuel 17). In contrast, during periods of anguish, like his flight from Absalom, David poured out his heart in laments, expressing his fears and sorrows yet always returning to a place of trust in God (2 Samuel 15, Psalm 3). David's Psalms teach us that in every circumstance, whether joy or sorrow, we can turn to God with honesty and faith.

The Psalms of praise and lament offer a model for how we can approach God in every season of life. Psalms of praise, like Psalm 150, encourage us to celebrate God's goodness and mighty works, reminding us of His greatness and our reason to hope. On the other hand, Psalms of lament, such as Psalm 22, give voice to our pain, confusion, and longing, allowing us to bring our deepest struggles before God. These Psalms teach us that it's okay to express our true feelings to God, whether they are of joy or sorrow. They remind us that God is present in every aspect of our lives.

Prayer Point:

Heavenly Father, thank You for the Psalms that teach me to praise You in joy and cry out to You in sorrow. Let my life be a continuous Psalm of praise, acknowledging Your goodness and grace in every situation.

Friday June 28

Topic: The Christian Response to Suffering

Memory Verse: "I consider that our present sufferings are not worth comparing with the glory that will be revealed in us." - **Romans 8:18**

Bible Reading: 1 Peter 4:12-19

Read & Learn:

The story of Job is a profound example of the Christian response to suffering. Despite losing his wealth, his children, and his health, Job maintained his faith in God. He wrestled with deep questions and emotions, yet he did not sin by charging God with wrongdoing. Job's story teaches us that it is natural to question and grieve in our suffering, but through it all, we can hold onto our faith, trusting in God's sovereignty and goodness, even when we do not understand our circumstances.

Suffering is an inevitable part of the human experience, and the Christian response is unique in its perspective and approach. Romans 8:18 encourages believers to view present sufferings in light of the future glory in Christ. 1 Peter 4:12-19 reminds Christians not to be surprised by fiery trials but to rejoice in sharing Christ's sufferings. The Christian response to suffering involves acknowledging our pain and grief, leaning into our community for support, and maintaining our hope and trust in God. It's about seeing our trials as opportunities for spiritual growth and deeper reliance on God, knowing that He is with us in our suffering and has a purpose in it.

Prayer Point:

Father, grant me the strength to endure hardships, seeing them as opportunities to grow closer to You and to be refined in my faith. Comfort me in my pain, and use my experiences to help others who suffer, sharing the hope and love found in You.

Saturday June 29

Topic: Biblical Insights on Health and Wellness

Memory Verse: "Do you not know that your bodies are temples of the Holy Spirit, who is in you, whom you have received from God? You are not your own; you were bought at a price. Therefore honour God with your bodies." - **1 Corinthians 6:19-20**

Bible Reading: 3 John 1:2

Read & Learn:

Daniel 1:8-16 show that despite being in a foreign land and under pressure to conform, Daniel chose to honour God by maintaining dietary practices that aligned with his faith. This decision, which could have resulted in severe consequences, instead led to Daniel and his friends appearing healthier and better nourished than those who ate the royal food. This story demonstrates the importance of honouring God with our bodies and making choices that promote our physical well-being.

1 Corinthians 6:19-20 reminds us that our bodies are not our own but are to be used to honour God. This includes how we eat, exercise, rest, and avoid harmful behaviours. 3 John 1:2 expresses the desire for good health and a prosperous life, indicating that physical well-being is a valid concern for believers. Biblical insights on health and wellness are not just about physical health but encompass mental, emotional, and spiritual well-being, encouraging a holistic approach to living a life that honours God.

Prayer Point:
Father, help me to honour You with my body, making choices that promote holistic health and wellness. Guide me in caring for my physical, mental, emotional, and spiritual well-being, recognising my body as a temple of the Holy Spirit.

Sunday June 30

Topic: The Concept of Christian Stewardship

Memory Verse: "Each of you should use whatever gift you have received to serve others, as faithful stewards of God's grace in its various forms." **- 1 Peter 4:10**

Bible Reading: Genesis 1:26-28

Read & Learn:

The parable of the talents in Matthew 25:14-30 illustrates the concept of Christian stewardship vividly. In this parable, a man going on a journey entrusts his property to his servants according to their abilities. Upon his return, he assesses how each servant managed his resources. The servants who diligently invested and multiplied their talents were commended and rewarded, while the servant who fearfully hid his talent was reprimanded. This story teaches the importance of responsible stewardship, using the gifts and resources God has given us for His glory and the benefit of others.

Christian stewardship extends beyond financial management; it encompasses the responsible use of all resources God has entrusted to us, including time, talents, the environment, and our bodies. 1 Peter 4:10 encourages us to use our gifts to serve others, highlighting that everything we have is a gift from God and should be used in service to Him and our fellow humans. Stewardship is rooted in the recognition that we are caretakers, not owners, of what we have. It's about making choices that reflect our values as followers of Christ and our commitment to God's purposes.

Prayer Point:
Father, help me to be a faithful steward of all the resources You have entrusted to me, using them for Your glory and the good of others.

Monday July 01

Topic: Understanding the Lord's Prayer

Memory Verse: "This is the confidence we have in approaching God: that if we ask anything according to his will, he hears us."

- 1 John 5:14

Bible Reading: Luke 11:1-4

Read & Learn:

The Lord's Prayer, as taught by Jesus to His disciples, is more than a prayer; it's a framework for understanding how to approach God in prayer. In Luke 11:1-4 Jesus provided a prayer that encompasses praise, submission to God's will, reliance on Him for daily needs, seeking forgiveness, and guidance in spiritual warfare. This prayer reflects the heart of Jesus' teaching on prayer, emphasising a relationship with God as our Father, the desire for God's kingdom and will, dependence on God for provision, and the need for spiritual vigilance.

The Lord's Prayer is a model for Christian prayer that encapsulates key aspects of our relationship with God. It begins with acknowledging God's holiness and sovereignty ("hallowed be your name"), expressing a desire for His kingdom and will. It then shifts to our daily needs ("give us today our daily bread"), reminding us of our dependence on God for all things. The prayer also emphasises forgiveness, both receiving it from God and extending it to others, and concludes with a plea for spiritual protection.

Prayer Point:
Father, help me to understand and embody the principles of the Lord's Prayer in my daily life and communion with You. Teach me to rely on You for my daily needs, to forgive and be forgiven, and to seek Your guidance and protection from temptation.

Tuesday July 02

Topic: The Journey of Faith and Doubt

Memory Verse: "Immediately the boy's father exclaimed, 'I do believe; help me overcome my unbelief!'" **- Mark 9:24**

Bible Reading: James 1:5-6

Read & Learn:

The story of Thomas, often called "Doubting Thomas," in John 20:24-29, powerfully illustrates the journey of faith and doubt. After Jesus' resurrection, Thomas struggled to believe that Jesus had appeared to the other disciples in his absence. He expressed a desire for tangible proof of Jesus' resurrection. When Jesus later appeared and invited Thomas to touch His wounds, Thomas' doubt turned to faith, leading him to exclaim, "My Lord and my God!" This story shows that doubt is a part of the faith journey and that encountering Jesus can transform our doubts into deeper faith.

Faith and doubt are not necessarily opposites; rather, they can be part of the same journey. Doubt can lead to questions, exploration, and ultimately a deeper understanding of faith. The father's cry in Mark 9:24 embodies this tension between belief and unbelief. James 1:5-6 encourages believers to ask God for wisdom without doubting, indicating that seeking understanding is a part of faith.

Prayer Point:

Lord, in my moments of doubt, help me to seek You earnestly, trusting that You will guide me to a deeper understanding and stronger faith.

Wednesday July 03

Topic: The Impact of Christian Art and Culture

Memory Verse: "He has filled him with the Spirit of God, with wisdom, with understanding, with knowledge and with all kinds of skills - to make artistic designs for work in gold, silver and bronze."
                                                                    - Exodus 35:31-32

Bible Reading: Psalm 96:9-12

Read & Learn:

The construction of the Tabernacle in Exodus 35-36 is a testament to the impact of Christian art and culture. Bezalel, appointed by God, was endowed with the Holy Spirit to create artistic designs in the Tabernacle. His work, along with that of other skilled artisans, was not merely decorative but served to create a space that reflected God's glory and beauty. This story illustrates how art and culture, inspired, and guided by the Spirit, can be powerful expressions of faith, drawing people into a deeper understanding and appreciation of God's character and truths.

Christian art and culture encompass a wide range of creative expressions that communicate and reflect the truths of the Christian faith. Exodus 35:31-32 shows that God values and empowers artistic skills and creativity. These creative expressions can impact both believers and non-believers by conveying the beauty of the Gospel, inspiring worship, and providing a tangible representation of spiritual truths. Christian art and culture can bridge gaps, open dialogues, and enrich our understanding of God and His work in the world.

Prayer Point:
Father, help me to discover and express the creative gift in me and use them to honour you. Bless the artists and creators within Your church, that through their work, Your beauty and truth may be revealed.

Thursday July 04

Topic: Lessons from the Early Church

Memory Verse: "They devoted themselves to the apostles' teaching and to fellowship, to the breaking of bread and to prayer." - **Acts 2:42**

Bible Reading: Acts 4:32-35

Read & Learn:

In Acts 4:32-35, the believers shared everything they had, ensuring that no one among them was in need. This radical generosity was a tangible expression of their love for one another and their commitment to Christ's teachings. Their lifestyle of sharing and caring for each other was a powerful testimony to the surrounding community, attracting many to the faith. The early church's example challenges us to consider how our lives and communities reflect the love and unity that should characterise followers of Christ.

The early church provides valuable lessons for Christians today. Their devotion to the apostles' teaching, fellowship, breaking of bread, and prayer, as mentioned in Acts 2:42, highlights the importance of sound doctrine, community, sacraments, and prayer in the life of the church. Their example of sharing resources and supporting one another speaks to the need for practical expressions of love and generosity within the Christian community. The unity and authenticity they displayed were instrumental in the growth and impact of the early church. These principles remain relevant for contemporary Christian communities, calling us to live out our faith in tangible, communal, and transformative ways.

Prayer Point:

Father, inspire our church communities to embody the unity, generosity, and devotion of the early church. May our lives reflect the love, generosity, and authenticity that marked the early church, drawing others to Your grace and truth.

Friday July 05

Topic: When God Does Not Make Sense

Memory Verse: "In all this, Job did not sin by charging God with wrongdoing." **- Job 1:22**

Bible Reading: Job 42:10-15

Read & Learn:

The story of Job is a powerful example of when God's ways do not make sense to us. Job was a righteous man who experienced immense suffering and loss, including the deaths of his children and the deterioration of his health. Job questioned God and wrestled with the apparent injustice of his circumstances. However, in the end, God revealed His sovereignty and wisdom to Job, reminding him that His ways are higher and beyond human comprehension. Job learned to trust God's wisdom and goodness even when he couldn't understand the reasons behind his suffering.

There are moments in life when we encounter situations that seem confusing, painful, and beyond our understanding. During such times, it's essential to remember that God's ways are not always our ways, and His thoughts are far above our thoughts. We may not always grasp the reasons behind our circumstances, but we can trust in God's character and sovereignty.

The story of Job teaches us that even in our moments of doubt and suffering, God is in control. Though we may not understand His ways, we can choose to trust in His goodness and wisdom, knowing that He works all things together for our good.

Prayer Point:
Father, I confess that Your ways are higher than my, and I trust in Your wisdom. Grant me the faith to trust You even when I cannot understand or comprehend Your ways.

Saturday July 06

Topic: The Dynamics of Faith and Science

Memory Verse: "The LORD by wisdom founded the earth; by understanding He established the heavens." - **Proverbs 3:19**

Bible Reading: Genesis 1:1-31

Read & Learn:

The relationship between faith and science has often been seen as contentious, but it need not be. The story of creation in Genesis 1 presents a framework where the natural world is a product of divine design. It shows that the universe, in all its complexity and wonder, is a reflection of God's creativity and power. Throughout history, many scientists who were also people of faith, like Isaac Newton and Gregor Mendel, viewed scientific exploration as a way to understand God's handiwork. Their discoveries did not diminish their faith but rather enhanced their awe of the Creator. This synergy between faith and science can inspire contemporary believers to appreciate and study the natural world as a manifestation of God's glory.

Faith provides a foundation of moral and ethical values, while science offers a method for understanding the natural world. The Biblical narrative doesn't contradict scientific discovery; instead, it gives it context and meaning. Embracing both faith and science enriches our understanding of the universe and our place in it. For Christians, this means acknowledging God's sovereignty in creation while valuing scientific inquiry as a means to discover the intricacies of His work.

Prayer Point:
Lord, grant us wisdom to see Your hand in the beauty and complexity of the universe. Help us to embrace both faith and scientific inquiry, using each to deepen our understanding of Your creation.

Sunday July 07

Topic: The Gifts of the Holy Spirit

Memory Verse: "Now to each one the manifestation of the Spirit is given for the common good." **- 1 Corinthians 12:7**

Bible Reading: 1 Corinthians 12:4-11

Read & Learn:

The disciples received the Holy Spirit, who bestowed upon them various gifts like speaking in tongues, prophecy, and healing. These gifts were not for personal glory but for building up the church and spreading the Gospel. This event marked a significant transformation in the disciples, empowering them to carry out God's work with boldness and effectiveness. The story of Pentecost is a powerful reminder of how the Holy Spirit equips believers with diverse gifts to fulfil God's purposes and to serve one another in love.

The gifts of the Holy Spirit, as outlined in 1 Corinthians 12:4-11, include wisdom, knowledge, faith, healing, miraculous powers, prophecy, discernment, speaking in tongues, and interpretation of tongues. These gifts are given by the same Spirit to different individuals for the benefit of the entire church. They are not a measure of one's spirituality or favour with God but are intended for the common good and to edify the body of Christ. Understanding and embracing these gifts helps believers to contribute to the church's mission and to foster unity and growth within the Christian community.

Prayer Point:
Holy Spirit, guide me to understand and use the gifts You have bestowed upon me for the benefit and edification of the church. Lord, help me to value and respect the diverse gifts within the body of Christ, using mine to serve others and glorify Your name.

Monday July 08

Topic: Nurturing Spiritual Gifts in the Church

Memory Verse: "Now to each one the manifestation of the Spirit is given for the common good." - **1 Corinthians 12:7**

Bible Reading: Romans 12:3-8

Read & Learn:

Consider the story of Bezalel in Exodus 31:1-5. God chose Bezalel and filled him with the Spirit of God, granting him abilities in artistic craftsmanship to construct the Tabernacle. Bezalel's story is a powerful example of how God equips individuals with specific gifts for His purposes. His gift was not preaching or prophecy, typically highlighted in spiritual contexts, but a creative skill used to glorify God and serve the community. Bezalel's role in building the Tabernacle reminds us that every gift, no matter how unconventional it may seem, is valuable and can be used to further God's kingdom. His story challenges us to recognise and celebrate the diverse gifts within our church community, understanding that each plays a crucial part in God's plan.

The nurturing of spiritual gifts in the church is vital for its health and mission. Recognising and nurturing these gifts is not just the responsibility of church leaders but of the entire congregation. It involves creating an environment where individuals are encouraged to discover, develop, and deploy their gifts for the benefit of the church and the glory of God.

Prayer Point:
Father, help us to recognise and nurture the spiritual gifts You have given to each of us. Empower us by the Holy Spirit, to serve one another with the gifts You have bestowed, building up the body of Christ in love.

Tuesday July 09

Topic: The Challenge of Christian Discernment

Memory Verse: "But solid food is for the mature, who by constant use have trained themselves to distinguish good from evil."

- Hebrews 5:14

Bible Reading: 1 Kings 3:16-28

Read & Learn:

Two women came to Solomon, each claiming to be the mother of the same baby. Solomon, faced with an impossible decision, displayed extraordinary wisdom by suggesting to cut the baby in two, each woman to receive half. His unconventional approach revealed the true mother, as she was willing to give up her child to save its life. This story demonstrates the need for God given discernment in complex situations. Solomon's wisdom, a gift from God, allowed him to see beyond the surface, making a decision that revealed truth and upheld justice. His example is a powerful reminder of the importance of seeking divine guidance and wisdom in our decision-making processes.

Christian discernment is the ability to make wise choices and understand the difference between right and wrong, as guided by the Holy Spirit. It involves more than just intellectual understanding; it requires spiritual sensitivity and a deep connection with God's Word. The challenge for believers is to cultivate this discernment through prayer, study of the Scriptures, and reliance on the Holy Spirit to distinguishing truth from deception.

Prayer Point:
Lord, grant us the wisdom to discern Your will in every situation we face. Guide us in our decision-making processes, that we may reflect Your wisdom and justice.

Wednesday July 10

Topic: Exploring Biblical Prophecy Today

Memory Verse: "We also have the prophetic message as something completely reliable, and you will do well to pay attention to it, as to a light shining in a dark place, until the day dawns and the morning star rises in your hearts." **- 2 Peter 1:19**

Bible Reading: Daniel 2:20-23

Read & Learn:

The book of Daniel, particularly in chapter 2, narrates an intriguing account of King Nebuchadnezzar's dream and Daniel's interpretation of it. Nebuchadnezzar had a troubling dream that none of his wise men could interpret. Daniel, with God's revelation, not only described the dream but also explained its meaning, which foretold the rise and fall of empires and the establishment of God's eternal kingdom. This event shows the precision and reliability of biblical prophecy. Daniel's ability to interpret the dream when no one else could highlights the divine origin of true prophecy. This story invites us to consider how biblical prophecy, though ancient, still offers insight and hope for today's world, reminding us of God's sovereignty over history and the future.

Prophecies in the Bible, like those in Daniel and Revelation, often speak to future events and divine plans. 2 Peter 1:19 encourages believers to pay attention to these prophecies, viewing them as reliable and illuminating guides. Biblical prophecy encourages believers to live with hope and faithfulness, looking forward to the fulfilment of God's promises.

Prayer Point:
Father, help us to see Your prophecies as beacons of hope, reminding us of Your control over history and the future.

Thursday July 11

Topic: The Importance of Integrity in Leadership

Memory Verse: "The integrity of the upright guides them, but the unfaithful are destroyed by their duplicity." **- Proverbs 11:3**

Bible Reading: 2 Samuel 12:1-14

Read & Learn:

The story of King David and his encounter with the prophet Nathan in 2 Samuel 12:1-14 highlights the critical importance of integrity in leadership. David, after committing adultery with Bathsheba and arranging the death of her husband, was confronted by Nathan through a powerful parable. Nathan's parable led David to recognise his own sin, prompting him to repent. This narrative underscores how integrity, or the lack thereof, profoundly impacts a leader's effectiveness and moral authority. David's initial failure, followed by his heartfelt repentance, teaches that integrity involves accountability, honesty, and the courage to face one's mistakes. It's a sobering reminder that leaders are held to high standards and that their actions have significant consequences for themselves and those they lead.

Leaders with integrity inspire confidence and loyalty in their followers, create a positive and ethical work culture, and are more likely to make decisions that benefit the greater good. The challenge for leaders is to maintain their integrity even in the face of difficult choices or potential personal gain. This involves self-awareness, accountability, and a commitment to a set of moral and ethical principles that guide one's decisions and actions.

Prayer Point:
Lord, grant us the strength to lead with integrity, upholding truth and justice in all our actions. Help us to be accountable for our actions and to lead by example, inspiring others through our conduct.

Friday July 12

Topic: The Christian Approach to Conflict Resolution

Memory Verse: "Blessed are the peacemakers, for they will be called children of God." - **Matthew 5:9**

Bible Reading: Matthew 18:15-17

Read & Learn:

The narrative of Paul and Barnabas in Acts 15:36-41 presents a practical example of conflict resolution in the early church. They had a disagreement over John Mark's role in their ministry, leading to a sharp dispute. Instead of letting this conflict hinder their mission, they chose to part ways amicably, with each continuing to spread the gospel in different areas. This story illustrates that conflicts, when approached with a Christ-like attitude, can lead to constructive outcomes. Paul and Barnabas respected each other's perspectives and separated on good terms, demonstrating that even in disagreements, Christians can maintain love and respect for one another. Their example teaches us the importance of addressing conflicts directly, seeking mutual understanding, and always prioritising the mission of the church and the unity of believers.

In Matthew 18:15-17, Jesus provides a framework for resolving conflicts within the church: addressing the issue directly with the individual, seeking reconciliation, and involving others only if necessary for resolution. Christian conflict resolution is not about proving oneself right, but about restoring relationships and preserving unity in the body of Christ.

Prayer Point:
Father, grant us wisdom and patience to resolve conflicts in a manner that honours You. Help us to approach disagreements with a spirit of humility and a desire for reconciliation.

Saturday July 13

Topic: Understanding the Concept of God's Kingdom

Memory Verse: "But seek first his kingdom and his righteousness, and all these things will be given to you as well." **- Matthew 6:33**

Bible Reading: Luke 17:20-21

Read & Learn:

In Luke 13:18-21, Jesus teaches about the Kingdom of God using the parables of the mustard seed and the yeast. He compares the Kingdom to a mustard seed, which, though small when sown, grows into a large tree. Similarly, He likens it to yeast that a woman mixes into a large amount of flour until it works all through the dough. These parables illustrate how the Kingdom of God starts small within us and expands, influencing every part of our lives and the world around us. The Kingdom is not just a future reality but is also present in the here and now, growing and transforming lives in often unseen but profound ways. This teaches us that the Kingdom of God is not always about grandiose manifestations, but about the gradual and transformative work of God's presence and principles in our daily lives.

The concept of God's Kingdom is central to Jesus' teaching and the Christian faith. Understanding the Kingdom of God requires recognising it as a spiritual realm where God's values - love, justice, peace, and grace - prevail. It's about the redemptive work of Christ, bringing reconciliation and restoration. It's a call to be agents of God's Kingdom, influencing the world through our lives and actions.

Prayer Point:
Father, guide us in understanding and living out the principles of Your Kingdom in our daily lives. Empower us by the Holy Spirit, to be agents of transformation, bringing the values of Your Kingdom to our world.

Sunday July 14

Topic: Faith and Environmental Responsibility

Memory Verse: "The Lord God took the man and put him in the Garden of Eden to work it and take care of it." **- Genesis 2:15**

Bible Reading: Psalm 24:1-2

Read & Learn:

In the book of Jonah, particularly in chapters 3 and 4, there is an interesting aspect often overlooked: Jonah's concern for the plant that provided him shade. After his mission in Nineveh, Jonah becomes upset when a worm destroys the plant that was giving him shelter from the sun. This story, while primarily about God's mercy and Jonah's attitudes, also touches on a subtle but important point: our relationship with and care for the environment. Jonah's distress over the loss of a single plant serves as a metaphor for the broader responsibility humans have towards the natural world.

Genesis 2:15 shows that from the beginning, humanity was tasked with caring for creation. This stewardship is not merely about utilising resources but about maintaining and preserving the natural world. Psalm 24:1-2 declares that the earth is the Lord's, and everything in it, emphasising that we are caretakers of God's creation, not its owners. As Christians, acknowledging the intrinsic value of the environment and actively working to protect and preserve it is a reflection of our reverence for the Creator, fulfillment of our God-given mandate and ensuring a sustainable and flourishing world for future generations.

Prayer Point:
Father, help us to be mindful stewards of the beautiful world You have entrusted to us. Give us the wisdom and commitment to care for the environment, reflecting our respect and love for You.

Monday July 15

Topic: The Role of Praise in Overcoming Challenges

Memory Verse: "I will extol the Lord at all times; his praise will always be on my lips." - **Psalm 34:1**

Bible Reading: Acts 16:25-34

Read & Learn:

The account of Paul and Silas in Acts 16:25-34 powerfully illustrates the role of praise in overcoming challenges. Imprisoned and facing dire circumstances in Philippi, Paul and Silas chose to pray and sing hymns to God, despite their situation. Their praise was so fervent that it led to a miraculous earthquake, which opened the prison doors and unshackled all the prisoners. This act of praise not only brought about their physical liberation but also led to the spiritual awakening of the jailer and his family. This story highlights how praise can be a powerful tool in the midst of trials, not just as a means of seeking divine intervention, but as an expression of trust and faith in God's sovereignty, regardless of our circumstances. It teaches us that praising God in difficult times can shift our focus from our problems to God's power and presence.

Praise is a vital aspect of the Christian life, especially in the context of overcoming challenges. As stated in Psalm 34:1, praising God is a continuous action, not limited to times of ease and comfort. In difficult situations, praise can shift our perspective, helping us to see beyond our immediate problems and focus on God's strength and faithfulness.

Prayer Point:
Lord, help us to maintain a spirit of praise, even in the midst of our challenges and trials. Teach us to focus on Your strength and faithfulness through our praises, regardless of our circumstances.

Tuesday July 16

Topic: Biblical Perspectives on Human Rights

Memory Verse: "So God created mankind in his own image, in the image of God he created them; male and female he created them."
                                                            - Genesis 1:27

Bible Reading: Micah 6:8

Read & Learn:

The story of the Good Samaritan in Luke 10:25-37 offers profound insights into the biblical perspective on human rights. In this parable, a Samaritan, considered an outsider and enemy by the Jews, shows compassion to a beaten and robbed Jewish man, while others, including a priest and a Levite, pass by without helping. This story challenges societal norms and prejudices, emphasising the inherent value and dignity of every individual, irrespective of their nationality, race, or social status. Jesus uses this parable to teach the importance of loving and caring for our neighbours as a fundamental expression of justice and human rights. It illustrates that respect for human rights, according to the Bible, is rooted in the recognition of every person's worth as being created in the image of God.

According to Genesis 1:27, all people are made in God's image, granting each individual inherent worth and rights. Micah 6:8 calls for acting justly, loving mercy, and walking humbly with God, which includes advocating for and upholding the rights of others. Christians are called to see and treat others as God sees them, Recognising the God-given dignity and rights inherent in every person.

Prayer Point:

Heavenly Father, guide us in recognising and respecting the inherent dignity You have bestowed on every person. Empower us, Lord, to be advocates for justice and mercy, reflecting Your love and righteousness in our treatment of others.

Wednesday July 17

Topic: The Power of Christian Hospitality

Memory Verse: "Do not forget to show hospitality to strangers, for by so doing some people have shown hospitality to angels without knowing it." **- Hebrews 13:2**

Bible Reading: Genesis 18:1-15

Read & Learn:

The account of Abraham hosting three strangers in Genesis 18:1-15 provides a profound example of Christian hospitality. Abraham, without knowing their true identity, welcomed these visitors with great respect and generosity. He offered them food, rest, and comfort, demonstrating a deep sense of hospitality that was common in his culture but also reflective of his character. This act of kindness led to a remarkable encounter where one of the visitors, revealed to be the Lord, promised the birth of Isaac to Sarah. This story illustrates the power of hospitality to bring blessings and divine encounters. It shows that when we open our homes and hearts to others, especially strangers, we not only provide for their needs but also open ourselves to be blessed and used by God in ways we might not expect.

Christian hospitality is more than just a social courtesy; it's a powerful expression of love and service. Hospitality in the Christian context involves creating a space where people feel valued, cared for, and part of a community. It's an opportunity to demonstrate God's love and grace. In a world where many are isolated and lonely, Christian hospitality can be a powerful tool for connection and ministry.

Prayer Point:
Father, inspire us to practice hospitality, opening our homes and hearts to others as a reflection of Your love. Help us to recognise the opportunities for ministry and connection that hospitality provides.

Thursday July 18

Topic: Cultivating a Heart of Servitude

Memory Verse: "Just as the Son of Man did not come to be served, but to serve, and to give his life as a ransom for many."
- Matthew 20:28

Bible Reading: Acts 9:36-42

Read & Learn:

The life of Dorcas (also known as Tabitha) in Acts 9:36-42 is a compelling example of a heart of servitude. Dorcas was known for her good works and acts of charity, particularly making clothes for the widows in her community. Her acts of service were so impactful that, upon her death, the widows showed Peter the garments she had made, a testament to her selfless devotion. Her story illustrates the profound impact that acts of service, no matter how seemingly small, can have on a community. Dorcas' legacy was not about grandiose deeds but about consistent, humble service that met the needs of those around her.

As Jesus states in Matthew 20:28, He came to serve, setting an example for His followers. Philippians 2:3-8 further emphasises this by encouraging believers to have the same mindset as Christ, who humbled Himself and served others selflessly. Developing a heart of servitude involves shifting focus from self to others, seeking to meet their needs and showing love through practical actions. In practicing servitude, Christians can experience the joy of being Christ-like and make a tangible difference in the world.

Prayer Point:
Father, grant us the humility and compassion to serve others selflessly, reflecting Your love in our actions. Help us to recognise the needs around us and respond with the same kindness and generosity that You show us.

Friday July 19

Topic: Embracing God's Plan in Uncertain Times

Memory Verse: "Trust in the Lord with all your heart and lean not on your own understanding; in all your ways submit to him, and he will make your paths straight." **- Proverbs 3:5-6**

Bible Reading: Jeremiah 29:11-13

Read & Learn:

The story of Joseph, spanning from Genesis 37 to 50, vividly illustrates embracing God's plan in uncertain times. Joseph faced numerous challenges: he was sold into slavery by his brothers, falsely accused by Potiphar's wife, and imprisoned. Despite these circumstances, Joseph continued to trust in God. His faith and integrity eventually led him to a position of power in Egypt, where he was instrumental in saving many lives during a famine, including those of his own family.

Joseph's journey from the pit to the palace was riddled with uncertainty and hardship, yet he remained faithful, Recognising God's hand at work even in his darkest moments. His story teaches us that, in times of uncertainty, embracing God's plan involves trusting His sovereignty and believing that He can bring good out of our trials.

Embracing God's plan in uncertain times requires a deep trust in His wisdom and timing. It calls for a perspective that sees beyond immediate circumstances to the bigger picture of God's redemptive work. In uncertain times, this trust and surrender bring peace and hope, anchoring us in the truth of God's faithful presence and promises.

Prayer Point:
Father, in times of uncertainty, help us to trust in Your love, plan, and timing. Give us the peace that comes from surrendering our worries and plans to Your sovereign will.

Saturday July 20

Topic: The Significance of Old Testament Covenants

Memory Verse: "I will establish my covenant as an everlasting covenant between me and you and your descendants after you for the generations to come, to be your God and the God of your descendants after you." **- Genesis 17:7**

Bible Reading: Genesis 12:1-3

Read & Learn:

The covenant God made with Abraham in Genesis 12:1-3 is a pivotal moment in the Old Testament. God promised Abraham that He would make him into a great nation, bless him, and make his name great, so that he would be a blessing. This covenant was not only significant for Abraham but also set the stage for God's relationship with humanity. It was a promise of blessing and redemption, a foreshadowing of the coming Messiah who would bless all nations. The story of Abraham's covenant shows the depth of God's commitment to His people and His proactive plan for salvation.

The covenants in the Old Testament are crucial for understanding the story of salvation and God's relationship with humanity. They foreshadow the New Covenant established through Jesus Christ, which fulfils and transcends the Old Testament covenants, offering salvation and a restored relationship with God to all who believe. Understanding these covenants provides a deeper appreciation for the continuity and fulfilment of God's redemptive plan through history.

Prayer Point:
Father, help us to understand the depth and significance of Your covenants and guide us in living out the truths of Your New Covenant.

Sunday July 21

Topic: Christian Perspectives on Wealth and Poverty

Memory Verse: "For who makes you different from anyone else? What do you have that you did not receive? And if you did receive it, why do you boast as though you did not?" **- 1 Corinthians 4:7**

Bible Reading: 1 Timothy 6:17-19

Read & Learn:

The parable of the Rich Man and Lazarus in Luke 16:19-31 offers a striking perspective on wealth and poverty. In this story, a rich man lives in luxury while Lazarus, a poor man, suffers at his gate. After their deaths, their roles are reversed; Lazarus is comforted in Abraham's bosom, while the rich man is tormented. This parable is not a condemnation of wealth itself but a warning against indifference and selfishness.

Christian perspectives on wealth and poverty focus on stewardship, compassion, and the dangers of materialism. According to 1 Timothy 6:17-19, wealth is not inherently negative, but the love of money and the neglect of moral and spiritual responsibilities are.

Poverty, on the other hand, is not seen as a sign of spiritual favour or moral superiority, but as a situation requiring the compassion and support of those who can help. The Christian approach to wealth and poverty is rooted in the understanding that all resources are provided by God and should be used in ways that honour Him and reflect His love and care for all people.

Prayer Point:
Heavenly Father, guide us in using our resources wisely and compassionately to honour You. Teach us to be generous and to care for those in need, reflecting Your love and kindness.

Monday July 22

Topic: Overcoming Anxiety through Faith

Memory Verse: "Do not be anxious about anything, but in every situation, by prayer and petition, with thanksgiving, present your requests to God. And the peace of God, which transcends all understanding, will guard your hearts and your minds in Christ Jesus."
                                          - Philippians 4:6-7

Bible Reading: Matthew 6:25-34

Read & Learn:

In 1 Samuel 1, the story of Hannah's deep anxiety and her subsequent faith-filled response offers insight into overcoming anxiety through faith. Hannah, who was deeply distressed by her inability to conceive a child, poured out her heart to God in prayer instead of succumbing to her anxiety. Her faith and persistence in prayer brought her peace and eventually led to the birth of her son, Samuel. Hannah's experience teaches us that in moments of anxiety and distress, turning to God in honest prayer can bring comfort and peace. Her story exemplifies how faith can lead us to surrender our anxieties to God, trusting in His care and timing, even when the outcome is uncertain.

Overcoming anxiety through faith involves trusting in God's sovereignty and goodness, as highlighted in Philippians 4:6-7. It's about shifting our focus from our worries to God's promises and power. Jesus addresses this in Matthew 6:25-34, urging us not to worry about our lives, as God knows our needs and cares for us deeply.

Prayer Point:
Father, grant us peace that transcends understanding as we surrender our worries and fears to You, trusting in Your care and plan for our lives.

Tuesday July 23

Topic: The Biblical Concept of Justice

Memory Verse: "He has shown you, O mortal, what is good. And what does the Lord require of you? To act justly and to love mercy and to walk humbly with your God." **- Micah 6:8**

Bible Reading: 2 Samuel 12:1-15

Read & Learn:

The account of the prophet Nathan confronting King David in 2 Samuel 12:1-15 is a powerful illustration of the biblical concept of justice. This narrative highlights the importance of accountability and justice, even for the powerful. Nathan's courage to confront the king, and David's subsequent repentance, exemplify the principles of justice: standing up for the wronged, holding those in power accountable, and seeking restoration and forgiveness when wrongs have been committed.

As stated in Micah 6:8, God requires His people to act justly, love mercy, and walk humbly with Him. Isaiah 1:16-17 further emphasises this by instructing us to seek justice, encourage the oppressed, defend the cause of the fatherless, and plead the case of the widow. Biblical justice involves more than fairness and legal equity; it encompasses compassion, empathy, and action on behalf of those who are vulnerable. It calls for a proactive stance in correcting injustices and promoting righteousness. This concept challenges believers to be agents of justice in their communities, reflecting God's heart for justice in their actions and attitudes.

Prayer Point:
Father, guide us to act justly and to be voices for the voiceless in our world. Help us to embody your love and mercy, standing up against injustice wherever we see it.

Wednesday July 24

Topic: Understanding and Experiencing God's Grace

Memory Verse: "For it is by grace you have been saved, through faith—and this is not from yourselves, it is the gift of God—not by works, so that no one can boast." **- Ephesians 2:8-9**

Bible Reading: Luke 15:11-32

Read & Learn:

The story of the Prodigal Son in Luke 15:11-32 beautifully illustrates the concept of God's grace. This parable demonstrates the nature of God's grace: unconditional love and forgiveness, not based on our merits or actions. The father's response to his wayward son is a powerful depiction of how God receives us when we turn to Him, regardless of our past. This story encourages us to understand that God's grace is about His generous love and mercy, freely given to us, not because we deserve it, but because of His profound love for us.

Understanding and experiencing God's grace is fundamental to the Christian faith. Ephesians 2:8-9 emphasises that salvation is a gift of grace through faith, not a result of our works. This means that grace is unearned and undeserved; it is freely given by God out of His immense love and mercy. It is transformative, empowering us to live in a way that honours God. Experiencing God's grace often leads to a profound sense of gratitude and a desire to extend grace to others. It reminds us of our worth in God's eyes and our identity as His beloved children. Embracing God's grace means accepting His forgiveness and love, and allowing it to transform our lives.

Prayer Point:
Lord, thank You for Your amazing grace, which saves and transforms us. Help us to fully embrace Your grace in our lives, understanding its depth and the freedom it offers.

Thursday July 25

Topic: The Role of Christian Parents

Memory Verse: "Train up a child in the way he should go, and when he is old he will not depart from it." **- Proverbs 22:6**

Bible Reading: 1 Samuel 1:21-28

Read & Learn:

In 1 Samuel 1-2, the story of Hannah, the mother of the prophet Samuel, offers insight into the role of Christian parents. Hannah's commitment to raising Samuel in the ways of the Lord, even before his birth, and her dedication to fulfilling her promise, reflect the profound responsibility of Christian parents. Her story teaches that parenting is not just about providing for physical needs but also about guiding children spiritually and setting a foundation in faith.

This guidance is not merely about enforcing rules but about modelling godly character, teaching biblical principles, and encouraging a personal relationship with God. Christian parenting is a stewardship responsibility, recognising that children are a gift from God and that parents are entrusted with their spiritual, emotional, and physical development. This role is carried out not in human wisdom but through prayer, reliance on God's grace, and the guidance of the Holy Spirit.

Prayer Point:
Heavenly Father, grant wisdom and guidance to Christian parents in their vital role of raising children in Your ways. Help parents to lovingly and effectively nurture their children's faith, character, and overall well-being.

Friday July 26

Topic: Navigating Christian Singleness

Memory Verse: "Nevertheless, each person should live as a believer in whatever situation the Lord has assigned to them, just as God has called them. This is the rule I lay down in all the churches."

- 1 Corinthians 7:17

Bible Reading: 1 Corinthians 7:32-35

Read & Learn:

The life of the Apostle Paul, as depicted in the New Testament, particularly in his epistles, provides a profound example of navigating Christian singleness. Paul, who was single, used his status to fully dedicate himself to the ministry and service of the early church. His life exemplifies the potential of singleness to be a time of undivided devotion to God and His work. Paul's teachings in 1 Corinthians 7:32-35 highlight the advantages of singleness in serving the Lord without distraction.

Navigating Christian singleness involves understanding and embracing singleness as a unique and valuable season of life. It's an opportunity for personal growth, ministry, and service without the added responsibilities of a marital relationship. Singleness is not a lesser state but a different one, with its own opportunities and challenges. Embracing singleness in a Christian context means seeking fulfilment and purpose in Christ, cultivating a vibrant personal and communal spiritual life, and contributing actively to the church and community.

Prayer Point:

Father, guide those who are single in Your ways, helping them to embrace and utilise this season for Your glory. Grant them peace, fulfilment, and a sense of purpose in their singleness.

Saturday July 27

Topic: Biblical Insights into Work Ethic

Memory Verse: "Whatever you do, work at it with all your heart, as working for the Lord, not for human masters, since you know that you will receive an inheritance from the Lord as a reward. It is the Lord Christ you are serving." - **Colossians 3:23-24**

Bible Reading: Proverbs 6:6-11

Read & Learn:

The account of Nehemiah rebuilding the walls of Jerusalem in the book of Nehemiah provides a compelling example of a strong work ethic rooted in a biblical perspective. Nehemiah faced significant opposition and challenges, but his commitment to the task, motivated by his faith and sense of calling, led him to persevere. He organised the people, dealt with threats and challenges, and completed the rebuilding in a remarkably short period. Nehemiah's leadership and dedication demonstrate the value of a work ethic that combines diligence, integrity, and a sense of purpose. His story shows that work, when undertaken with a commitment to excellence and as an act of service to God, is both rewarding and impactful.

Biblical insights into work ethic emphasise the value of hard work, integrity, and serving God through our labour. Colossians 3:23-24 encourages believers to work wholeheartedly, as if serving the Lord, not just human employers. This perspective transforms our approach to work, making it a form of worship and stewardship.

Prayer Point:
Heavenly Father, help us to embrace our work as an opportunity to serve and honour You. Guide us to work with integrity, diligence, and excellence, reflecting Your character in our professional lives.

Sunday July 28

Topic: The Power of Forgiving and Forgetting

Memory Verse: "Get rid of all bitterness, rage and anger, brawling and slander, along with every form of malice. Be kind and compassionate to one another, forgiving each other, just as in Christ God forgave you." - Ephesians 4:31-32 -

Bible Reading: Matthew 18:21-35

Read & Learn:

The story of Joseph and his brothers, spanning from Genesis 37 to Genesis 50, vividly illustrates the power of forgiving and forgetting. Despite being sold into slavery by his own brothers, falsely accused, and imprisoned, Joseph rose to a position of power in Egypt. When a famine led his brothers to seek help in Egypt, unaware of Joseph's identity, he responded not with revenge but with forgiveness. Joseph's decision to forgive his brothers, provide for them, and reconcile, despite their betrayal, highlights the transformative power of forgiveness. His ability to let go of the past and embrace the future without bitterness demonstrates the concept of "forgetting" in a biblical sense - not erasing the memory, but choosing not to let it dictate one's actions or attitudes.

Biblical forgiveness is not just a one-time act but a continual process of releasing resentment and choosing compassion. This kind of forgiveness and forgetting is liberating and healing, both for the one who forgives and the one forgiven, reflecting the grace and forgiveness offered to us through Christ.

Prayer Point:
Lord, grant us the strength to forgive those who have wronged us, following the example of Your boundless forgiveness. Help us to let go of bitterness and resentment, choosing a path of compassion and reconciliation.

Monday July 29

Topic: Living a Life of Spiritual Discipline

Memory Verse: "Have nothing to do with godless myths and old wives' tales; rather, train yourself to be godly. For physical training is of some value, but godliness has value for all things, holding promise for both the present life and the life to come." - **1 Timothy 4:7-8**

Bible Reading: Hebrews 12:11-13

Read & Learn:

The life of Daniel, as depicted in the Book of Daniel, particularly in chapters 1 and 6, provides an inspiring example of living a life of spiritual discipline. Despite being in exile and facing tremendous pressure to conform to the culture and practices of Babylon, Daniel remained steadfast in his commitment to God. Daniel's disciplined spiritual life, marked by regular prayer and adherence to God's commandments, not only maintained his personal integrity but also led to divine favour and influence. His story demonstrates how spiritual discipline is not a burdensome duty but a means of deepening one's relationship with God and standing firm in one's faith, even in challenging circumstances.

Spiritual disciplines, such as prayer, fasting, reading and meditating on Scripture, worship, and service, are not about earning God's favour but about aligning ourselves more closely with Him. They help in cultivating a godly character, discerning God's will, and becoming resilient in the face of life's challenges. The practice of these disciplines may require sacrifice and effort, but they ultimately lead to spiritual growth and a deeper sense of joy in one's walk with God.

Prayer Point:
Heavenly Father, help us to embrace the discipline of a spiritual life, strengthen us in our commitment to practices that deepen our faith and character.

Tuesday July 30

Topic: The Importance of Patience in Faith

Memory Verse: "Let perseverance finish its work so that you may be mature and complete, not lacking anything." **- James 1:4**

Bible Reading: Hebrews 11:1-12

Read & Learn:

The story of Abraham and Sarah in Genesis, particularly in chapters 12 through 21, illustrates the importance of patience in faith. God promised Abraham that he would be the father of many nations, but years passed without the fulfilment of this promise. Despite their advanced age and moments of doubt and frustration, Abraham and Sarah eventually witnessed the fulfilment of God's promise with the birth of their son Isaac. Their journey was marked not only by their faith but also by their patience in waiting for God's timing. Their story teaches us that patience is an integral part of faith, involving trust in God's promises and timing, even when circumstances seem impossible or when there are long delays in the fulfilment of His promises.

Hebrews 11:1-12, often referred to as the "faith chapter," recounts the faith of various biblical figures, including Abraham, who waited patiently for God's promises. Patience in faith is about trusting in God's plan and His timing, even when it differs from our expectations or desires. It involves enduring challenges and persevering in faithfulness, even when the fulfilment of God's promises is not immediately evident. Patience is also about maintaining hope and continuing to serve God diligently, despite delays or obstacles. It is a testament to our trust in God's sovereignty and goodness.

Prayer Point:
Father, teach us to be patient in our faith, trusting in Your timing and Your promises.

Wednesday July 31

Topic: Christian Responses to Global Issues

Memory Verse: "He has shown you, O mortal, what is good. And what does the Lord require of you? To act justly and to love mercy and to walk humbly with your God." **- Micah 6:8**

Bible Reading: Matthew 25:31-46

Read & Learn:

The story of the Good Samaritan in Luke 10:25-37 offers a timeless model for Christian responses to global issues. This parable challenges Christians to transcend cultural, national, and religious boundaries to respond with compassion and action to those in need. It exemplifies a proactive approach to global issues such as poverty, injustice, and suffering, encouraging believers to not only recognise these problems but also actively engage in providing solutions, reflecting Christ's love and mercy to all, regardless of their background or status.

Christians are called to respond to global challenges, not as distant observers, but as active participants. This response can take various forms, including advocacy, humanitarian aid, sustainable development, and fighting against injustices like poverty, inequality, and environmental degradation. It's about being the hands and feet of Jesus in a broken world, showing God's love through practical actions.

Prayer Point:
Father, inspire us to respond to global issues with compassion and action, reflecting Your heart for justice and mercy.

Thursday August 01

Topic: The Role of Faith in Healing

Memory Verse: "And the prayer offered in faith will make the sick person well; the Lord will raise them up. If they have sinned, they will be forgiven." **- James 5:15**

Bible Reading: Mark 5:25-34

Read & Learn:

The story of the woman with the issue of blood in Mark 5:25-34 provides a profound example of the role of faith in healing. Her story shows that faith is not just a passive belief but an active trust in God's power and willingness to heal, which can lead to profound physical and spiritual restoration.

The role of faith in healing, as depicted in the Bible, involves a deep trust in God's power and a willingness to seek Him for restoration. James 5:15 highlights that prayers offered in faith can lead to healing and forgiveness. While faith is a crucial component, it's also important to recognise that healing can occur in various forms – physical, emotional, and spiritual – and sometimes in ways that we do not expect. It's essential to understand that while faith can lead to miraculous healing, the absence of physical healing does not indicate a lack of faith. Healing is ultimately under God's sovereign will, and faith involves trusting in His decisions, whether it leads to immediate healing, gradual recovery, or strength in enduring ongoing trials. Faith in healing also includes seeking wisdom in utilising medical resources, viewing them as part of God's provision for health and restoration.

Prayer Point:

Heavenly Father, we ask for Your healing touch in our lives and we trust in Your power and grace.

Friday August 02

Topic: Building a Personal Relationship with God

Memory Verse: "Draw near to God, and He will draw near to you. Cleanse your hands, you sinners, and purify your hearts, you double-minded." **- James 4:8**

Bible Reading: Psalm 63:1-8

Read & Learn:

The life of King David, particularly as expressed in the Psalms, exemplifies building a personal relationship with God. Psalm 63:1-8 reflects David's deep yearning for and intimate experience with God. Despite his status as king, David consistently sought a personal, heartfelt connection with God, expressing his desires, fears, joys, and sorrows openly. His relationship with God was not built on formalities or religious rituals alone but on genuine, raw, and honest communication. David's life demonstrates that building a personal relationship with God involves more than just knowledge about God; it's about experiencing His presence, sharing every aspect of life with Him, and finding satisfaction and strength in His love.

Building a personal relationship with God is a fundamental aspect of Christian faith. This relationship is nurtured through practices such as prayer, reading and meditating on Scripture, worship, and obedience. It's about open and honest communication with God, acknowledging Him as a constant presence in our lives. This relationship is not static but dynamic, growing deeper through life's experiences, both in times of joy and in challenges.

Prayer Point:

Lord, help us to draw near to You with open hearts, seeking a deeper, more personal relationship with you.

Saturday August 03

Topic: Understanding Biblical Eschatology

Memory Verse: "But about that day or hour no one knows, not even the angels in heaven, nor the Son, but only the Father."
                                                          - Matthew 24:36

Bible Reading: Revelation 21:1-4

Read & Learn:

The Book of Revelation, written by the Apostle John, provides a rich and complex vision of the end times, embodying the essence of biblical eschatology. This book, filled with symbolic imagery and prophetic visions, describes the ultimate victory of good over evil, the second coming of Christ, the final judgment, and the establishment of a new heaven and a new earth. Revelation 21:1-4, in particular, offers a hopeful picture of a future where God dwells with humanity, wiping away every tear, with no more death, mourning, crying, or pain. This portrayal of eschatology does not just focus on the end of the world, but more importantly, on the renewal and restoration of all things.

As Matthew 24:36 states, the exact timing of these events is unknown, emphasising the importance of being spiritually prepared rather than fixating on dates. Biblical eschatology offers hope and encouragement, reminding believers of God's sovereignty and the ultimate victory of Christ over evil. It also serves as a call to live righteously, to share the Gospel, and to be active participants in God's kingdom work, knowing that our actions have eternal significance.

Prayer Point:

Heavenly Father, help us to live in readiness for Christ's return, actively serving and loving in Your kingdom.

Sunday August 04

Topic: The Virtue of Humility in Christian Life

Memory Verse: "Do nothing out of selfish ambition or vain conceit. Rather, in humility value others above yourselves, not looking to your own interests but each of you to the interests of the others."
- Philippians 2:3-4

Bible Reading: John 13:1-17

Read & Learn:

The example of Jesus washing His disciples' feet in John 13:1-17 is a profound illustration of the virtue of humility in Christian life. In this act, Jesus, the Son of God and Lord, took the position of a servant, performing a task that was typically reserved for the lowest servant in a household. This powerful gesture was not just a lesson in humility but also a demonstration of love and service. Jesus' action challenged the conventional hierarchy and expectations of His time. It showed that true greatness in God's kingdom is not about status or power, but about serving others with a humble heart. Jesus' life and teachings consistently highlighted humility as a core virtue for His followers, encouraging them to live selflessly and to consider others before themselves.

Humility in Christian life is a fundamental principle that calls for a genuine recognition of our dependence on God and the value of others. Humility is not about self-degradation but about having a right understanding of our position before God and others. Humility also enables us to be teachable, open to correction, and willing to admit our mistakes.

Prayer Point:
Lord, teach us to embrace humility, following the example of Jesus in loving and serving others.

Monday August 05

Topic: The Dynamics of Faith and Reason

Memory Verse: "Come now, let us reason together," says the Lord. "Though your sins are like scarlet, they shall be as white as snow; though they are red like crimson, they shall become like wool."

- Isaiah 1:18

Bible Reading: Hebrews 11:1-3

Read & Learn:

The life of the Apostle Paul, as chronicled in the Book of Acts and his epistles, exemplifies the dynamics of faith and reason. Paul, a well-educated Pharisee, adept in religious law and reasoning, underwent a dramatic conversion experience on the road to Damascus. Post-conversion, he did not abandon his intellectual rigor; instead, he used his understanding and reasoning skills to articulate and defend the Christian faith. His sermons and writings in places like Athens, where he reasoned with Jews and Greeks alike, illustrate that faith and reason are not mutually exclusive but complementary. Paul's approach shows that Christianity welcomes inquiry and intellectual engagement, and that reason can be a tool to understand and articulate one's faith more profoundly.

This relationship encourages Christians to explore and understand their faith intellectually, while recognising that some aspects of faith transcend human understanding.

Prayer Point:
Heavenly Father, guide us in harmonising our faith with reason, deepening our understanding of You.

Tuesday August 06

Topic: Developing Effective Christian Communication

Memory Verse: "Do not let any unwholesome talk come out of your mouths, but only what is helpful for building others up according to their needs, that it may benefit those who listen." **- Ephesians 4:29**

Bible Reading: James 1:19-20

Read & Learn:

The interaction between Jesus and the Samaritan woman at the well, as recounted in John 4:1-26, exemplifies effective Christian communication. In this encounter, Jesus demonstrates key aspects of effective communication: He engages the woman in a respectful and non-judgmental manner, listens attentively, and speaks truthfully and insightfully. His approach leads to a deep and meaningful conversation that not only reveals her own needs and struggles but also offers her the message of living water - the Gospel. This story highlights the importance of empathy, active listening, and speaking truth in love. Through this respectful and compassionate dialogue, Jesus transforms the woman's life and, subsequently, that of her community.

Developing effective Christian communication involves more than just speaking about one's faith. As Ephesians 4:29 suggests, it includes speaking in ways that build up others, addressing their needs, and offering benefit to the listeners. James 1:19-20 emphasises the importance of being quick to listen, slow to speak, and slow to become angry. This approach not only applies to sharing the Gospel but also to everyday interactions, reflecting a Christ-like attitude in all forms of communication.

Prayer Point:
Lord, help us to communicate effectively, reflecting Your love and grace in our words and actions.

Wednesday August 07

Topic: The Importance of Accountability in Faith

Memory Verse: "Carry each other's burdens, and in this way you will fulfill the law of Christ." - **Galatians 6:2**

Bible Reading: James 5:16

Read & Learn:

The story of David and the prophet Nathan in 2 Samuel 12 provides a striking example of the importance of accountability in faith. After David sinned by taking Bathsheba and arranging the death of her husband, Uriah, Nathan confronted him with a parable that led David to recognise his wrongdoing. This encounter shows the vital role of accountability in helping individuals recognise and repent from their sins. Nathan's approach was both direct and compassionate, providing David with the opportunity to confess and seek forgiveness. This story highlights that accountability within a faith community is essential for spiritual growth and integrity. It encourages individuals to be open to correction and to provide gentle, yet honest, feedback to others.

Accountability helps to foster spiritual growth, maintain moral integrity, and provide support in overcoming temptations and trials. It's not about judgment or condemnation, but about encouraging one another to live in accordance with God's word.

Prayer Point:
Father, grant us strength to uphold accountability, bear each other's burdens, and live true to Christ's teachings.

Thursday August 08

Topic: Guard Your Heart

Memory Verse: "Above all else, guard your heart, for everything you do flows from it." **- Proverbs 4:23**

Bible Reading: Matthew 15:10-20

Read & Learn:

In Matthew 15:10-20, Jesus teaches about the importance of guarding our hearts. He emphasises that what comes out of our mouths is a reflection of what is in our hearts. Just as a spring produces water of its kind, our hearts produce words and actions that reveal our true character. Jesus reminds us that external rituals or behaviours alone cannot make us clean; it is the condition of our hearts that truly matters. This lesson encourages us to be vigilant in guarding our hearts against negativity, malice, and impurity, and to cultivate a heart that reflects the love, grace, and goodness of God.

"Guard your heart" is a biblical exhortation found in Proverbs 4:23. It underscores the significance of protecting the innermost core of our being, which shapes our thoughts, emotions, and actions. The passage in Matthew 15:10-20 reinforces this teaching by revealing that the state of our hearts determines the words we speak and the deeds we perform. As Christians, we are called to examine our hearts regularly, seeking God's transformation and renewal. We must be cautious of negative influences and sinful attitudes that can corrupt our hearts. Guarding our hearts involves filling them with God's Word, prayer, and a desire for righteousness, which leads to a life that reflects Christ's love and purity.

Prayer Point:

Father, help us to guard our hearts diligently, knowing that everything flows from it.

Friday August 09

Topic: The Power of a Renewed Mind

Memory Verse: "Do not conform to the pattern of this world, but be transformed by the renewing of your mind. Then you will be able to test and approve what God's will is - his good, pleasing and perfect will." **- Romans 12:2**

Bible Reading: Ephesians 4:22-24

Read & Learn:

The transformation of the Apostle Paul, as described in Acts 9, dramatically showcases the power of a renewed mind. Before his conversion, Paul, then Saul, was a fervent persecutor of Christians, firmly convinced in his beliefs and actions. However, his encounter with Jesus on the road to Damascus led to a complete transformation of his mindset. This change was not just a shift in beliefs but a total renewal of his perspective, values, and priorities. Paul's renewed mind led him to become one of the most influential figures in the early church, spreading the Gospel with passion and clarity. His life illustrates that renewing our minds can lead to profound changes in our actions and attitudes, aligning us more closely with God's will and purposes.

A renewed mind affects how we perceive ourselves, others, and the world around us, influencing our decisions and actions. It involves adopting a mindset grounded in scriptural truths, leading to a life that reflects Christ's character. The renewal of the mind is essential for spiritual growth and effective Christian living, as it transforms us from the inside out, enabling us to live in a way that honours God and impacts the world positively.

Prayer Point:

Heavenly Father, guide us in the process of renewing our minds, that we may embrace Your truth and wisdom.

Saturday August 10

Topic: Christian Perspectives on Human Dignity

Memory Verse: "So God created mankind in his own image, in the image of God he created them; male and female he created them."

- **Genesis 1:27**

Bible Reading: James 3:9-10

Read & Learn:

The encounter of Jesus with the woman caught in adultery, as narrated in John 8:1-11, powerfully illustrates the Christian perspective on human dignity. Despite the woman's situation and the accusations against her, Jesus responded not with condemnation, but with compassion and respect for her dignity as a person. His statement, "Let any one of you who is without sin be the first to throw a stone at her," and His subsequent act of forgiveness highlights the value Jesus places on each individual. This story teaches that every person is valuable and deserving of dignity, regardless of their past or present circumstances.

Christian perspectives on human dignity are rooted in the belief that all people are created in the image of God, as stated in Genesis 1:27.

This call for the respect, protection, and care of all individuals, advocating for justice, compassion, and empathy in our interactions.

Prayer Point:
Father, help us to see the worth and value of all individuals and to treat them with love and compassion.

Sunday August 11

Topic: Overcoming Prejudice with Love

Memory Verse: "Whoever claims to love God yet hates a brother or sister is a liar. For whoever does not love their brother and sister, whom they have seen, cannot love God, whom they have not seen."
- 1 John 4:20

Bible Reading: Luke 10:25-37

Read & Learn:

The parable of the Good Samaritan in Luke 10:25-37 powerfully addresses the issue of overcoming prejudice with love. In this story, a Jewish man who is left beaten on the road is ignored by his own people but is helped by a Samaritan, a group despised by the Jews. This Samaritan not only provides immediate aid but also ensures ongoing care for the injured man. This act of compassion and kindness transcends deep-seated ethnic and religious prejudices. The Samaritan's actions exemplify how love can break down barriers of prejudice and bias. Jesus used this story to teach that love for one's neighbour should have no boundaries or limitations, challenging us to show love and kindness to all, irrespective of their background or identity.

Overcoming prejudice with love is a fundamental Christian teaching. According to 1 John 4:20, professing love for God while harbouring hate or prejudice against others is contradictory.

Love, as the cornerstone of Christian faith, empowers believers to conduct self-examination, show understanding, challenge and dismantle prejudice, building communities that reflect God's inclusive and unconditional love.

Prayer Point:
Father, empower us to overcome prejudice and bias with Your love, seeing each person as You see them.

Monday August 12

Topic: The Concept of Biblical Fellowship

Memory Verse: "But if we walk in the light, as he is in the light, we have fellowship with one another, and the blood of Jesus, his Son, purifies us from all sin." **- 1 John 1:7**

Bible Reading: Acts 2:42-47

Read & Learn:

The early church's practice of fellowship as described in Acts 2:42-47 provides a clear and powerful example of the concept of biblical fellowship. The believers devoted themselves to the apostles' teaching, to fellowship, to the breaking of bread, and to prayer. They met together in homes for meals with glad and sincere hearts, sharing everything they had, and ensuring that no one was in need. This communal life was more than just social interaction; it was a sharing of life, resources, and spiritual growth. Their fellowship was marked by a deep sense of unity, generosity, and a commitment to each other's well-being, rooted in their shared faith and love for Christ. This example challenges contemporary Christians to view fellowship not just as a social gathering, but as a vital and active part of living out our faith in community.

The concept of biblical fellowship goes beyond mere socialising; it is about sharing life together in a community of faith. In Acts 2:42-47, fellowship is seen as an integral part of the believers' daily lives, encompassing teaching, worship, breaking of bread, prayer, and mutual support. Biblical fellowship is essential for personal growth and the strengthening of the church, fostering a sense of belonging, unity, and purpose in the body of Christ.

Prayer Point:
Father, guide us to embrace true biblical fellowship, fostering deep connections and shared life within our faith community.

Tuesday August 13

Topic: Christian Views on Government and Authority

Memory Verse: "Let everyone be subject to the governing authorities, for there is no authority except that which God has established. The authorities that exist have been established by God."
- Romans 13:1

Bible Reading: 1 Peter 2:13-17

Read & Learn:

The story of Daniel in Babylon, especially as recounted in Daniel 6, offers a compelling view of a Christian's interaction with government and authority. Daniel, while living under a foreign government, displayed respect and submission to the authority, but not at the expense of his faith and obedience to God. When a law was passed that contradicted God's commands, Daniel chose to obey God rather than man, leading to his trial in the lion's den. His faithfulness and integrity not only led to his miraculous deliverance but also to a royal decree that glorified God.

Christian views on government and authority are grounded in the understanding that all authority is established by God.

This perspective encourages respect for and submission to governing authorities, as long as it does not conflict with God's commandments. We are called to engage with government and authority in a way that demonstrates our primary allegiance to God, while also being exemplary citizens who promote justice, peace, and the common good.

Prayer Point:
Father, guide us in navigating our relationship with government and authority, balancing respect for laws with our ultimate allegiance to You.

Wednesday August 14

Topic: The Role of Women in the Church

Memory Verse: "There is neither Jew nor Gentile, neither slave nor free, nor is there male and female, for you are all one in Christ Jesus."
- Galatians 3:28

Bible Reading: Romans 16:1-16

Read & Learn:

In Romans 16:1-16, the Apostle Paul mentions numerous women who played significant roles in the early Church. Among them is Phoebe, a deaconess of the church in Cenchreae, whom Paul commends for her service. Also mentioned are Priscilla (along with her husband, Aquila), who was instrumental in teaching and guiding new believers, including Apollos. These examples, along with others in the passage, highlight the active and vital role women played in the early Christian community. They were leaders, teachers, supporters, and significant contributors to the growth and establishment of the church.

The role of women in the church, as seen in the New Testament, involves active participation and leadership in various aspects of church life. The Bible presents numerous instances where women are acknowledged for their roles in teaching, leading, and supporting the church. Understanding the role of women in the church requires a holistic view of Scripture, acknowledging cultural contexts while recognising the timeless principle of equality and unity in Christ.

Prayer Point:
Lord, we thank You for the gifts and contributions of women in Your church. Help us to recognise and value their vital role in our faith communities.

Thursday August 15

Topic: Navigating Faith in a Digital Age

Memory Verse: "And whatever you do, whether in word or deed, do it all in the name of the Lord Jesus, giving thanks to God the Father through him." **- Colossians 3:17**

Bible Reading: James 1:22-25

Read & Learn:

In today's digital age, the story of the Bereans in Acts 17:11-12 offers valuable insights. The Bereans were commended for their discerning approach to Paul's teachings. They did not accept his words at face value but searched the Scriptures daily to verify the truth. This example is particularly relevant in an era where information, including religious teachings, is readily accessible online. Just as the Bereans critically examined Paul's teachings, Christians today are called to discernment in their digital interactions. They should critically evaluate online content, discern its alignment with biblical truths, and thoughtfully engage with digital media.

Navigating faith in a digital age involves using technology responsibly and discerningly as a tool to enhance one's faith journey, while being aware of its potential pitfalls. The digital age offers tremendous opportunities for learning, connecting with fellow believers, and sharing the Gospel. However, it also requires a commitment to authenticity, integrity, and intentional Christian living, ensuring that digital engagement is a reflection of your faith and values.

Prayer Point:
Father, guide us as we navigate our faith in this digital age, to use technology in ways that honour You and strengthen our walk with Christ.

Friday August 16

Topic: Understanding the Gifts of the Spirit

Memory Verse: "There are different kinds of gifts, but the same Spirit distributes them. There are different kinds of service, but the same Lord. There are different kinds of working, but in all of them and in everyone it is the same God at work." - **1 Corinthians 12:4-6**

Bible Reading: 1 Corinthians 12:1-11

Read & Learn:

In the early church, as depicted in the Book of Acts, the outpouring of the Holy Spirit at Pentecost led to the manifestation of various spiritual gifts among believers. These gifts, including speaking in tongues, prophecy, and healing, were not just for individual edification but for the building up of the church. An example of this is Peter's transformation from a fisherman into a bold preacher, empowered by the Holy Spirit. His sermon in Acts 2, which led to the conversion of about three thousand people, demonstrates how the gifts of the Spirit can significantly impact the church and its mission. This event highlights the diversity and purpose of spiritual gifts: they are granted by the same Spirit for the common good, equipping believers to serve effectively in God's kingdom.

As stated in 1 Corinthians 12:4-6, these gifts are diverse but originate from the same Spirit. These gifts are intended for the common good, to build up the body of Christ, and to advance the church's mission. They are not a measure of spiritual maturity or favouritism but are distributed as the Spirit determines. The proper use of spiritual gifts requires humility, love, and a desire to serve others, avoiding division or a sense of superiority.

Prayer Point:
Father, help me to discover and use the Spiritual Gifts you have given me to honour you and to edify the body of Christ.

Saturday August 17

Topic: The Biblical Approach to Conflict and Reconciliation

Memory Verse: "If your brother or sister sins, go and point out their fault, just between the two of you. If they listen to you, you have won them over." **- Matthew 18:15**

Bible Reading: 2 Corinthians 5:18-19

Read & Learn:

The reconciliation between Esau and Jacob in Genesis 33 offers a profound example of the biblical approach to conflict and reconciliation. After years of conflict and estrangement stemming from Jacob's deception, the brothers' reunion is marked by humility, forgiveness, and restoration. Jacob approaches Esau with gifts and a posture of humility, while Esau, despite having every reason to hold a grudge, greets Jacob with a warm embrace. This story demonstrates the power of seeking forgiveness and extending grace in resolving conflicts. It shows the importance of taking the initiative for reconciliation, acknowledging wrongdoings, and the willingness to forgive. Their encounter is a testament to the transformation that can occur when individuals approach conflicts with a heart of repentance and forgiveness.

Matthew 18:15 provides guidance on dealing with offenses within the Christian community, highlighting the value of direct and private conversations aimed at reconciliationIn handling conflicts, Christians are called to mirror God's grace and love, striving for reconciliation that restores relationships and fosters harmony within the body of Christ.

Prayer Point:
Lord, grant us wisdom and grace to handle conflicts in a manner that honours You and reflects Your heart for reconciliation.

Sunday August 18

Topic: Faith as a Foundation for Marriage

Memory Verse: "Husbands, love your wives, just as Christ loved the church and gave himself up for her." - **Ephesians 5:25**

Bible Reading: 1 Corinthians 13:4-7

Read & Learn:

The story of Ruth and Boaz in the Book of Ruth offers a poignant example of faith as a foundation for marriage. Ruth, a Moabite widow, chose to stay with her Israelite mother-in-law, Naomi, demonstrating faith and loyalty. Her decision led her to Boaz, a man of strong faith and integrity. Their marriage was rooted not only in mutual love and respect but also in a shared commitment to God and His principles. This union, blessed by faith and devotion, became part of the lineage of Jesus Christ. Ruth and Boaz's story illustrates how faith can guide individuals to make marital choices that honour God.

Faith as a foundation for marriage is about building a relationship that is centred on mutual trust in and commitment to God. Ephesians 5:25 calls husbands to love their wives sacrificially, as Christ loved the church, setting a standard of selfless love for both partners in the marriage.

A marriage rooted in faith views love not just as a feeling but as a choice and commitment to act in the best interest of the other person. Such a marriage is marked by mutual support, open communication, shared values, and a commitment to grow together spiritually. Faith becomes the anchor that helps couples navigate challenges, make decisions, and cultivate a loving, respectful, and enduring relationship.

Prayer Point:
Father, bless our marriages and relationships, anchoring them in faith and Your love.

Monday August 19

Topic: The Art of Biblical Storytelling

Memory Verse: "We will not hide them from their descendants; we will tell the next generation the praiseworthy deeds of the Lord, his power, and the wonders he has done." **- Psalm 78:4**

Bible Reading: Luke 10:25-37

Read & Learn:

The parable of the Good Samaritan in Luke 10:25-37 is a masterful example of Jesus' use of storytelling to convey deep spiritual truths. In this story, Jesus used a simple yet powerful narrative to redefine the concept of 'neighbour' and to teach about love and compassion. Through the characters of the priest, Levite, and Samaritan, Jesus challenged social norms and religious prejudices. His storytelling did not just inform, but it transformed the understanding and perspective of His listeners. This parable, like many others, shows how storytelling can effectively communicate complex truths in an engaging and memorable way, encouraging listeners to think deeply and reflect on their own lives in the light of God's truth.

The art of biblical storytelling is a powerful tool for conveying spiritual truths and ethical teachings. It involves the use of narratives, parables, and accounts to illustrate and bring to life the principles and lessons of the Bible. These stories, while often simple, carry profound meanings and invite listeners or readers to engage with the text on a deeper level. As a Christian, learning the art of biblical storytelling can enhance personal study, teaching, and evangelism, making the timeless truths of the Bible accessible and relevant to all.

Prayer Point:

Lord, help us to embrace and share the art of biblical storytelling, making Your truths vivid and relatable.

Tuesday August 20

Topic: Christian Ethics in Business

Memory Verse: "The Lord detests dishonest scales, but accurate weights find favour with him." **- Proverbs 11:1**

Bible Reading: Colossians 3:23-24

Read & Learn:

The biblical account of Lydia in Acts 16:14-15 provides an insightful example of Christian ethics in business. Lydia, a merchant dealing in expensive purple cloth, was known for her integrity and fairness in business. After she became a believer, her home became a place of fellowship and support for Paul and his companions. This account highlights how Lydia's faith influenced her business practices. Her ethical conduct, coupled with her hospitality and support of the ministry, shows that Christian ethics in business go beyond mere transactions; they encompass honesty, integrity, fairness, and using one's resources for the betterment of the community and advancement of God's work.

Christian ethics in business involve applying biblical principles to all aspects of business conduct. As Proverbs 11:1 suggests, God values honesty and integrity, not just in personal life but also in business dealings. Christian ethics in business encompass more than avoiding unethical practices; they include conducting business in a way that reflects Christ's values, such as fairness, generosity, and care for others. This approach challenges the conventional business mindset of profit maximisation at any cost, promoting instead a model that values people, ethical practices, and positive contributions to society, all done in a way that honours God.

Prayer Point:

Father, guide us in our business endeavours to uphold Your principles of honesty and integrity.

Wednesday August 21

Topic: The Journey of Personal Transformation

Memory Verse: "Do not conform to the pattern of this world, but be transformed by the renewing of your mind. Then you will be able to test and approve what God's will is - his good, pleasing and perfect will." - **Romans 12:2**

Bible Reading: Act 9:1-15

Read & Learn:

The transformation of the Apostle Paul, from a persecutor of Christians to one of the most influential apostles of Christ, is a profound example of personal transformation. Paul's encounter with Jesus on the road to Damascus, as recounted in Acts 9, was a pivotal moment that changed the course of his life. This dramatic conversion was not just a change in beliefs but a complete transformation of his character, purpose, and actions. His life afterward was marked by a fervent commitment to spreading the Gospel, enduring hardships, and making significant contributions to the early church.

The journey of personal transformation in the Christian context involves a profound change that begins with the heart and mind. It is about allowing God's Spirit to renew, reshape, and reform our thoughts, attitudes, and behaviours. 2 Corinthians 5:17 speaks of this transformation as becoming a new creation in Christ, where old things have passed away, and all things have become new. Personal transformation is a lifelong journey that includes developing Christ-like qualities, overcoming sinful patterns, and actively pursuing a life that reflects God's love and righteousness.

Prayer Point:
Heavenly Father, guide us on our journey of personal transformation, renewing our minds and hearts in You.

Thursday August 22

Topic: Embracing Diversity in the Body of Christ

Memory Verse: " For we were all baptised by one Spirit so as to form one body - whether Jews or Gentiles, slave or free - and we were all given the one Spirit to drink." **- 1 Corinthians 12:13**

Bible Reading: Revelation 7:9-10

Read & Learn:

The account of Pentecost in Acts 2 is a vivid illustration of embracing diversity in the body of Christ. On this day, the Holy Spirit descended upon the disciples, enabling them to speak in various tongues. This miraculous event attracted a diverse crowd from different nations, each hearing the wonders of God proclaimed in their own language. This phenomenon not only signifies the outpouring of the Holy Spirit but also symbolises the inclusivity and diversity of the kingdom of God. People from varied cultural and linguistic backgrounds were united by the Gospel, reflecting the universal nature of Christ's message. The story of Pentecost encourages the modern church to embrace diversity, recognising the beauty and strength that comes from varied perspectives, cultures, and backgrounds, all unified in Christ.

In the church, diversity should be celebrated and leveraged for the enrichment and effectiveness of its ministry. It involves creating an environment where differences are respected and where everyone can contribute their gifts and talents. Embracing diversity in the body of Christ is not about erasing distinctions but about fostering unity in diversity, reflecting the inclusive and reconciling heart of God.

Prayer Point:

Lord, help us to embrace the beautiful diversity within Your body, Recognising the value and contribution of each member.

Friday August 23

Topic: Understanding the Book of Revelation

Memory Verse: "Blessed is the one who reads aloud the words of this prophecy, and blessed are those who hear it and take to heart what is written in it, because the time is near." **- Revelation 1:3**

Bible Reading: Revelation 21:1-4

Read & Learn:

The Book of Revelation, with its rich symbolism and prophetic imagery, can often seem daunting and enigmatic. The story of John, the author of Revelation, exiled on the island of Patmos, provides context to this intriguing book. John's vision, given in a time of persecution and struggle for the early church, offers hope and encouragement. Revelation 21:1-4, with its depiction of a new heaven and a new earth where God dwells with His people, wiping away every tear, is a powerful promise of God's ultimate triumph and the restoration of all things. This passage, and the book as a whole, is not just about future events, but it is also a source of comfort and hope, reminding believers of God's sovereignty and the ultimate victory of good over evil.

Revelation uses symbolic language to convey truths about God's plan for humanity and the cosmic battle between good and evil. Revelation 1:3 highlights the blessing that comes from reading and heeding its words, underscoring its importance in the Christian faith. The book encourages perseverance and faithfulness, offering hope in the ultimate realisation of God's kingdom.

Prayer Point:
Father, as we study the Book of Revelation, grant us insight and understanding of its message and let it inspire us to live a life that honours you.

Saturday August 24

Topic: The Power of Christian Creativity

Memory Verse: "And he has filled him with the Spirit of God, with wisdom, with understanding, with knowledge and with all kinds of skills—to make artistic designs for work in gold, silver and bronze."

Exodus 35:31-32

Bible Reading: Ephesians 2:10

Read & Learn:

The construction of the Tabernacle in Exodus 35-36 exemplifies the power of Christian creativity. God appointed Bezalel and filled him with the Holy Spirit, granting him extraordinary skill, ability, and knowledge in all kinds of crafts. His task was to design and create the Tabernacle, a dwelling place for God among His people

The power of Christian creativity lies in Recognising and using our God-given talents and abilities to glorify Him and serve others. Ephesians 2:10 reminds us that we are God's handiwork, created in Christ Jesus to do good works, which God prepared in advance for us to do. Christian creativity is not just about arts and crafts; it encompasses all forms of creative expression and innovation, used in a way that honours God and furthers His kingdom. It's about seeing our creative gifts as a means to worship God, serve others, and express the truth of the Gospel in diverse and impactful ways.

Prayer Point:

Lord, inspire us to recognise and use our creative gifts as a reflection of Your creativity and for Your glory.

Sunday August 25

Topic: Exploring the Life of Jesus

Memory Verse: "The Word became flesh and made his dwelling among us. We have seen his glory, the glory of the one and only Son, who came from the Father, full of grace and truth." **-John 1:14**

Bible Reading: Luke 4:16-21

Read & Learn:

The account of Jesus in the synagogue of Nazareth, as described in Luke 4:16-21, provides a profound insight into His life and mission. Returning to his hometown, Jesus read from the scroll of Isaiah, proclaiming Himself as the fulfilment of the prophecy about the Messiah. This moment marked the beginning of His public ministry, highlighting His role as a teacher, a prophet, and the promised Saviour. Jesus' declaration that the scripture was fulfilled in their hearing was a defining moment, revealing His identity and purpose. His life, from His miraculous birth to His ministry, death, and resurrection, was a testament to God's love and plan for humanity. Exploring the life of Jesus is not just about understanding historical events but is about discovering the person of Jesus Christ - His character, teachings, and the transformative impact He has on the lives of individuals and the world.

Jesus' life exemplifies perfect obedience to God, compassionate service to others, and the ultimate sacrifice for human redemption.

Prayer Point:

Lord Jesus, as we explore Your life, open our hearts and minds to the depths of Your love, grace, and truth.

Monday August 26

Topic: The Significance of Christian Symbols

Memory Verse: "For the message of the cross is foolishness to those who are perishing, but to us who are being saved it is the power of God." **- 1 Corinthians 1:18**

Bible Reading: John 6:35

Read & Learn:

Among the most recognised Christian symbols is the fish, often called the "Ichthys." During the early days of Christianity, when followers of Christ were persecuted, the fish symbol served as a secret sign for believers to identify each other. The Greek word for fish, "Ichthys," was used as an acronym for "Jesus Christ, God's Son, Saviour." This symbol was a quiet yet powerful declaration of faith, representing believers' allegiance to Jesus. It demonstrated the early Christians' creativity and resilience in maintaining their faith and fellowship under oppressive circumstances.

The significance of Christian symbols lies in their ability to convey profound spiritual truths and historical aspects of the Christian faith. The cross, as noted in 1 Corinthians 1:18, symbolises the power of salvation through Jesus' sacrifice. In John 6:35, Jesus describes Himself as the "Bread of Life," symbolising His role in sustaining spiritual life.

Prayer Point:

Heavenly Father, thank You for the rich heritage of symbols in our faith that remind us of Your truths and promises.

Tuesday August 27

Topic: Biblical Insights on Aging and Wisdom

Memory Verse: "Grey hair is a crown of splendour; it is attained in the way of righteousness." **- Proverbs 16:31**

Bible Reading: Job 12:12

Read & Learn:

The life of Moses offers profound insights into the biblical view of aging and wisdom. Moses' most significant contributions to the Israelites occurred during the latter part of his life. At the age of eighty, he confronted Pharaoh, led the Israelites out of Egypt, and received the Ten Commandments from God. His later years were marked by strong leadership, deep communion with God, and the impartation of wisdom to an entire nation. Moses' story demonstrates that aging in the biblical sense is not about decline but about the accumulation of experience, wisdom, and an opportunity to make impactful contributions. His life encourages us to view aging not as a diminishing phase but as a time rich with potential for spiritual growth, wisdom, and continued service to God and others.

Biblical insights on aging and wisdom offer a perspective that honours and values the elderly, seeing age not as a detriment but as a source of wisdom and experience. As stated in Proverbs 16:31, aging is portrayed as a mark of honour and dignity. Job 12:12 affirms, "Is not wisdom found among the aged? Does not long life bring understanding?"

Prayer Point:

Heavenly Father, help us to honour and value the wisdom and experience that come with aging, as You do.

Wednesday August 28

Topic: The Role of Silence and Solitude in Faith

Memory Verse: "Be still, and know that I am God; I will be exalted among the nations, I will be exalted in the earth." - **Psalm 46:10**

Bible Reading: Mark 1:35

Read & Learn:

The life of Jesus Christ provides numerous examples of the role of silence and solitude in faith. In Mark 1:35, we find Jesus rising early in the morning, while it was still dark, to go to a solitary place where he prayed. This practice of withdrawing to quiet places was a regular part of Jesus' life, providing Him with moments of communion with the Father, away from the busyness and demands of His ministry. These times of solitude and silence were not mere escapes but were foundational to His spiritual strength and clarity. This aspect of Jesus' life invites believers to recognise the importance of integrating moments of solitude and silence into their spiritual practice, as a means of deepening their relationship with God and finding strength and guidance.

As Psalm 46:10 suggests, being still and knowing God requires intentional pauses in our busy lives. In these moments, one can listen more attentively to God's voice, engage in contemplative prayer, and gain spiritual insight and peace. Silence and solitude also offer opportunities for self-examination, leading to spiritual growth and renewal.

Prayer Point:

Lord, guide us to seek moments of silence and solitude, where we can be still and know You more deeply.

Thursday August 29

Topic: Christian Perspectives on Human Sexuality

Memory Verse: "Do you not know that your bodies are temples of the Holy Spirit, who is in you, whom you have received from God? You are not your own; you were bought at a price. Therefore honour God with your bodies." - **1 Corinthians 6:19-20**

Bible Reading: Genesis 2:24-25

Read & Learn:

The creation narrative in Genesis provides foundational insights into the Christian perspective on human sexuality. Genesis 2:24-25 describes the union of Adam and Eve, highlighting the significance of the marital bond as a deep, intimate, and sacred union designed by God. This union is portrayed as more than just a physical connection; it is a spiritual and emotional bond that reflects unity, mutual respect, and love. The Biblical account of creation sets the framework for understanding sexuality as a gift from God, intended to be expressed within the covenant of marriage.

Christian perspectives on human sexuality emphasise that it is a gift from God, intended to be cherished and honoured within the context of marriage. As stated in 1 Corinthians 6:19-20, our bodies are temples of the Holy Spirit, and we are called to honour God with them. This perspective views sexuality not merely as a physical act but as an integral part of human identity and relational expression, deeply connected to spiritual and emotional aspects of life.

Prayer Point:

Heavenly Father, help us to understand and honour the gift of sexuality as You have designed and intended.

Friday August 30

Topic: The Concept of Christian Leadership

Memory Verse: "Whoever wants to become great among you must be your servant, and whoever wants to be first must be slave of all. For even the Son of Man did not come to be served, but to serve, and to give his life as a ransom for many." **- Mark 10:43-45**

Bible Reading: Philippians 2:3-5

Read & Learn:

The leadership style of Jesus Christ provides the perfect model for Christian leadership. One of the most compelling examples is found in John 13, where Jesus washes His disciples' feet. In this act, Jesus demonstrates servant leadership, reversing the conventional norms of power and authority. He took on the role of a servant, humbly washing the feet of His followers, including Judas, who would betray Him. This profound act illustrated that true leadership in the Christian context is characterised by humility, service, and sacrificial love. Jesus' approach to leadership challenges traditional concepts of power and authority, calling Christian leaders to lead by example, to serve others selflessly, and to prioritise the well-being and growth of those they lead.

Christian leadership, as shown in Philippians 2:3-5, involves adopting the mindset of Christ, valuing others above oneself, and looking out for their interests. It's about leading with love, integrity, and humility, and being willing to sacrifice for the good of others.

Prayer Point:

Lord, guide us to embrace Your model of servant leadership, prioritising the service and well-being of others.

Saturday August 31

Topic: Overcoming Materialism with Contentment

Memory Verse: "Keep your lives free from the love of money and be content with what you have, because God has said, 'Never will I leave you; never will I forsake you.'" **- Hebrews 13:5**

Bible Reading: 1 Timothy 6:6-10

Read & Learn:

The story of the rich young ruler in Matthew 19:16-22 offers a poignant lesson on overcoming materialism with contentment. This young man approached Jesus, asking what he must do to inherit eternal life. Despite his adherence to the commandments, his heart was tied to his great wealth. When Jesus invited him to sell his possessions, give to the poor, and follow Him, the young man went away sad, unable to part with his riches. This encounter highlights the danger of allowing material possessions to dominate one's life, overshadowing spiritual and eternal values.

1 Timothy 6:6-10 teaches that godliness with contentment is great gain, warning against the temptation to pursue wealth for its own sake. These scriptures suggest that contentment is not about complacency or lack of ambition but about an inner sense of satisfaction and peace, regardless of external circumstances. It involves prioritising spiritual and eternal values over material gain and recognising that true security and joy are found in a relationship with God.

Prayer Point:

Heavenly Father, help us to find true contentment in Your love and provision, not in the accumulation of material wealth.

Sunday September 01

Topic: The Power of Prayerful Intercession

Memory Verse: "Therefore confess your sins to each other and pray for each other so that you may be healed. The prayer of a righteous person is powerful and effective." - **James 5:16**

Bible Reading: Colossians 4:12-13

Read & Learn:

The story of Moses interceding for the Israelites in Exodus 32:9-14 provides a profound example of the power of prayerful intercession. After the Israelites sinned by worshipping the golden calf, God's anger burned against them. Moses, however, interceded on their behalf, pleading with God to spare them and remember His promises. His intercession showcased his deep concern for the people and his trust in God's mercy. Remarkably, God relented and did not bring the disaster He had threatened. This incident illustrates how intercessory prayer is not just a passive act but a robust engagement with God, where one stands in the gap for others, pleading for mercy, guidance, and intervention.

Prayerful intercession is a vital aspect of Christian life, where believers pray on behalf of others, seeking God's intervention and blessing in their lives. Intercession involves empathy, love, and a willingness to bear the burdens of others in prayer. It reflects the heart of Christ, who intercedes for believers at the right hand of God.

Prayer Point:

Lord, guide us to be faithful intercessors, praying earnestly for the needs and healing of those around us.

Monday September 02

Topic: Understanding the Parables of the Kingdom

Memory Verse: "He replied, 'Because the knowledge of the secrets of the kingdom of heaven has been given to you, but not to them.'"

Matthew 13:11

Bible Reading: Matthew 13:24-30, 36-43

Read & Learn:

One of Jesus' most illustrative parables about the kingdom of heaven is the Parable of the Weeds (Matthew 13:24-30, 36-43). In this story, Jesus describes a farmer who sows good seed in his field. But while everyone is sleeping, his enemy comes and sows weeds among the wheat. The servants ask if they should pull up the weeds, but the farmer says no, explaining that in doing so, they might uproot the wheat as well. At harvest, the wheat and weeds will be separated, with the weeds being burned and the wheat gathered into the barn. This parable, explained by Jesus to His disciples, teaches about the coexistence of good and evil in the world and the ultimate judgment at the end of the age. It highlights God's patience and the assurance of His just and righteous judgment

Understanding these parables is crucial for believers, as they provide guidance on how to live a life that aligns with God's kingdom.

Prayer Point:

Heavenly Father, grant us wisdom and insight as we seek to understand the profound truths of Your kingdom through the parables of Jesus.

Tuesday September 03

Topic: The Role of Prophecy in Today's World

Memory Verse: "We also have the prophetic message as something completely reliable, and you will do well to pay attention to it, as to a light shining in a dark place, until the day dawns and the morning star rises in your hearts." **- 2 Peter 1:19**

Bible Reading: 1 Corinthians 14:1-5

Read & Learn:

The New Testament provides insights into the role of prophecy in the early church, particularly in the teachings of Paul. In 1 Corinthians 14:1-5, Paul emphasises the importance of prophecy for the edification, encouragement, and comfort of the church community.

An example from contemporary times could be the guidance and encouragement believers receive in their church communities, where prophetic words are shared that align with Biblical truth and uplift the body of Christ. This underscores the relevance of prophecy in today's world as a means of spiritual edification and a tool for reinforcing faith and godliness, always in alignment with Scriptural truths.

The gift of prophecy should be exercised under the guidance of the Holy Spirit and with accountability within the church community.

Prayer Point:

Lord, guide us in understanding and valuing the gift of prophecy as a means of edification and encouragement in our faith journey.

Wednesday September 04

Topic: Cultivating Spiritual Resilience

Memory Verse: "Consider it pure joy, my brothers and sisters, whenever you face trials of many kinds, because you know that the testing of your faith produces perseverance." **- James 1:2-3**

Bible Reading: Romans 5:3-5

Read & Learn:

The life of Joseph, as detailed from Genesis 37 to 50, is a remarkable story of spiritual resilience. Joseph faced numerous challenges, including being sold into slavery by his brothers, unjustly imprisoned in Egypt, and forgotten by those he helped. Despite these hardships, Joseph maintained his faith in God. His resilience was not just a stoic acceptance of his fate; it was an active trust in God's sovereignty and goodness. This trust was ultimately rewarded when he rose to a position of power in Egypt and was able to save many lives, including those of his family. Joseph's story teaches that spiritual resilience is grounded in unwavering faith and trust in God, even in the midst of trials, and it bears fruit in both personal growth and God's broader purposes.

Cultivating spiritual resilience involves developing a steadfast faith that endures through difficulties and grows stronger through trials. It requires a deep-rooted faith that trusts in God's plans and timing, even when circumstances seem overwhelming.

Prayer Point:

Heavenly Father, help us to cultivate spiritual resilience, trusting in Your love and purpose even in challenging times.

Thursday September 05

Topic: Biblical Teachings on Restitution and Justice

Memory Verse: "Then it shall be, because he has sinned and is guilty, that he shall restore what he has stolen, or the thing which he has extorted, or what was delivered to him for safekeeping, or the lost thing which he found, or all that about which he has sworn falsely. He shall restore its full value, add one-fifth more to it, and give it to whomever it belongs, on the day of his trespass offering."

Leviticus 6:4-5

Bible Reading: Luke 19:1-10

Read & Learn:

Zacchaeus' encounter with Jesus in Luke 19:1-10 illustrates the biblical principle of restitution and justice. As a chief tax collector, Zacchaeus had become wealthy by extorting money from his fellow citizens. However, after meeting Jesus and experiencing a transformation of heart, Zacchaeus demonstrated true repentance by pledging to give half of his possessions to the poor and to restore fourfold to anyone he had cheated. This act of restitution was a tangible expression of Zacchaeus' changed heart and commitment to justice. It shows that biblical restitution is not just about returning what was wrongfully taken but also about restoring relationships and ensuring justice. Zacchaeus' story teaches that true repentance involves making amends wherever possible, aligning actions with the principles of righteousness and justice.

Prayer Point:

Lord, help us to understand and apply the principles of restitution and justice in our lives, reflecting Your righteousness and mercy.

Friday September 06

Topic: The Christian Approach to Modern Science

Memory Verse: "It is the glory of God to conceal a matter; to search out a matter is the glory of kings." **- Proverbs 25:2**

Bible Reading: Psalm 111:2

Read & Learn:

Throughout history, many Christians have contributed significantly to the field of science, seeing their work as a means to understand God's creation more deeply. A notable example is Sir Isaac Newton, a devout Christian, whose groundbreaking work in physics laid the foundations for classical mechanics. Newton saw his scientific pursuits not as separate from his faith, but as a way to explore and marvel at the intricacies of God's universe. His approach demonstrates that faith and science need not be in conflict; rather, they can be complementary paths to understanding the truth. The pursuit of scientific knowledge, when approached with humility and reverence, can lead to a greater appreciation of the Creator's wisdom and power.

The Christian approach to modern science is one that embraces the pursuit of knowledge and understanding of the natural world as a reflection of God's creative order. Psalm 111:2 celebrates the works of the Lord as great and studied by all who delight in them, indicating that scientific inquiry can be an act of worship and reverence.

Prayer Point:

Heavenly Father, grant us wisdom and discernment as we navigate the relationship between faith and science.

Saturday September 07

Topic: Nurturing Faith in Youth

Memory Verse: "Start children off on the way they should go, and even when they are old they will not turn from it." **- Proverbs 22:6**

Bible Reading: 1 Timothy 4:12

Read & Learn:

The story of Timothy in the New Testament is an inspiring example of nurturing faith in youth. Timothy was mentored by the Apostle Paul, who recognised his young protégé's faith and potential for ministry. Paul's letters to Timothy (1 Timothy and 2 Timothy) are filled with advice, encouragement, and guidance, helping him to grow in faith and leadership. Despite Timothy's youth, Paul urged him to set an example for believers in speech, in conduct, in love, in faith, and in purity (1 Timothy 4:12). This mentorship shows the importance of nurturing faith in young people by investing time, sharing wisdom, and providing guidance

Nurturing faith in youth is a crucial aspect of Christian discipleship and community life. As Proverbs 22:6 suggests, guiding young people in their spiritual journey lays a foundation that endures throughout their lives. Encouraging young Christians in their faith involves more than just imparting knowledge; it's about modelling a genuine life of faith, providing opportunities for them to explore and express their faith, and listening to their perspectives.

Prayer Point:

Lord, guide us in nurturing the faith of young people, providing them with the wisdom, love, and support they need.

Sunday September 08

Topic: Christian Views on Social Media Use

Memory Verse: "Finally, brothers and sisters, whatever is true, whatever is noble, whatever is right, whatever is pure, whatever is lovely, whatever is admirable - if anything is excellent or praiseworthy - think about such things." **- Philippians 4:8**

Bible Reading: James 1:19-20

Read & Learn:

In today's digital age, the story of Daniel provides a relevant parallel for responsible social media use. Living in Babylon, a place of diverse cultures and practices, Daniel was faced with many influences that contradicted his faith. However, he chose to engage with his surroundings in a way that was respectful, wise, and aligned with his beliefs. He did not isolate himself from the society but instead found ways to be a part of it without compromising his principles. Daniel's story teaches the importance of maintaining one's values and integrity in all forms of interaction, including digital ones.

As Philippians 4:8 suggests, what Christians consume and how they interact online should reflect whatever is true, noble, right, pure, lovely, and admirable. Social media offers both opportunities and challenges for Christians. It can be a platform for positive communication, evangelism, and community building, but it also poses risks of distraction, negative influences, and ungodly interactions.

Prayer Point:

Heavenly Father, guide us to use social media in ways that honour You and reflect our Christian values.

Monday September 09

Topic: The Importance of Christian Missions

Memory Verse: "Therefore go and make disciples of all nations, baptising them in the name of the Father and of the Son and of the Holy Spirit, and teaching them to obey everything I have commanded you. And surely I am with you always, to the very end of the age."

Matthew 28:19-20

Bible Reading: Acts 1:8

Read & Learn:

The early Christian mission movement, particularly the journeys of the Apostle Paul, vividly illustrates the importance of Christian missions. Acts 13-28 details Paul's missionary journeys, where he travelled extensively, preaching the Gospel in various cities across the Roman Empire. Despite facing persecution, imprisonment, and numerous hardships, Paul remained committed to his mission of spreading the message of Christ. His efforts, along with other early Christian missionaries, were instrumental in establishing the church in diverse cultural contexts.

Christian missions involve proclaiming the Gospel, making disciples, and establishing churches. It's about sharing the love, hope, and salvation found in Jesus Christ and addressing spiritual, physical, and social needs. The goal is to reflect God's love to the world and to bring people into a life-transforming relationship with Christ.

Prayer Point:

Heavenly Father, inspire and equip us to fulfil the Great Commission, sharing Your love and Gospel with all nations.

Tuesday September 10

Topic: Understanding the Fruit of the Spirit

Memory Verse: "But the fruit of the Spirit is love, joy, peace, forbearance, kindness, goodness, faithfulness, gentleness and self-control. Against such things there is no law." **- Galatians 5:22-23**

Bible Reading: Galatians 5:22-23

Read & Learn:

The transformation of the Apostle Paul is a powerful testament to the work of the Holy Spirit and the fruit it bears in a believer's life. Before his conversion, Paul, then Saul, was known for his zealous persecution of Christians. However, after his encounter with Christ on the road to Damascus, there was a dramatic change in his character and actions. The man who once was driven by anger and violence became a paragon of the fruits of the Spirit, exhibiting love, peace, patience, kindness, and self-control in his ministry. Paul's life is a vivid illustration of how the Spirit transforms believers, producing qualities that reflect the character of Christ.

The Fruit of the Spirit, as listed in Galatians 5:22-23, encompasses the characteristics that are produced in the life of a believer through the work of the Holy Spirit. These qualities are not just moral virtues; they are manifestations of the character of Christ being formed in a believer.

Prayer Point:

Heavenly Father, fill us with Your Spirit, that we may bear the fruit that reflects Your love and character.

Wednesday September 11

Topic: The Role of Prayer in Social Change

Memory Verse: "If my people, who are called by my name, will humble themselves and pray and seek my face and turn from their wicked ways, then I will hear from heaven, and I will forgive their sin and will heal their land." - **2 Chronicles 7:14**

Bible Reading: James 5:16

Read & Learn:

The civil rights movement in the United States, particularly the leadership of Dr. Martin Luther King Jr., offers a compelling example of the role of prayer in social change. Dr. King, a Baptist minister, emphasised prayer not only as a spiritual practice but also as a powerful tool for social activism. His faith and prayer life fuelled his nonviolent approach to combating racial injustice. Prayer meetings and church services were central to the movement, providing spiritual strength, guidance, and community solidarity. Dr. King's approach illustrates how prayer can be foundational in inspiring and sustaining movements for social change, fostering courage, unity, and resilience among those fighting for justice.

The role of prayer in social change is multifaceted. It involves seeking divine guidance and intervention while also cultivating personal and communal strength and wisdom to address social injustices.

Prayer Point:

Lord, guide us in using prayer as a powerful instrument for social change, aligning our actions with Your will for justice and peace.

Thursday September 12

Topic: Biblical Perspectives on Justice and Equality

Memory Verse: "He has shown you, O mortal, what is good. And what does the Lord require of you? To act justly and to love mercy and to walk humbly with your God." - **Micah 6:8**

Bible Reading: Isaiah 1:17

Read & Learn:

The story of the Good Samaritan in Luke 10:25-37 offers a profound insight into the biblical perspective on justice and equality. In this parable, Jesus responds to a lawyer's question about who qualifies as a neighbour by telling the story of a Samaritan who helped a Jewish man beaten by robbers. Samaritans and Jews typically held deep prejudices against each other, yet the Samaritan in the story shows compassion and care, transcending cultural and ethnic boundaries. His actions contrast with those of the priest and Levite who passed by the injured man. This parable challenges the listeners to rethink their understanding of justice and equality, emphasising that love and compassion should extend beyond societal barriers, and that true righteousness involves actively working for the welfare of all, regardless of their background or status.

Biblical perspectives on justice and equality are deeply rooted in the nature of God and His teachings. The Bible presents justice as integral to God's character and His expectations for human conduct

Prayer Point:

Heavenly Father, inspire us to embody Your heart for justice and equality in our actions and attitudes.

Friday September 13

Topic: The Power of Testimony in Evangelism

Memory Verse: "They triumphed over him by the blood of the Lamb and by the word of their testimony; they did not love their lives so much as to shrink from death." **- Revelation 12:11**

Bible Reading: Acts 22:1-21

Read & Learn:

The Apostle Paul's conversion and subsequent testimony provide a powerful example of the impact of personal testimony in evangelism. Acts 22:1-21 records Paul sharing his conversion experience before a hostile crowd in Jerusalem. He recounts his previous zeal in persecuting Christians, his transformative encounter with Jesus on the road to Damascus, and the radical change in his life that followed. Paul's testimony was a powerful tool in his evangelistic efforts, as it demonstrated the life-changing power of Christ in a personal and relatable way. Through his story, many were able to see the reality of Jesus' transformative power, bridging gaps of understanding and disbelief. Paul's experience shows that personal testimony can be an effective means of sharing the Gospel, as it provides a tangible example of how God can transform a life.

Sharing one's personal journey of faith can help break down barriers and preconceptions, making the message of the Gospel more accessible and understandable.

Prayer Point:

Lord, empower us to share our testimonies with courage and authenticity, revealing Your transformative work in our lives.

Saturday September 14

Topic: Living a Balanced Christian Life

Memory Verse: "To everything there is a season, a time for every purpose under heaven." - **Ecclesiastes 3:1**

Bible Reading: Luke 10:38-42

Read & Learn:

The account of Mary and Martha in Luke 10:38-42 provides a valuable lesson on living a balanced Christian life. Martha, busy with the preparations to host Jesus, becomes frustrated with her sister Mary, who sits at Jesus' feet, listening to His teaching. When Martha complains to Jesus, He gently reminds her that Mary has chosen what is better. This story highlights the balance between active service and spiritual nourishment. It's not that Jesus dismisses the importance of Martha's service, but He emphasises the priority of being spiritually fed and rested. The narrative teaches the importance of balancing practical responsibilities with spiritual growth and rest, ensuring that neither aspect of life is neglected.

Living a balanced Christian life involves managing various aspects of life - spiritual, physical, social, and emotional – in harmony with God's will. As Ecclesiastes 3:1 suggests, there is a time and season for every activity under heaven. A balanced Christian life recognises the need for time devoted to spiritual growth, such as prayer and Bible study, alongside fulfilling daily responsibilities and nurturing relationships.

Prayer Point:

Heavenly Father, help us to find balance in our lives, aligning our priorities with Your will and purpose.

Sunday September 15

Topic: The Impact of Faith on Community Building

Memory Verse: "And let us consider how we may spur one another on toward love and good deeds, not giving up meeting together, as some are in the habit of doing, but encouraging one another—and all the more as you see the Day approaching." **- Hebrews 10:24-25**

Bible Reading: Acts 2:42-47

Read & Learn:

The early Christian community, as described in Acts 2:42-47, is a striking example of the impact of faith on community building. The believers devoted themselves to the apostles' teaching, fellowship, breaking of bread, and prayer. They shared their possessions, provided for those in need, and met together regularly with glad and sincere hearts. This communal life was marked by a strong sense of unity, generosity, and commitment to one another, stemming from their shared faith in Christ. Their actions had a profound impact not only on the members of the community but also on the wider society, as more people were drawn to the faith by their example. This early Christian community illustrates how faith can be a powerful catalyst for building a supportive, loving, and dynamic community, where members care for each other and work together for the common good.

The impact of faith on community building is evident in the way it fosters unity, love, and mutual support among believers.

Prayer Point:

Lord, bless our communities with the unity, love, and commitment exemplified in the early church.

Monday September 16

Topic: Exploring the Proverbs of Wisdom

Memory Verse: "The beginning of wisdom is this: Get wisdom. Though it cost all you have, get understanding." **- Proverbs 4:7**

Bible Reading: Proverbs 3:1-8

Read & Learn:

The book of Proverbs, traditionally attributed to King Solomon, is a rich collection of wisdom sayings that offer guidance on various aspects of life. Solomon's wisdom, as described in 1 Kings 4:29-34, was a gift from God that drew people from all nations to hear his wise words. His proverbs cover diverse topics from personal conduct to social justice, emphasising the fear of the Lord as the foundation of wisdom. For example, Proverbs 3:1-8 advises on trusting in the Lord, honouring Him, and the importance of kindness and truth. These teachings have transcended time, providing timeless principles for living a life of wisdom, integrity, and godliness. The proverbs encourage reflection, discernment, and a pursuit of wisdom that aligns with God's will and character.

They address themes such as discipline, speech, relationships, work ethics, and righteousness, offering guidance on navigating life's complexities with discernment and integrity. The fear of the Lord, a central theme in Proverbs, is depicted as the foundation of true wisdom – a reverential awe and respect for God that influences one's actions and decisions.

Prayer Point:

Heavenly Father, grant us the desire and diligence to seek wisdom as instructed in Your Proverbs.

Tuesday September 17

Topic: The Dynamics of Faith and Culture

Memory Verse: "To the weak I became weak, to win the weak. I have become all things to all people so that by all possible means I might save some." **- 1 Corinthians 9:22**

Bible Reading: Acts 17:22-28

Read & Learn:

The Apostle Paul's approach to preaching in Athens, as recorded in Acts 17:22-28, provides a profound example of navigating the dynamics of faith and culture. Addressing the Areopagus, Paul did not dismiss the Athenians' beliefs and cultural practices. Instead, he started by acknowledging their religiosity and then used their altar to an 'unknown god' as a point of connection to introduce the Christian God. He quoted their own poets and philosophers to bridge the cultural gap and make the message of Christ relevant to their context. Paul's method in Athens is a model of how Christians can engage with different cultures: by understanding and respecting the culture, finding common ground, and presenting the Gospel in a way that is understandable and relatable within that cultural framework.

As stated in 1 Corinthians 9:22, effective ministry often requires adaptability and cultural sensitivity. This does not mean compromising the core message of the Gospel.

Prayer Point:

Lord, give us wisdom and sensitivity as we navigate the dynamics of faith and culture in our efforts to share Your Gospel.

Wednesday September 18

Topic: Christian Responses to Poverty and Inequality

Memory Verse: "Speak up for those who cannot speak for themselves, for the rights of all who are destitute. Speak up and judge fairly; defend the rights of the poor and needy."

Proverbs 31:8-9

Bible Reading: James 2:14-17

Read & Learn:

The story of the early church's response to poverty, as described in Acts 4:32-35, provides a compelling model for Christian responses to poverty and inequality. The believers in the early church shared their possessions and ensured that none among them was needy. Those who owned land or houses sold them and brought the proceeds to the apostles, who distributed to each as any had need. This radical approach to community and generosity demonstrates how faith in Christ translates into practical action to address economic disparities. The early Christians did not merely offer prayers and well-wishes but took concrete steps to ensure equitable distribution and care for the vulnerable.

Christian responses to poverty and inequality are rooted in the biblical mandate to care for the marginalised and speak up for justice. Proverbs 31:8-9 urges believers to be advocates for the destitute and defend the rights of the poor and needy

Prayer Point:

Heavenly Father, inspire us to be Your hands and feet in serving the poor and advocating for justice and equality.

Thursday September 19

Topic: The Importance of Christian Fellowship

Memory Verse: "And let us consider how to stir up one another to love and good works, not neglecting to meet together, as is the habit of some, but encouraging one another, and all the more as you see the Day drawing near." - **Hebrews 10:24-25**

Bible Reading: Acts 2:42-47

Read & Learn:

The early Christian community, as depicted in Acts 2:42-47, exemplifies the importance and power of Christian fellowship. The believers devoted themselves to the apostles' teaching, fellowship, breaking of bread, and prayer. They shared their possessions, met together in the temple courts daily, and broke bread in their homes with glad and sincere hearts. This deep sense of community and shared life was instrumental in their spiritual growth and the rapid expansion of the early church. Their fellowship was marked by mutual support, joy, and a powerful witness to the surrounding community. This example from the early church highlights how Christian fellowship is essential not just for individual spiritual growth, but also for building a supportive and dynamic faith community that can effectively share Christ's love with the wider world.

Through fellowship, Christians can experience the tangible presence and love of Christ as they interact with one another

Prayer Point:

Heavenly Father, help us to value and engage in Christian fellowship, drawing us closer to You and to one another.

Friday September 20

Topic: Navigating Doubts in Faith

Memory Verse: "But when you ask, you must believe and not doubt, because the one who doubts is like a wave of the sea, blown and tossed by the wind." - **James 1:6**

Bible Reading: Mark 9:24

Read & Learn:

The narrative of the father who brought his demon-possessed son to Jesus in Mark 9:14-29 provides a poignant example of navigating doubts in faith. When Jesus asked if the father believed He could heal his son, the father exclaimed, "I do believe; help me overcome my unbelief!" This honest confession of mixed faith and doubt is a powerful expression of the human experience. The father's plea for help in his unbelief shows that doubt does not have to be a barrier to faith, but rather an opportunity for growth and deeper understanding. His story teaches that it is normal to experience doubts and that being honest about them with God can be a step towards strengthening faith.

Navigating doubts in faith is a common experience for many believers. James 1:6 speaks to the importance of asking in faith without doubting, yet the Bible also acknowledges that doubt is part of the human condition. Faith that has been tested and has wrestled with doubt can often emerge stronger and more resilient.

Prayer Point:

Lord, in moments of doubt, help us to seek You honestly and openly, trusting that You will guide us to greater understanding.

Saturday September 21

Topic: The Role of Miracles in Christianity

Memory Verse: "Very truly I tell you, whoever believes in me will do the works I have been doing, and they will do even greater things than these, because I am going to the Father." **- John 14:12**

Bible Reading: Acts 3:1-10

Read & Learn:

The healing of the lame beggar at the Beautiful Gate by Peter and John, as recorded in Acts 3:1-10, is a vivid illustration of the role of miracles in Christianity. This event demonstrates the continuation of Jesus' miraculous works through His disciples, reinforcing the message of the Gospel with tangible signs of God's power. When Peter said to the beggar, "Silver or gold I do not have, but what I do have I give you. In the name of Jesus Christ of Nazareth, walk," it was not just the physical healing that was remarkable, but also the clear attribution of this miracle to Jesus' power and authority. This miracle, along with many others in the Acts of the Apostles, illustrates that miracles serve as a testament to the reality of Jesus' message and kingdom, encouraging faith in believers and often sparking curiosity and openness to the Gospel among non-believers.

While miracles are not the foundation of Christian faith, they are confirmations of the faith's truth and power.

Prayer Point:

Heavenly Father, help us to recognise and appreciate the miracles that reveal Your power and love in our world.

Sunday September 22

Topic: Christian Ethics in Daily Life

Memory Verse: "And whatever you do, whether in word or deed, do it all in the name of the Lord Jesus, giving thanks to God the Father through him." - **Colossians 3:17**

Bible Reading: James 1:22-25

Read & Learn:

The life of Joseph, particularly during his time in Egypt as recorded in Genesis 39-41, offers a compelling example of living out Christian ethics in daily life. Despite facing unjust treatment, temptation, and imprisonment, Joseph consistently displayed integrity, faithfulness, and trust in God. His refusal to succumb to Potiphar's wife's advances, his honest and wise management of resources, and his humble acknowledgment of God's power in interpreting Pharaoh's dreams illustrate a steadfast commitment to ethical living, guided by his faith. Joseph's story demonstrates how Christian ethics can be applied in various aspects of life, including personal decisions, workplace conduct, and dealing with adversity, highlighting that living ethically is a powerful testimony of one's faith in God.

As Colossians 3:17 advises, believers are called to do everything in the name of the Lord Jesus, which encompasses all areas of life including work, relationships, communication, and personal conduct.

Prayer Point:

Lord, guide us to live out our faith with integrity and love in every aspect of our daily lives.

Monday September 23

Topic: The Significance of Jesus' Resurrection

Memory Verse: "And if Christ has not been raised, your faith is futile; you are still in your sins." **- 1 Corinthians 15:17**

Bible Reading: Luke 24:1-12

Read & Learn:

The discovery of the empty tomb by the women followers of Jesus, as recorded in Luke 24:1-12, marks a pivotal moment in Christian faith - the resurrection of Jesus Christ. The women, who went to the tomb to anoint Jesus' body, found the stone rolled away and the tomb empty. They encountered angels who reminded them of Jesus' prophecy that He would rise on the third day. This event was not just a miraculous occurrence but a foundational truth for Christian faith. The resurrection proved that Jesus had overcome death, validating His claims and teachings. It demonstrated God's power over sin and death, providing believers with hope for eternal life. The significance of the resurrection lies in its affirmation of Jesus as the Son of God and its implications for salvation, forgiveness, and the promise of resurrection for believers.

The resurrection also empowers Christians to live a new life in Christ, characterised by faith, hope, and love, and it motivates them to share the Gospel message with others. It validates the truth of Jesus' teachings and His identity as the Messiah.

Prayer Point:

Lord Jesus, we thank You for Your resurrection, which brings us hope, forgiveness, and the promise of eternal life.

Tuesday September 24

Topic: The Challenge of Living a Holy Life

Memory Verse: "But just as he who called you is holy, so be holy in all you do; for it is written: 'Be holy, because I am holy.'"

1 Peter 1:15-16

Bible Reading: Romans 12:1-2

Read & Learn:

The life of Daniel in the Old Testament provides a powerful example of the challenge of living a holy life, especially in an environment not conducive to such a lifestyle. Taken into Babylonian captivity, Daniel was surrounded by a culture and practices that were often at odds with his faith. Despite these challenges, he remained committed to living a life that honoured God. Daniel's refusal to eat the king's food, which likely violated dietary laws, and his persistence in prayer despite the threat of the lion's den, are testaments to his dedication to holiness. His story demonstrates that living a holy life is not about withdrawing from the world but about maintaining integrity and faithfulness to God's standards within it.

Living a holy life in a Christian context means living in a way that is set apart and reflects God's character. As 1 Peter 1:15-16 urges, believers are called to be holy in all aspects of their lives, following the example of God's holiness.

Prayer Point:

Heavenly Father, help us to embrace the challenge of living a holy life, seeking to reflect Your holiness in all we do.

Wednesday September 25

Topic: The Power of Persistent Prayer

Memory Verse: "Then Jesus told his disciples a parable to show them that they should always pray and not give up." **- Luke 18:1**

Bible Reading: Luke 11:5-10

Read & Learn:

The parable of the persistent widow in Luke 18:1-8 exemplifies the power of persistent prayer. In this parable, Jesus describes a widow who repeatedly approaches an unjust judge to get justice against her adversary. Despite his initial reluctance, the judge eventually grants her request, worn down by her persistence. Jesus uses this story to encourage His followers to continually pray and not lose heart. This parable teaches that persistence in prayer is not about changing God's mind but about deepening our trust and dependence on Him. It emphasises that persistent prayer fosters a stronger relationship with God, aligns our hearts with His will, and demonstrates our faith and commitment to seeking His guidance and intervention in our lives.

Persistent prayer is an expression of steadfast faith and trust in God's timing and wisdom. It involves continually coming before God with our requests, concerns, and desires, while also being open to His guidance and sovereignty. Persistent prayer is not merely about repeated requests; it is about maintaining a continuous, open line of communication with God.

Prayer Point:

Lord, teach us to be persistent in prayer, trusting in Your perfect timing and wisdom.

Thursday September 26

Topic: The Role of the Church in Society

Memory Verse: "You are the salt of the earth; but if the salt loses its flavour, how shall it be seasoned? You are the light of the world. A city that is set on a hill cannot be hidden." **- Matthew 5:13-14**

Bible Reading: 1 Peter 2:9-12

Read & Learn:

The impact of the early church on its society is a profound example of the role of the church in society. The Book of Acts records how the early Christians, filled with the Holy Spirit, boldly proclaimed the Gospel and addressed various needs in their communities. Their radical love and generosity, as seen in Acts 2:42-47 and Acts 4:32-37, were transformative, leading to the growth of the church and favour among the people. They did not conform to the prevailing societal norms but set a new standard of community, compassion, and moral integrity. Their engagement in society was not limited to spiritual matters; they also addressed social, economic, and justice issues, reflecting Jesus' holistic mission.

According to 1 Peter 2:9-12, the church is a chosen people, called to declare God's praises and live exemplary lives among the nations.

Prayer Point:

Heavenly Father, empower Your church to be salt and light in society, positively influencing and transforming the world around us.

Friday September 27

Topic: Christian Perspectives on Human Nature

Memory Verse: "So God created mankind in his own image, in the image of God he created them; male and female he created them."

Genesis 1:27

Bible Reading: Romans 3:23-24

Read & Learn:

The story of King David, as depicted in the Bible, encapsulates the complexity of human nature from a Christian perspective. David, anointed as a young shepherd to be king of Israel, was a man after God's own heart, displaying profound faith and courage. Yet, he was also flawed, committing grave sins like adultery and murder. David's life exemplifies the dual aspects of human nature in Christian theology: the dignity and goodness from being made in God's image, and the propensity to sin due to the fallen state of humanity. His eventual repentance and seeking of God's forgiveness in Psalm 51 show the potential for redemption and restoration in human nature.

Christian perspectives on human nature are grounded in the belief that humans are created in the image of God (Genesis 1:27), endowed with dignity, worth, and the capacity for relationship with God and others.

Prayer Point:

Heavenly Father, help us to understand and embrace our nature as beings created in Your image, yet in need of Your grace.

Saturday September 28

Topic: Overcoming Adversity with Faith

Memory Verse: "Consider it pure joy, my brothers and sisters, whenever you face trials of many kinds, because you know that the testing of your faith produces perseverance." **- James 1:2-3**

Bible Reading: 2 Corinthians 12:9-10

Read & Learn:

The apostle Paul's life is a compelling testimony to overcoming adversity with faith. His experiences, as chronicled in 2 Corinthians 11:23-29 and other passages, include imprisonments, beatings, shipwrecks, and constant danger. Despite these challenges, Paul's faith remained steadfast. His perspective on adversity is powerfully articulated in 2 Corinthians 12:9-10, where he speaks of boasting in his weaknesses because Christ's power is made perfect in weakness. Paul's approach to adversity was not one of defeat or despair but of embracing trials as opportunities for God's strength to be displayed. His life exemplifies how faith in Christ can provide the resilience and perspective needed to endure hardships, transforming adversity into a platform for spiritual growth and testimony.

Overcoming adversity with faith is a key theme in Christian living. As James 1:2-3 suggests, trials are seen not as meaningless sufferings but as opportunities for developing perseverance and maturing in faith.

Prayer Point:

Heavenly Father, in our adversities, help us to find strength and hope in You, trusting in Your grace and power.

Sunday September 29

Topic: The Significance of Holy Ghost Baptism

Memory Verse: "But you will receive power when the Holy Spirit comes on you; and you will be my witnesses in Jerusalem, and in all Judea and Samaria, and to the ends of the earth." **- Acts 1:8**

Bible Reading: Acts 2:1-4

Read & Learn:

The Day of Pentecost, as recounted in Acts 2:1-4, marks a significant event in Christian history – the baptism of the Holy Ghost. On this day, the apostles, along with other believers, were gathered in a room when suddenly they heard a sound like a mighty rushing wind, and tongues of fire appeared and rested on each of them. They were all filled with the Holy Spirit and began to speak in other tongues as the Spirit enabled them. This event was not only a fulfilment of Jesus' promise to send the Holy Spirit (John 16:7) but also a transformative moment for the early church

The significance of Holy Ghost baptism in Christianity lies in its role in empowering and transforming believers. As Acts 1:8 indicates, the Holy Spirit's coming brings power for witness and ministry.

It signifies the presence and power of the Holy Spirit in a believer's life, marking a dynamic shift in their relationship with God and their effectiveness in ministry.

Prayer Point:

Lord, we seek the empowering presence of Your Holy Spirit in our lives, to be effective witnesses for Your kingdom.

Monday September 30

Topic: The Concept of Christian Sacrifice

Memory Verse: "Therefore, I urge you, brothers and sisters, in view of God's mercy, to offer your bodies as a living sacrifice, holy and pleasing to God this is your true and proper worship."- **Romans 12:1**

Bible Reading: Philippians 2:3-8

Read & Learn:

The ultimate example of Christian sacrifice is found in the life and death of Jesus Christ. Philippians 2:3-8 beautifully encapsulates this, describing how Jesus, being in very nature God, did not consider equality with God something to be used to His own advantage. Instead, He humbled Himself by becoming obedient to death—even death on a cross. This act of selflessness and obedience is the foundation of Christian sacrifice. It's not about losing oneself but about giving oneself for the greater good, following Christ's example of love, humility, and service. Jesus' sacrifice on the cross exemplifies the depth and breadth of sacrificial love, calling believers to live lives that reflect this same self-giving love in their relationships, choices, and actions.

Christian sacrifice involves giving of oneself for the benefit of others and for the glory of God. Christian sacrifice is not confined to grand, life-altering acts but is often expressed in daily decisions and interactions—choosing to serve others, putting others' needs above one's own, and living a life of obedience and humility. It is about aligning one's will with God's will, embracing a life of service, and being willing to forego personal rights and comforts for the sake of Christ.

Prayer Point:

Heavenly Father, inspire us to embrace the concept of sacrifice, following the example of Jesus Christ in our daily lives.

Tuesday October 01

Topic: The Role of Worship in Daily Life

Memory Verse: "I will bless the Lord at all times; His praise shall continually be in my mouth." **- Psalm 34:1**

Bible Reading: Romans 12:1-2

Read & Learn:

The life of King David, exemplified in the Psalms, vividly portrays the role of worship in daily life. Despite facing various trials, including political unrest, personal failings, and family strife, David consistently turned to worship. Whether he was experiencing victory, despair, or mundane daily activities, his life was a tapestry of worship woven into every circumstance. Psalm 34:1, penned by David, reflects his commitment to constant worship, showing that worship for him was not confined to religious rituals or specific times, but was a continuous expression of his relationship with God. David's example teaches that worship is a lifestyle, an ongoing attitude of reverence, gratitude, and adoration towards God, shaping our responses to every situation in life.

Worship in daily life goes beyond formal church services and encompasses a continuous attitude of honouring God in all aspects of life. Romans 12:1-2 calls believers to present their bodies as a living sacrifice, holy and pleasing to God, which is an act of spiritual worship. This implies that worship is not just singing praises or participating in religious ceremonies, but living in a way that glorifies God, whether in work, leisure, relationships, or decision-making.

Prayer Point:

Lord, help us to embrace worship as a vital part of our daily lives, honouring You in all that we do.

Wednesday October 02

Topic: Understanding the Nature of God

Memory Verse: "And he passed in front of Moses, proclaiming, 'The Lord, the Lord, the compassionate and gracious God, slow to anger, abounding in love and faithfulness, maintaining love to thousands, and forgiving wickedness, rebellion, and sin. Yet he does not leave the guilty unpunished; he punishes the children and their children for the sin of the parents to the third and fourth generation.'"

Exodus 34:6-7

Bible Reading: John 4:24

Read & Learn:

The encounter between Jesus and the Samaritan woman at the well, as narrated in John 4, provides deep insights into the nature of God. Jesus, in His conversation with the woman, reveals crucial aspects of God's character. He speaks of God as Spirit, emphasising that true worshipers must worship in spirit and truth (John 4:24). This encounter illustrates God's desire for genuine, heartfelt worship rather than mere religious formalities. It also shows God's accessibility and willingness to engage with individuals across cultural and societal barriers. This story reveals God as compassionate, personal, and seeking an authentic relationship with His creation. It underlines that understanding the nature of God is not just an intellectual exercise but involves a personal experience of His presence and character.

Understanding the nature of God is fundamental to Christian faith. It involves comprehending His attributes and how He relates to the world.

Prayer Point:

Heavenly Father, grant us a deeper understanding of Your nature, that we may know You more truly and worship You more fully.

Thursday October 03

Topic: Discovering Your Divine Calling

Memory Verse: "For I know the plans I have for you, declares the Lord, plans to prosper you and not to harm you, plans to give you hope and a future." - **Jeremiah 29:11**

Bible Reading: Exodus 3:1-12

Read & Learn:

The encounter between Moses and the burning bush in Exodus 3:1-12 serves as a powerful example of discovering one's divine calling. Moses, a shepherd in the wilderness, encountered a burning bush that was not consumed by the flames. When he drew near to investigate, God spoke to him from the bush and revealed His divine plan. Despite his initial hesitation and self-doubt, Moses eventually embraced his calling to lead the Israelites out of Egypt. This story teaches us that divine callings often come unexpectedly and may require us to step out of our comfort zones. Like Moses, we may doubt our abilities, but when God calls, He equips and empowers us to fulfil His purposes.

Discovering your divine calling is a journey of discerning God's unique plan and purpose for your life. Jeremiah 29:11 reminds us that God has plans for us that are filled with hope and a future. The story of Moses demonstrates that God can call us in unexpected ways and places. It's essential to be attuned to God's leading, just as Moses paid attention to the burning bush. When we encounter moments of divine calling, we may feel inadequate or unworthy, as Moses did. However, God assures us, as He assured Moses, that He will be with us and equip us for the task.

Prayer Point:

Heavenly Father, thank You for having a unique calling and purpose for each of us.

Friday October 04

Topic: The Importance of Christian Identity

Memory Verse: "I have been crucified with Christ and I no longer live, but Christ lives in me. The life I now live in the body, I live by faith in the Son of God, who loved me and gave himself for me."

Galatians 2:20

Bible Reading: 1 Peter 2:9-10

Read & Learn:

The transformation of Saul to Paul vividly illustrates the importance of Christian identity. Saul, originally a persecutor of Christians, experienced a radical transformation after encountering Jesus on the road to Damascus (Acts 9:1-19). This encounter not only changed his name from Saul to Paul but also redefined his entire identity and purpose. From a fierce opponent, he became a passionate apostle of Christ, dedicating his life to spreading the Gospel. Paul's letters often reflect on his identity in Christ, emphasising that it's not his past or his achievements that define him, but his relationship with Jesus. This change in identity was the driving force behind his ministry and writings, highlighting that Christian identity is rooted in who we are in Christ, not in our past, accomplishments, or societal labels.

Christian identity is fundamental to understanding one's purpose and place in the world as a believer. As 1 Peter 2:9-10 describes, Christians are chosen people, a royal priesthood, a holy nation, and God's special possession. This identity transcends all other labels and affiliations, shaping how believers view themselves, their life purposes, and their interactions with others.

Prayer Point:

Lord, help us to embrace our identity in You, finding our true worth and purpose in Your love and sacrifice.

Saturday October 05

Topic: Biblical Teachings on Stewardship

Memory Verse: "The earth is the Lord's, and everything in it, the world, and all who live in it." **- Psalm 24:1**

Bible Reading: Matthew 25:14-30

Read & Learn:

The Parable of the Talents in Matthew 25:14-30 provides a foundational teaching on stewardship from a biblical perspective. In this parable, a man going on a journey entrusts his property to his servants. Each servant receives a different amount of talents (a form of currency), and upon the master's return, they are accountable for how they have used these resources. The servants who diligently utilised and increased their talents were commended, while the servant who hid his talent was reprimanded. This parable illustrates the principle that all we have is entrusted to us by God, and we are accountable to Him for how we use our resources, talents, and time.

Biblical stewardship encompasses the responsible management of everything God has entrusted to our care. This includes not only financial resources but also our abilities, time, the environment, and our own bodies. Psalm 24:1 reminds us that everything belongs to God, reinforcing the idea that we are caretakers, not owners, of the resources we possess. Stewardship from a biblical standpoint is an act of worship, acknowledging God's sovereignty and our role as His stewards. It involves using resources wisely, caring for the environment, helping those in need, and investing in God's work.

Prayer Point:

Heavenly Father, help us to be faithful stewards of all that You have entrusted to us, using our resources, talents, and time for Your glory.

Sunday October 06

Topic: The Impact of Faith on Personal Development

Memory Verse: "Being confident of this, that he who began a good work in you will carry it on to completion until the day of Christ Jesus." **- Philippians 1:6**

Bible Reading: 2 Peter 1:5-8

Read & Learn:

The life of Joseph, as narrated in the Book of Genesis (chapters 37-50), vividly illustrates the impact of faith on personal development. Joseph's journey from a favored but naive young man to a wise and compassionate leader of Egypt demonstrates how faith can shape character and life direction. Despite facing betrayal, slavery, and imprisonment, Joseph's steadfast faith in God was crucial in his personal growth and resilience. He developed qualities such as patience, integrity, forgiveness, and wisdom, which were instrumental in his rise to prominence and in his actions during the famine. Joseph's story shows that faith is not just a private spiritual matter but a dynamic force that influences personal development, equipping individuals to navigate life's challenges with grace and strength.

The impact of faith on personal development is a key theme in Christian teaching. Faith is seen as a transformative force that shapes character, values, and behaviour. 2 Peter 1:5-8 encourages believers to supplement their faith with virtues like goodness, knowledge, self-control, perseverance, godliness, mutual affection, and love. This process of adding to one's faith demonstrates that Christian development is an active, ongoing pursuit.

Prayer Point:

Heavenly Father, guide us in our journey of faith, that it may continually shape and enrich our personal development.

Monday October 07

Topic: The Role of the Church in Global Issues

Memory Verse: "He has shown you, O mortal, what is good. And what does the Lord require of you? To act justly and to love mercy and to walk humbly with your God." - **Micah 6:8**

Bible Reading: Matthew 28:19-20

Read & Learn:

The global impact of the church can be seen in the history of Christian missions, exemplified by figures like William Carey, known as the father of modern missions. Carey, a British Christian missionary in the late 18th and early 19th centuries, felt a strong call to spread the Gospel in India. His work went beyond evangelism; he engaged in social reform, including fighting against the practice of sati (widow burning) and promoting education. Carey's approach to missions showcased how the church can address global issues: by combining the proclamation of the Gospel with actions that seek justice, elevate human dignity, and address societal ills. His life illustrates that the role of the church in global issues involves both sharing the Christian faith and actively working to improve societal conditions, based on the principles of justice, mercy, and humility.

As Matthew 28:19-20, the Great Commission, mandates, the church is called to make disciples of all nations, teaching them to obey Christ's commands. This global mandate encompasses addressing social, economic, and environmental issues, as fulfilling the Great Commission involves caring for the whole person, both spiritually and physically.

Prayer Point:

Heavenly Father, guide Your church to be a light in addressing global issues, reflecting Your justice, mercy, and love.

Tuesday October 08

Topic: Christian Perspectives on Mental Health

Memory Verse: "Dear friend, I pray that you may enjoy good health and that all may go well with you, even as your soul is getting along well." **- 3 John 1:2**

Bible Reading: Psalm 34:17-18

Read & Learn:

The story of Elijah in 1 Kings 19 provides a poignant biblical perspective on mental health. After a significant victory at Mount Carmel, Elijah faced threats from Queen Jezebel, leading him to flee into the wilderness. There, Elijah experienced despair and exhaustion to the point of wishing for death. God's response to Elijah was not one of condemnation but of care and restoration. God provided for Elijah's physical needs, allowed him time to rest, and then gently guided him back to his mission. This story demonstrates the importance of acknowledging mental health struggles, the need for holistic care and the understanding that mental health issues do not equate to a lack of faith or spiritual failure.

Christian perspectives on mental health recognise that mental and emotional well-being are essential aspects of overall health. The Bible offers numerous examples of individuals who experienced emotional distress, anxiety, and depression, treating these experiences with compassion and understanding. This perspective acknowledges that mental health issues are complex and can be influenced by various factors, including biological, environmental, psychological, and spiritual elements.

Prayer Point:

Heavenly Father, grant us wisdom and compassion in understanding and addressing mental health, Recognising its importance in our overall well-being.

Wednesday October 09

Topic: The Importance of Spiritual Renewal

Memory Verse: "But those who hope in the Lord will renew their strength. They will soar on wings like eagles; they will run and not grow weary, they will walk and not be faint." - **Isaiah 40:31**

Bible Reading: Romans 12:2

Read & Learn:

The experience of the prophet Elijah in 1 Kings 19 beautifully illustrates the importance of spiritual renewal. After his dramatic confrontation with the prophets of Baal on Mount Carmel, Elijah found himself exhausted and disillusioned, fleeing from Queen Jezebel's threats. In his moment of despair, God met Elijah not in dramatic displays like wind, earthquake, or fire, but in a gentle whisper. This encounter, along with rest and sustenance provided by God, led to Elijah's spiritual renewal. It's a powerful reminder that spiritual renewal often happens in quiet, reflective moments rather than in spectacular events. This renewal gave Elijah the strength to continue his prophetic mission, showing that regular spiritual renewal is essential for sustaining faith and purpose in one's spiritual journey.

Spiritual renewal is a vital aspect of Christian life, involving the revitalisation of one's relationship with God and rejuvenation of one's spirit. Romans 12:2 emphasises the transformation that comes from renewing the mind, indicating that spiritual renewal is as much about internal change as it is about external experiences. It is about letting go of old, unhelpful patterns of thinking and embracing God's perspective and will.

Prayer Point:

Heavenly Father, guide us in our journey of spiritual renewal, that we may find new strength and inspiration in You.

Thursday October 10

Topic: The Dynamics of Faith and Tradition

Memory Verse: "You have let go of the commands of God and are holding on to human traditions." **- Mark 7:8**

Bible Reading: Colossians 2:6-8

Read & Learn:

The interaction between Jesus and the Pharisees in Mark 7:1-13 offers a critical look at the dynamics of faith and tradition. The Pharisees and some teachers of the law questioned Jesus about why His disciples didn't follow the traditional ritual of hand washing before eating. Jesus responded by highlighting the danger of allowing traditions to supersede God's commandments. He emphasised that the heart of faith is not found in rigid adherence to traditions, but in a relationship with God and obedience to His word. This incident teaches that while traditions can be valuable, they should not overshadow the core principles of faith. It challenges believers to discern whether their traditions support or hinder their faith and relationship with God.

Traditions can play a significant role in guiding worship, fostering a sense of community, and connecting believers with the historical church. However, as Colossians 2:6-8 and Mark 7:8 caution, there is a risk of traditions becoming ends in themselves, losing their meaning, or even contradicting the core values of the Christian faith. The key is to ensure that traditions serve to deepen one's understanding and practice of faith, rather than replace or dilute the essence of the Gospel.

Prayer Point:

Heavenly Father, help us to discern the role of traditions in our faith, ensuring they honour You and align with Your word.

Friday October 11

Topic: The Significance of the Lord's Supper

Memory Verse: "For whenever you eat this bread and drink this cup, you proclaim the Lord's death until he comes." **- 1 Corinthians 11:26**

Bible Reading: Luke 22:19-20

Read & Learn:

The Last Supper, as described in Luke 22:19-20, is a foundational event for understanding the significance of the Lord's Supper in Christian practice. During this meal, Jesus shared bread and wine with His disciples, symbolising His body and blood, respectively. This act was not just a shared meal; it was a profound declaration of the new covenant through Jesus' sacrifice. The Lord's Supper serves as a continual reminder of Christ's sacrifice for humanity's sins and His promise of salvation. It's a sacred moment of communion with Christ and with other believers, reinforcing the unity of the church, the forgiveness of sins, and the hope of eternal life. The practice of the Lord's Supper is a testament to the faith's continuity, from Jesus' time to the present, and a powerful symbol of the Christian faith's core truths.

The Lord's Supper, also known as Communion or the Eucharist, holds deep spiritual significance in Christianity. It's a sacrament that commemorates Jesus' Last Supper with His disciples, signifying the sacrifice He made for mankind. It is an act of worship, remembrance, and thanksgiving. The Lord's Supper is a means of grace, where believers reflect on the cost of their salvation and their relationship with Christ and one another.

Prayer Point:

Lord Jesus, as we partake in the Lord's Supper, help us to truly comprehend and cherish the depth of Your sacrifice for us.

Saturday October 12

Topic: The Challenge of Christian Discipleship

Memory Verse: "Then he said to them all: 'Whoever wants to be my disciple must deny themselves and take up their cross daily and follow me.'" - **Luke 9:23**

Bible Reading: Matthew 16:24-26

Read & Learn:

The story of Peter's journey as a disciple, from his initial call to follow Jesus to his eventual denial and restoration (Matthew 4:18-19, Matthew 26:69-75, John 21:15-19), vividly illustrates the challenges of Christian discipleship. Peter, who left everything to follow Christ, shows both the dedication and the struggle inherent in being a disciple. His bold declarations of faith, his failures, and his ultimate reaffirmation of love for Jesus after the resurrection depict the complex path of discipleship. It involves not just the initial enthusiasm of following Christ but also facing trials, understanding and accepting difficult teachings, personal failures, and continual growth.

Christian discipleship is the process of following Jesus Christ and growing in faith and obedience. As described in Luke 9:23 and Matthew 16:24-26, it involves self-denial, bearing one's cross, and prioritising Christ above all else. The challenge of discipleship includes understanding and applying Jesus' teachings, transforming one's character and actions, and engaging in the mission of spreading the Gospel. It often requires sacrifices, such as giving up certain comforts, confronting personal sins and weaknesses, and sometimes facing opposition or misunderstanding from others.

Prayer Point:

Lord Jesus, strengthen us in the challenging journey of discipleship, that we may faithfully follow You and grow in Your likeness.

Sunday October 13

Topic: Understanding God's Love for Humanity

Memory Verse: "For God so loved the world that he gave his one and only Son, that whoever believes in him shall not perish but have eternal life." - **John 3:16**

Bible Reading: Romans 5:6-8

Read & Learn:

The parable of the Prodigal Son in Luke 15:11-32 beautifully illustrates God's love for humanity. In this story, a young man demands his inheritance, leaves his father's house, and squanders his wealth in reckless living. When he hits rock bottom, he decides to return to his father, expecting punishment or rejection. Instead, his father welcomes him with open arms, celebrating his return. This parable, told by Jesus, reveals the depth of God's love and forgiveness. It shows that God's love is unconditional, not based on human merit or behaviour. The father's response in the story mirrors God's eagerness to forgive and embrace anyone who turns back to Him. This parable teaches that God's love is enduring, patient, and full of grace, inviting all to experience reconciliation and the fullness of His love.

John 3:16 and Romans 5:6-8 express the essence of this love - that God loved the world so profoundly that He sent Jesus Christ to die for humanity's sins, offering salvation and eternal life. God's love is characterised by its unconditional nature, extending to all people regardless of their status, actions, or beliefs. This divine love is not merely an emotional expression but is active and sacrificial, demonstrated through Christ's life, death, and resurrection.

Prayer Point:

Heavenly Father, help us to grasp the magnitude of Your love for us, revealed through Jesus Christ.

Monday October 14

Topic: The Power of Christian Unity

Memory Verse: "Make every effort to keep the unity of the Spirit through the bond of peace." **- Ephesians 4:3**

Bible Reading: 1 Corinthians 12:12-27

Read & Learn:

The early church, as depicted in Acts 2:42-47, serves as a powerful example of Christian unity. In these verses, the believers devoted themselves to the apostles' teaching, fellowship, breaking of bread, and prayer. They shared their possessions, met together daily, and praised God with one heart. This unity was not just a superficial agreement but a deep, spiritual bond that transcended differences. It resulted in a powerful witness to the surrounding community and contributed to the rapid growth of the church. Their example demonstrates how unity among believers can lead to a stronger community, effective ministry, and a vibrant witness to Christ's love and power. It shows that Christian unity is more than just getting along; it's a profound expression of our shared faith and purpose in Christ.

The power of Christian unity is rooted in the belief that despite diverse backgrounds, traditions, and perspectives, believers are one in Christ. Ephesians 4:3 and 1 Corinthians 12:12-27 emphasise the importance of unity in the body of Christ. This unity is not based on uniformity in all beliefs and practices but on a shared commitment to Christ and the Gospel. It involves valuing each other's differences, supporting one another, and working together for the common good and the mission of the church.

Prayer Point:

Heavenly Father, guide us in fostering unity within the body of Christ, that we may reflect Your love and grace.

Tuesday October 15

Topic: Biblical Perspectives on Human Responsibility

Memory Verse: "For each one should carry their own load." Galatians 6:5

Bible Reading: James 2:14-17

Read & Learn:

The story of the Good Samaritan in Luke 10:25-37 highlights the importance of human responsibility from a biblical perspective. A man traveling from Jerusalem to Jericho is robbed, beaten, and left for dead. Two religious leaders pass by without helping, but a Samaritan, considered an outsider, stops to assist. He treats the man's wounds and ensures his care. This parable, told by Jesus in response to the question "Who is my neighbour?", underscores the responsibility individuals have towards others, especially those in need. It challenges the notion of responsibility being limited to one's own community or group and expands it to include acts of compassion and assistance to all, regardless of their background or status. The Good Samaritan exemplifies taking personal responsibility to care for others, embodying the love and mercy that are central to Christian ethics.

Biblical perspectives on human responsibility encompass a range of duties and obligations that individuals have towards God, themselves, others, and creation. James 2:14-17 emphasises that faith without deeds is dead, indicating that responsibility includes actionable expressions of faith. In the Bible, human responsibility is often linked with stewardship, care for the needy, ethical conduct, and the pursuit of justice.

Prayer Point:

Lord, help us to embrace our responsibilities as Your followers, showing Your love through our actions and choices.

Wednesday October 16

Topic: The Importance of Biblical Authority

Memory Verse: "All Scripture is God-breathed and is useful for teaching, rebuking, correcting and training in righteousness, so that the servant of God may be thoroughly equipped for every good work." - **2 Timothy 3:16-17**

Bible Reading: Psalm 119:105

Read & Learn:

The Bereans' approach to Scripture, as described in Acts 17:11, serves as a model for understanding the importance of biblical authority. When Paul and Silas preached in Berea, the Bereans received the message with great eagerness but also examined the Scriptures daily to see if what Paul said was true. This practice highlights the vital role of the Bible in discerning truth and guiding faith. The Bereans didn't blindly accept teachings; instead, they relied on the authority of Scripture to verify and understand the teachings. Their example demonstrates the importance of grounding beliefs and practices in the Bible, ensuring that teachings and doctrines align with God's Word, and using Scripture as the ultimate standard for truth and guidance in the Christian life.

As 2 Timothy 3:16-17 and Psalm 119:105 suggest, Scripture is crucial for teaching, guiding, and correcting believers, providing a foundation for understanding God's will and living righteously. The authority of the Bible means that it holds precedence over traditions, personal experiences, or human reasoning when it comes to spiritual truths and moral guidance.

Prayer Point:

Heavenly Father, instil in us a deep respect for Your word as the ultimate authority in our lives, guiding us in truth and righteousness.

Thursday October 17

Topic: The Significance of Christ's Teachings

Memory Verse: "Therefore everyone who hears these words of mine and puts them into practice is like a wise man who built his house on the rock." **- Matthew 7:24**

Bible Reading: John 13:34-35

Read & Learn:

The Sermon on the Mount, as recorded in Matthew chapters 5 to 7, is a prime example of the profound impact of Christ's teachings. In this sermon, Jesus presents key principles of the Kingdom of Heaven, challenging traditional understandings of righteousness, justice, and personal conduct. He addresses topics such as the Beatitudes, love for enemies, the Lord's Prayer, and the call to be salt and light in the world. This sermon encapsulates the essence of Christ's teachings and presents a radical call to live out the values of the kingdom of God. The principles taught in the Sermon on the Mount have not only shaped Christian ethics and behaviour but have also significantly influenced Western moral and legal thought. This sermon demonstrates that Christ's teachings are foundational to Christian faith, providing guidance for personal conduct, community life, and understanding of God's kingdom.

The significance of Christ's teachings lies in their transformative power and timeless relevance. John 13:34-35, where Jesus gives the new commandment to love one another, exemplifies the heart of His teachings. Christ's teachings offer profound insights into the nature of God, the path to true fulfilment, and principles for living in harmony with God and others.

Prayer Point:

Lord Jesus, help us to deeply understand and faithfully apply Your teachings in our lives, building a firm foundation on Your word.

Friday October 18

Topic: The Dynamics of Christian Growth

Memory Verse: "Instead, speaking the truth in love, we will grow to become in every respect the mature body of him who is the head, that is, Christ." **- Ephesians 4:15**

Bible Reading: 2 Peter 3:18

Read & Learn:

The growth of the apostle Peter, from a fisherman to a foundational leader in the early church, illustrates the dynamics of Christian growth. Peter's journey is marked by several key moments: his initial call to follow Jesus, his impulsive actions and statements, his denial of Christ, and his restoration and powerful leadership in the early church (John 21:15-19, Acts 2). Each phase of Peter's journey reveals different aspects of Christian growth: the call to discipleship, learning from mistakes, the importance of forgiveness and restoration, and the development of faith and leadership. Peter's life shows that Christian growth is not a linear process but involves various experiences and challenges that contribute to spiritual maturity and effectiveness in serving God's purposes.

Christian growth is a lifelong process of becoming more like Christ in character, understanding, and practice. As Ephesians 4:15 and 2 Peter 3:18 suggest, it involves growing in knowledge, faith, and love. This growth is not just an individual endeavour but occurs within the context of the Christian community, where believers can support, teach, and encourage one another.

Prayer Point:

Heavenly Father, guide us on our journey of Christian growth, that we may increasingly reflect Christ in our thoughts, words, and actions.

Saturday October 19

Topic: The Role of Faith in Family Dynamics

Memory Verse: "But as for me and my household, we will serve the Lord." **- Joshua 24:15**

Bible Reading: Ephesians 5:21-6:4

Read & Learn:

The story of Lois and Eunice, the grandmother and mother of Timothy, showcases the impact of faith in family dynamics (2 Timothy 1:5). Timothy, who became a key figure in the early church and a close companion of Paul, was influenced significantly by the faith of his mother and grandmother. Their sincere faith laid a foundation for Timothy's own faith and ministry. This example highlights how faith within a family can shape values, behaviours, and the overall direction of the family. It demonstrates the role of faith in providing guidance, strength, and a sense of purpose for family members. The nurturing of faith within the family setting can lead to a strong, resilient, and spiritually grounded family unit.

Faith plays a vital role in shaping family dynamics in various ways. As depicted in Ephesians 5:21-6:4, faith influences how family members interact with each other, guiding them to treat each other with love, respect, and kindness. Faith provides a moral and ethical framework, helping families make decisions that align with Christian values. It offers a source of comfort, unity, and strength, especially during challenging times. Faith also encourages practices such as prayer, worship, and reading Scripture together, which can strengthen family bonds and foster a shared sense of purpose.

Prayer Point:

Lord, bless our families with Your presence, guiding us to live out our faith in love, respect, and unity.

Sunday October 20

Topic: The Power of the Resurrection in Daily Life

Memory Verse: "I want to know Christ—yes, to know the power of his resurrection and participation in his sufferings, becoming like him in his death." **- Philippians 3:10**

Bible Reading: Romans 6:4-5

Read & Learn:

The transformation of the disciples after the resurrection of Jesus powerfully illustrates the impact of the resurrection in daily life. Before the resurrection, the disciples were often fearful, uncertain, and even fled in Jesus' most challenging moments. However, after witnessing the resurrected Christ and receiving the Holy Spirit, they became bold, confident, and willing to face persecution and hardship for the sake of the Gospel. Their transformation showcases the profound effect of the resurrection on their understanding of life, purpose, and faith. It moved them from fear to courage, from doubt to faith, and from despair to hope. The disciples' lives, post-resurrection, serve as a testament to how the reality of the resurrection can embolden and transform believers, influencing their daily actions, decisions, and outlook on life.

The power of the resurrection in daily life lies in its profound implications for Christian living and identity. As Romans 6:4-5 and Philippians 3:10 suggest, the resurrection of Christ is not just a historical event to be celebrated, but a reality that deeply affects believers. It signifies victory over sin and death, offering new life and hope. The resurrection empowers believers to live with a sense of purpose and hope, knowing that their life is anchored in something eternal and transformative.

Prayer Point:

Heavenly Father, help us to grasp the incredible power of Christ's resurrection and its impact on our daily lives.

Monday October 21

Topic: Navigating the Challenges of Modern Parenting

Memory Verse: "Start children off on the way they should go, and even when they are old they will not turn from it." **- Proverbs 22:6**

Bible Reading: Ephesians 6:4

Read & Learn:

The story of Timothy in the New Testament provides a glimpse into effective parenting in a challenging environment. Timothy, a young leader in the early church, was raised by his mother, Eunice, and grandmother, Lois, who instilled in him a strong faith from an early age (2 Timothy 1:5). Despite the absence of a Christian father figure (Acts 16:1), Timothy's mother and grandmother were instrumental in his spiritual upbringing, laying a foundation that prepared him for significant roles in the church and in his mentorship with the Apostle Paul. Their example highlights the importance of a consistent and nurturing spiritual environment in the home, particularly in the face of societal pressures and challenges. It shows that modern parenting, while complex, can successfully integrate faith principles to guide and prepare children for the future.

Navigating the challenges of modern parenting from a Christian perspective involves balancing love and discipline while instilling faith and values in children. Ephesians 6:4 advises parents to bring up their children in the training and instruction of the Lord, emphasising the role of parents in spiritual guidance. Modern parenting challenges include dealing with technological influences, societal pressures, and often, a busier family schedule.

Prayer Point:

Heavenly Father, grant wisdom and guidance to parents as they navigate the complexities of modern parenting, instilling Your values and love in their children.

Tuesday October 22

Topic: Christian Ethics in Technology and Innovation

Memory Verse: "And whatever you do, whether in word or deed, do it all in the name of the Lord Jesus, giving thanks to God the Father through him." **- Colossians 3:17**

Bible Reading: 1 Corinthians 10:31

Read & Learn:

Daniel's story in the Old Testament, particularly in the context of his service in the Babylonian and Persian empires, offers insight into navigating ethics in a complex, secular environment. Despite being in a culture with advanced knowledge and practices, often at odds with his faith, Daniel remained committed to God's principles. He navigated ethical dilemmas, such as the king's diet (Daniel 1) and the edict to pray only to King Darius (Daniel 6), with wisdom and integrity. Daniel's example demonstrates how Christians can engage with contemporary culture, including technology and innovation, while maintaining their ethical standards and faith values.

His story encourages believers to be discerning, to seek God's wisdom, and to stand firm in their beliefs, even as they participate in and contribute to technological and societal advancements. Christian ethics in technology and innovation involves applying biblical principles to guide behaviour and decision-making in these fields.

Prayer Point:

Heavenly Father, guide us as we navigate the complex world of technology and innovation, helping us to use these tools in ways that honour You and benefit others.

Wednesday October 23

Topic: Biblical Perspectives on Wealth and Prosperity

Memory Verse: "For the love of money is a root of all kinds of evil. Some people, eager for money, have wandered from the faith and pierced themselves with many griefs." - **1 Timothy 6:10**

Bible Reading: Matthew 6:19-21

Read & Learn:

The encounter between Jesus and the rich young ruler in Mark 10:17-27 provides a profound insight into biblical perspectives on wealth and prosperity. The young man, who had great wealth, approached Jesus to ask what he must do to inherit eternal life. When Jesus told him to sell all he had and give to the poor, he went away sad, unable to part with his possessions. This story illustrates the potential spiritual danger of wealth when it becomes a priority over following Christ. It teaches that wealth and prosperity, while not inherently evil, can become obstacles to spiritual growth and devotion if they lead to excessive attachment or replace God as the ultimate focus in life.

The encounter challenges believers to examine their attitudes towards wealth and to prioritise their relationship with God above material possessions. Biblical perspectives on wealth and prosperity emphasise the responsible and ethical use of resources and caution against allowing wealth to become an idol. As 1 Timothy 6:10 and Matthew 6:19-21 suggest, the love of money and the pursuit of wealth can lead to many problems and divert one's focus from spiritual matters. The Bible does not condemn wealth itself but rather the improper attitude towards it.

Prayer Point:

Heavenly Father, help us to have a healthy perspective on wealth and prosperity, aligning our attitudes and actions with Your teachings.

Thursday October 24

Topic: The Role of Christians in Politics

Memory Verse: "You are the salt of the earth... You are the light of the world. A town built on a hill cannot be hidden."

Matthew 5:13-14

Bible Reading: Romans 13:1-7

Read & Learn:

The story of Joseph, who rose to become the second most powerful person in Egypt, provides a biblical perspective on the role of Christians in politics (Genesis 41). Joseph's journey from a slave to a ruler is marked by his steadfast faith in God and his wise and ethical conduct, even in a pagan society. His position in the Egyptian government was used not only to save Egypt from famine but also to preserve his own family and eventually the entire nation of Israel. Joseph's story shows that Christians can have a significant and positive impact in the political realm, using their influence for the common good, the preservation of justice, and the promotion of godly values. It demonstrates that involvement in politics can be a platform for serving God's purposes and bringing about societal change.

The role of Christians in politics is to influence society positively while maintaining their Christian values and integrity. Romans 13:1-7 and Matthew 5:13-14 emphasise the Christian's responsibility to be involved in societal matters, including politics. Christians are called to be 'salt and light,' preserving what is good and illuminating truth and justice in the public sphere. Their involvement can take various forms, from voting and advocacy to holding public office.

Prayer Point:

Heavenly Father, guide Your people as they navigate the complex world of politics, to be effective witnesses of Your truth and love.

Friday October 25

Topic: The Concept of God's Omnipresence

Memory Verse: "Where can I go from your Spirit? Where can I flee from your presence? If I go up to the heavens, you are there; if I make my bed in the depths, you are there." **- Psalm 139:7-8**

Bible Reading: Jeremiah 23:23-24

Read & Learn:

The story of Jonah's attempt to flee from God's presence powerfully illustrates the concept of God's omnipresence. Jonah, a prophet, was called to deliver a message to Nineveh but chose to run away. He boarded a ship headed in the opposite direction, only to find that he could not escape from God's presence. A great storm arose, and eventually, Jonah was swallowed by a large fish. During this time, Jonah realised the futility of trying to hide from God and recognised God's presence even in the depths of the sea. This story teaches that God is present everywhere and in all situations, whether one is obedient to His call or attempting to run away from it. It highlights the inescapable and comforting reality of God's omnipresence in all aspects of life.

The concept of God's omnipresence is a fundamental aspect of Christian theology, asserting that God is present in all places at all times. As expressed in Psalm 139:7-8 and Jeremiah 23:23-24, God's presence is not limited by physical space or human constraints. This omnipresence means that God is always with His creation, aware of all things, and actively involved in the universe. The understanding of God's omnipresence offers comfort and assurance to believers, knowing that they are never alone or beyond God's reach.

Prayer Point:

Heavenly Father, we are in awe of Your omnipresence, comforted by the truth that You are with us everywhere and at all times.

Saturday October 26

Topic: The Impact of Faith on Work and Career

Memory Verse: "Whatever you do, work at it with all your heart, as working for the Lord, not for human masters, since you know that you will receive an inheritance from the Lord as a reward. It is the Lord Christ you are serving." - **Colossians 3:23-24**

Bible Reading: Proverbs 16:3

Read & Learn:

The life of Joseph, particularly during his time in Egypt, provides a compelling example of how faith can impact work and career. Despite being sold into slavery, falsely accused, and imprisoned, Joseph consistently exhibited integrity, excellence, and trust in God in his work. His faith influenced his approach to work, leading him to excel and eventually rise to become the second most powerful person in Egypt. Joseph's attitude and work ethic, rooted in his faith, not only brought him personal success but also allowed him to be used by God to save many lives during a time of famine. His story illustrates how faith can transform one's work attitude and ethics, leading to both professional excellence and a greater purpose beyond personal achievement.

Faith shapes the way believers view their work, not merely as a means to earn a living but as an opportunity to serve God and contribute positively to society. Colossians 3:23-24 and Proverbs 16:3 suggest that Christians should approach their work with diligence, integrity, and a spirit of service, seeing their career as part of God's plan.

Prayer Point:

Lord, guide us in our work and careers, that we may serve You faithfully and with excellence in our professional lives.

Sunday October 27

Topic: Navigating Christian Adolescence

Memory Verse: "Don't let anyone look down on you because you are young, but set an example for the believers in speech, in conduct, in love, in faith and in purity." **- 1 Timothy 4:12**

Bible Reading: Proverbs 3:5-6

Read & Learn:

The story of the young boy David facing Goliath in 1 Samuel 17 vividly illustrates the journey of Christian adolescence. Despite his youth and inexperience, David demonstrated remarkable faith, courage, and wisdom. His trust in God, understanding of God's past faithfulness, and willingness to face challenges that even seasoned warriors hesitated to confront, set a powerful example. David's story is an encouragement to Christian adolescents, showing that age does not limit one's ability to live out faith courageously and impactfully. It also serves as a reminder that God equips and uses young people in significant ways, encouraging them to rely on Him, develop their gifts, and stand firm in their convictions even in the face of daunting challenges.

Navigating Christian adolescence involves growing in faith and developing a personal relationship with God while dealing with the unique challenges and changes of this life stage. escence is a critical time for forming identity, values, and beliefs. Christian adolescents are called to navigate these formative years by grounding themselves in biblical truths, actively participating in a faith community, and applying their faith to everyday decisions and challenges.

Prayer Point:

Heavenly Father, guide our young people as they navigate adolescence, empowering them to grow in faith and to be examples of Your love and truth.

Monday October 28

Topic: The Significance of the Holy Spirit in Believers' Lives

Memory Verse: "But the Advocate, the Holy Spirit, whom the Father will send in my name, will teach you all things and will remind you of everything I have said to you." - **John 14:26**

Bible Reading: Galatians 5:22-23

Read & Learn:

The transformation of the apostles at Pentecost vividly illustrates the significance of the Holy Spirit in believers' lives (Acts 2). Before the coming of the Holy Spirit, the apostles were often uncertain and fearful, even hiding after Jesus' crucifixion. However, once they received the Holy Spirit, they were transformed into bold and confident messengers of the Gospel, effectively communicating and performing wonders in Jesus' name. The Holy Spirit empowered them to preach with boldness, understand spiritual truths, and carry out God's mission with great impact. This transformation highlights the essential role of the Holy Spirit in providing guidance, courage, wisdom, and the ability to fulfil God's purposes.

The Holy Spirit is integral to the Christian experience, serving as a comforter, guide, teacher, and source of strength. As Jesus promised in John 14:26, the Holy Spirit teaches believers and reminds them of Christ's teachings, aiding in understanding and applying God's Word. In Galatians 5:22-23, the fruits of the Spirit love, joy, peace, patience, kindness, goodness, faithfulness, gentleness, and self-control – are described, indicating the transformative effect of the Holy Spirit in a believer's character and actions.

Prayer Point:

Heavenly Father, thank You for the gift of the Holy Spirit, our comforter, teacher, and guide.

Tuesday October 29

Topic: Christian Perspectives on Globalisation

Memory Verse: "From one man he made all the nations, that they should inhabit the whole earth; and he marked out their appointed times in history and the boundaries of their lands. God did this so that they would seek him and perhaps reach out for him and find him, though he is not far from any one of us." **- Acts 17:26-27**

Bible Reading: Matthew 28:19-20

Read & Learn:

The missionary journeys of the Apostle Paul, as recorded in the Book of Acts, provide a biblical perspective on the concept of globalisation from a Christian viewpoint. Paul's travels across various cultural, national, and ethnic boundaries to preach the Gospel illustrate the Christian mandate to engage with a globally interconnected world. His ability to adapt his message for different contexts, while maintaining the core truths of the Gospel, showcases how Christians can navigate the complexities of globalisation. Paul's journeys reflect the early church's recognition of the diverse, interconnected world they lived in and their commitment to sharing the Gospel across these boundaries. This example encourages Christians today to embrace globalisation as an opportunity to spread the Gospel, learn from diverse cultures, and promote unity and understanding among different peoples.

Christian perspectives on globalisation recognise both the opportunities and challenges presented by an increasingly interconnected world. Matthew 28:19-20, known as the Great Commission, calls Christians to make disciples of all nations, highlighting the global scope of the Christian mission.

Prayer Point: Father, Help us to embrace globalisation as an opportunity to spread the Gospel.

Wednesday October 30

Topic: Marriage Is Honourable

Memory Verse: "Marriage should be honoured by all, and the marriage bed kept pure, for God will judge the adulterer and all the sexually immoral." **- Hebrews 13:4**

Bible Reading: Genesis 2:18-25

Read & Learn:

The story of Ruth and Boaz, found in the Book of Ruth, exemplifies the honour and beauty of marriage. Ruth, a widow from Moab, chose to accompany her mother-in-law Naomi to Bethlehem, where she met Boaz, a righteous and honourable man. Boaz showed kindness to Ruth and eventually married her. Their union not only brought them personal happiness but also played a crucial role in God's plan, as they became ancestors of King David and, ultimately, Jesus Christ. Ruth and Boaz's commitment to each other and to God's principles of love, faithfulness, and loyalty is a testament to the honour of marriage.

The story of Ruth and Boaz reminds us that marriage is not only a source of companionship and joy but also a part of God's plan for His people. When marriages are built on love, faithfulness, and commitment, they can become a powerful reflection of God's love for His Church. We are called to honour and protect the covenant of marriage, recognising that it has significance not only for the individuals involved but also for God's greater purposes.

Prayer Point:

Father, help us honour marriage in our lives and communities by upholding its sanctity and purity. May our marriages be a reflection of Your love and faithfulness.

Thursday October 31

Topic: Love and Respect in Marriage

Memory Verse: "However, each one of you also must love his wife as he loves himself, and the wife must respect her husband."

- Ephesians 5:33

Bible Reading: Ephesians 5:21-33

Read & Learn:

The story of Aquila and Priscilla from the New Testament illustrates the beautiful dynamics of love and respect in marriage. Aquila and Priscilla were a couple who worked as tentmakers and were also dedicated followers of Christ. Their partnership extended beyond their trade; they opened their home to fellow believers, including the apostle Paul. Acts 18:26 tells us that when Apollos, a gifted speaker, only knew the baptism of John, Aquila and Priscilla took him aside and explained the way of God more adequately. They worked together in harmony, supporting each other and advancing God's kingdom.

Love and respect are foundational in a healthy marriage. Husbands are called to love their wives sacrificially, just as Christ loved the Church. This kind of love involves selflessness, care, and a willingness to serve. Wives are called to respect their husbands, acknowledging their leadership role in the family.

The story of Aquila and Priscilla reminds us that within the framework of love and respect, couples can work together as partners, growing spiritually and contributing to the kingdom of God. When both spouses prioritize the needs and well-being of each other, they create a strong and loving marriage that reflects Christ's love for the Church.

Prayer Points:

Father, help us to love and respect each other in our marriages in a way that reflects Your love for the Church. May our marriage be a testimony of Your grace and a source of blessing to others.

Friday November 01

Topic: Navigating Faith in Times of Crisis

Memory Verse: "God is our refuge and strength, an ever-present help in trouble." - **Psalm 46:1**

Bible Reading: 2 Corinthians 4:8-9

Read & Learn:

The story of Job is a powerful example of navigating faith in times of crisis. Job, a man of great faith, faced severe trials, including the loss of his wealth, the death of his children, and debilitating illness. Despite these overwhelming challenges and the advice of his friends to curse God, Job maintained his faith. He wrestled with deep questions about suffering and God's justice, yet he did not turn away from God. In the end, God restored Job's fortunes and blessed him more than before. Job's story teaches that faith in crisis is not about denying pain or suffering, but about trusting God's character and presence, even when we do not understand our circumstances. It reminds believers that it is okay to question and lament, and that faith can be refined and deepened through trials.

Navigating faith in times of crisis involves trusting in God's sovereignty and goodness, even when life's circumstances are difficult and confusing. As Psalm 46:1 and 2 Corinthians 4:8-9 suggest, God is a source of strength and comfort in times of trouble, and faith does not exempt believers from experiencing hardship. Rather, it provides a foundation to face challenges with hope and resilience. In crisis, faith can manifest as a steadfast trust in God, a continuous prayerful dialogue, and a reliance on the support of the faith community.

Prayer Point:

Lord, in times of crisis, be our refuge and strength, helping us to trust in Your unfailing love and sovereign care.

Saturday November 02

Topic: The Role of Music in Worship

Memory Verse: "Let the word of Christ dwell in you richly as you teach and admonish one another with all wisdom through psalms, hymns, and songs from the Spirit, singing to God with gratitude in your hearts." - Colossians 3:16

Bible Reading: Ephesians 5:19-20

Read & Learn:

The story of King David, a skilled musician and the writer of many Psalms, highlights the significant role of music in worship. David used music to express a wide range of emotions, from deep despair to exuberant joy, in his relationship with God. His use of the harp to soothe King Saul (1 Samuel 16:23) illustrates music's power to bring peace and comfort. Additionally, David z the musicians and singers for the temple worship (1 Chronicles 25), showing the importance of music in corporate worship settings. David's life reflects the idea that music is a powerful tool for connecting with God, expressing devotion, and facilitating spiritual experiences both personally and in the community.

Music plays a vital and multifaceted role in worship within the Christian tradition. As indicated in Colossians 3:16 and Ephesians 5:19-20, music is a means of teaching, encouraging, and expressing heartfelt worship to God. It allows for the expression of truths about God and the Christian faith in a way that engages the emotions and the spirit. Music in worship can be a form of prayer, a declaration of God's greatness, and a reflection of the believers' adoration and gratitude towards God

Prayer Point:

Heavenly Father, thank You for the gift of music in worship, which enables us to express our love and adoration for You.

Sunday November 03

Topic: Understanding the Book of Job

Memory Verse: "I know that my redeemer lives, and that in the end he will stand on the earth." - **Job 19:25**

Bible Reading: Job 1:1-22

Read & Learn:

The Book of Job is a profound exploration of suffering, faith, and the sovereignty of God. Job, a righteous and prosperous man, faces extreme trials, including the loss of his children, wealth, and health. Despite his intense suffering and the advice of his friends who suggest he must have sinned to deserve such punishment, Job maintains his innocence and his faith in God. Throughout the book, Job wrestles with the question of why the righteous suffer, seeking understanding and questioning God's justice. In the end, God responds, not by explaining the reasons for the suffering, but by revealing His sovereignty and the limits of human understanding.

Job's story is a powerful reminder that faith in God is not dependent on our circumstances and that God's ways and reasons often transcend human comprehension. It encourages believers to trust in God's wisdom and character, even when life's events are baffling or painful. The Book of Job offers valuable insights into the nature of suffering and the appropriate response of faith. It challenges the simplistic notion that suffering is always a direct result of personal sin. Job's persistence in seeking God amidst his pain demonstrates the depth and authenticity of his faith. The book invites readers to consider that suffering can be a mystery, part of the larger purposes of God that humans may not understand.

Prayer Point:

Lord, in our times of suffering, help us to hold onto faith as Job did, trusting in Your character and sovereignty.

Monday November 04

Topic: Christian Perspectives on Education and Learning

Memory Verse: "The fear of the Lord is the beginning of knowledge, but fools despise wisdom and instruction." **- Proverbs 1:7**

Bible Reading: 2 Timothy 3:16-17

Read & Learn:

The story of Daniel and his friends in Babylon provides a compelling example of Christian perspectives on education and learning. Taken into captivity and placed in a pagan educational system, Daniel, Shadrach, Meshach, and Abednego excelled in their studies while maintaining their faith and integrity. They engaged with the learning and culture around them, but they did so discerningly, choosing to abstain from practices that contradicted their faith, such as consuming the king's food (Daniel 1:8-16). Their story demonstrates that Christians can actively engage in secular education, gaining knowledge and skills, while still holding fast to their faith and values. It illustrates the balance between embracing learning and maintaining a distinct Christian worldview.

Christian perspectives on education and learning emphasise the pursuit of knowledge and wisdom grounded in a biblical worldview. As Proverbs 1:7 and 2 Timothy 3:16-17 suggest, true knowledge begins with a reverence for God and is nurtured by engaging with Scripture. Christian education involves developing one's intellect and skills while also cultivating moral and spiritual understanding. It encourages critical thinking, informed by faith, and the integration of biblical principles in all areas of study.

Prayer Point:

Heavenly Father, bless our pursuit of knowledge and wisdom, grounding us in Your truth as we learn and grow.

Tuesday November 05

Topic: The Challenge of Maintaining Spiritual Integrity

Memory Verse: "Whoever walks in integrity walks securely, but whoever takes crooked paths will be found out." **- Proverbs 10:9**

Bible Reading: Daniel 6:1-28

Read & Learn:

The story of Daniel in the lions' den (Daniel 6) powerfully illustrates the challenge of maintaining spiritual integrity. Daniel, known for his exceptional qualities and faithful service, faced jealousy and scheming from other officials in King Darius' court. They manipulated the king into issuing a decree that ultimately put Daniel at risk because of his commitment to praying to God daily. Despite the threat to his life, Daniel continued his practice of prayer, demonstrating unwavering integrity and faithfulness to God. His commitment led to his being thrown into the lions' den, yet God delivered him, demonstrating His faithfulness to those who maintain spiritual integrity. Daniel's story is an inspiring example of steadfastness in faith and integrity amidst pressure and adversity, encouraging believers to stay true to their convictions even when faced with significant challenges. Maintaining spiritual integrity is an ongoing challenge in a believer's life. It involves consistently aligning one's beliefs and values with actions, especially in the face of trials, temptations, and societal pressures. As Proverbs 10:9 and Daniel's story show, integrity brings security and favour from God, even though it may initially lead to difficulties. Spiritual integrity requires regular self-examination, commitment to God's Word, and reliance on the Holy Spirit for strength and guidance.

Prayer Point:

Lord, help us to maintain spiritual integrity in all areas of our lives, staying true to You and Your Word.

Wednesday November 06

Topic: Understanding the Significance of the Cross

Memory Verse: "For the message of the cross is foolishness to those who are perishing, but to us who are being saved it is the power of God." **- 1 Corinthians 1:18**

Bible Reading: Galatians 6:14

Read & Learn:

The conversion of Paul, formerly Saul of Tarsus, profoundly illustrates the significance of the cross. Paul, initially a persecutor of Christians, experienced a radical transformation after encountering Christ (Acts 9:1-19). This encounter led him to a deep understanding of the cross's meaning, which he later articulated in his epistles. Paul went from despising the message of the cross to embracing it as the central theme of his teaching and life. His letters often reflect on the cross's power and wisdom, contrasting it with human wisdom and strength. Paul's life and ministry demonstrate how the cross symbolises God's love and grace, the forgiveness of sins, and the reconciliation of humanity with God. His teachings help believers understand that the cross is not just a symbol of suffering, but the embodiment of God's redemptive plan and the source of spiritual life and hope.

The significance of the cross in Christianity goes beyond its historical and cultural context. As expressed in 1 Corinthians 1:18 and Galatians 6:14, the cross represents the ultimate sacrifice of Jesus Christ for the redemption of humanity. It symbolises the depth of human sin and the extraordinary extent of God's love.

Prayer Point:

Heavenly Father, thank You for the cross, a symbol of Your profound love and our salvation.

Thursday November 07

Topic: The Power of Christian Fellowship

Memory Verse: "And let us consider how we may spur one another on toward love and good deeds, not giving up meeting together, as some are in the habit of doing, but encouraging one another—and all the more as you see the Day approaching." - **Hebrews 10:24-25**

Bible Reading: Acts 2:42-47

Read & Learn:

The early Christian community as described in Acts 2:42-47 offers a compelling example of the power of Christian fellowship. This community was characterised by shared faith, regular gathering for teaching, breaking of bread, and prayer. They also shared their possessions, provided for those in need, and enjoyed the goodwill of all the people. Their fellowship led to spiritual growth, mutual support, and significant impact in their wider community. The way they lived together, supported each other, and reached out to others illustrates the transformative power of Christian fellowship. It shows how a community of believers, united in Christ, can not only grow in faith but also be a powerful witness of God's love and grace to the world.

Christian fellowship is more than just socialising; it's about sharing life in Christ and encouraging one another in faith. As Hebrews 10:24-25 and Acts 2:42-47 show, fellowship involves mutual edification, support, and accountability. It provides a context for believers to grow spiritually, to use their gifts in service, and to bear one another's burdens.

Prayer Point:

Lord, bless our efforts to cultivate true Christian fellowship, that we may encourage and support each other in love and good deeds.

Friday November 08

Topic: The Role of Faith in Personal Wellness

Memory Verse: "Dear friend, I pray that you may enjoy good health and that all may go well with you, even as your soul is getting along well." **- 3 John 1:2**

Bible Reading: Philippians 4:6-7

Read & Learn:

The account of the woman with the issue of blood in the Gospels (Mark 5:25-34) vividly demonstrates the role of faith in personal wellness. This woman, who had suffered from a debilitating condition for twelve years and had exhausted her resources on treatments without improvement, found healing when she reached out in faith to touch Jesus' cloak. Her story highlights the profound connection between faith, healing, and well-being. Her belief in Jesus' power to heal her reflects the deeper truth that faith can play a significant role in one's physical and emotional wellness. It is a powerful testament to the idea that faith and trust in God can bring peace, hope, and sometimes even physical healing in the midst of suffering and illness.

The role of faith in personal wellness involves Recognising the interconnectedness of physical, mental, and spiritual health. As seen in 3 John 1:2 and Philippians 4:6-7, the Bible suggests that spiritual well-being can influence overall health. Faith provides a source of comfort, strength, and hope, especially in times of illness or stress. It encourages a perspective of trust in God's sovereignty, reducing anxiety and promoting peace of mind.

Prayer Point:

Heavenly Father, guide us to understand the role of faith in our personal wellness, trusting in Your care and provision for our whole being.

Saturday November 09

Topic: Christian Perspectives on Human Suffering

Memory Verse: "I consider that our present sufferings are not worth comparing with the glory that will be revealed in us." **- Romans 8:18**

Bible Reading: 2 Corinthians 1:3-4

Read & Learn:

The life of Joseph, as depicted in the book of Genesis, offers a profound insight into the Christian perspective on human suffering. Joseph endured betrayal by his brothers, wrongful imprisonment, and numerous other hardships. Despite these challenges, he maintained his faith and integrity. Ultimately, God used Joseph's suffering for a greater purpose: to preserve many lives during a famine, including the lives of his own family. Joseph's story shows that while suffering can be bewildering and painful, it can also be used by God to bring about growth, character development, and to fulfil His larger purposes. His famous statement to his brothers, "You intended to harm me, but God intended it for good" (Genesis 50:20), highlights the redemptive possibilities within suffering.

Christian perspectives on human suffering emphasise that while suffering is a part of the fallen world, it can have purpose and be used by God for good. Romans 8:18 and 2 Corinthians 1:3-4 suggest that suffering can produce spiritual growth, deepen faith, and enable believers to comfort others with the comfort they have received from God. Christians are called to have a hopeful perspective on suffering, trusting in God's sovereignty and the eventual redemption of all creation. This perspective does not diminish the pain of suffering but offers a way to navigate it with faith and hope.

Prayer Point:

Heavenly Father, in our times of suffering, help us to find comfort in Your love and to trust in Your sovereign purposes.

Sunday November 10

Topic: The Role of Faith in Overcoming Addiction

Memory Verse: "No temptation has overtaken you except what is common to mankind. And God is faithful; he will not let you be tempted beyond what you can bear. But when you are tempted, he will also provide a way out so that you can endure it."

1 Corinthians 10:13

Bible Reading: Psalm 34:4-6

Read & Learn:

The story of the prodigal son in Luke 15:11-32 can be seen as a metaphor for the journey of overcoming addiction. The younger son, who squanders his inheritance in reckless living, represents someone caught in the grip of addiction. His eventual realisation of his desperate state and decision to return to his father symbolises the moment of acknowledging the need for change. The father's loving and open-armed reception of the son illustrates the grace and forgiveness available from God. This parable demonstrates the importance of humility, repentance, and the acceptance of God's grace in the process of recovery. It also highlights the role of faith in providing hope, strength, and a sense of being loved and accepted, which are crucial in overcoming the struggles of addiction.

Faith plays a significant role in the journey of overcoming addiction by offering spiritual strength, hope, and a sense of purpose. 1 Corinthians 10:13 and Psalm 34:4-6 reassure that God provides support in times of temptation and delivers from fears, which is encouraging for those battling addiction.

Prayer Point:

Heavenly Father, grant strength and courage to those battling addiction, reminding them of Your constant presence and love.

Monday November 11

Topic: Christian Views on Peace and Nonviolence

Memory Verse: "Blessed are the peacemakers, for they will be called children of God." - **Matthew 5:9**

Bible Reading: Romans 12:17-21

Read & Learn:

The story of Jesus' arrest in the Garden of Gethsemane (Matthew 26:47-56) powerfully illustrates Christian views on peace and nonviolence. When one of Jesus' disciples struck a servant of the high priest, cutting off his ear, Jesus rebuked him and healed the servant. This response to a violent situation highlights Jesus' commitment to peace and nonviolence, even in the face of betrayal and imminent danger. Jesus' teachings and actions consistently pointed to a way of life that embraced peace, love for enemies, and non-retaliation. His example and teachings have inspired countless Christians throughout history to adopt principles of nonviolence and to seek peaceful resolutions in conflicts, reflecting Jesus' message that peacemakers are truly the children of God.

Christian views on peace and nonviolence are rooted in the teachings of Jesus and the New Testament. As Matthew 5:9 and Romans 12:17-21 suggest, Christians are called to be peacemakers and to overcome evil with good. This perspective is not about passivity in the face of injustice, but rather actively seeking ways to promote reconciliation, justice, and the well-being of others, including enemies. It involves forgiving others, refusing to seek revenge, and showing love and compassion even in challenging situations.

Prayer Point:

Heavenly Father, guide us to be peacemakers, reflecting Your love and compassion in our interactions and responses to conflict.

Tuesday November 12

Topic: The Challenge of Biblical Interpretation

Memory Verse: "Do your best to present yourself to God as one approved, a worker who does not need to be ashamed and who correctly handles the word of truth." **- 2 Timothy 2:15**

Bible Reading: 2 Peter 1:20-21

Read & Learn:

The encounter between Philip and the Ethiopian eunuch in Acts 8:26-40 provides an insightful example of the challenges of biblical interpretation. The Ethiopian eunuch, a high-ranking official, was reading a passage from Isaiah but struggled to understand its meaning. Philip, guided by the Holy Spirit, joined him and explained the scripture, revealing how the passage spoke of Jesus Christ. This interaction highlights the importance of seeking understanding and guidance in interpreting the Bible. It shows that while scripture is inspired and powerful, comprehension often requires diligent study, the guidance of the Holy Spirit, and sometimes the insight of others who have studied the Word. This story encourages believers to approach biblical interpretation with humility, seeking wisdom and clarity to understand the depths of God's Word.

The challenge of biblical interpretation lies in faithfully understanding and applying scripture in various contexts. As 2 Timothy 2:15 and 2 Peter 1:20-21 suggest, interpreting the Bible requires careful study, an acknowledgment of its divine inspiration, and consideration of historical and cultural contexts.

Prayer Point:

Lord, help us to approach Your Word with reverence, seeking Your wisdom and understanding in its interpretation.

Wednesday November 13

Topic: The Power of Living a Mission-Driven Life

Memory Verse: "Therefore go and make disciples of all nations, baptising them in the name of the Father and of the Son and of the Holy Spirit, and teaching them to obey everything I have commanded you. And surely I am with you always, to the very end of the age." - **Matthew 28:19-20**

Bible Reading: 2 Timothy 1:7-9

Read & Learn:

The life of the Apostle Paul is a remarkable example of the power of living a mission-driven life. After his dramatic conversion on the road to Damascus, Paul dedicated his life to spreading the Gospel. His missionary journeys, as documented in the Acts of the Apostles and his epistles, reveal his unwavering commitment to his mission. Despite facing immense challenges, including imprisonment, shipwreck, and opposition, Paul continued to preach, teach, and establish churches. His mission-driven life was not about personal ambition, but about fulfilling the call to share the message of Christ. Paul's example demonstrates how a life dedicated to a higher purpose can bring about significant impact and change, not just in one's personal life, but in the lives of many others.

Living a mission-driven life in a Christian context means aligning one's life purpose with God's will and mission. As Matthew 28:19-20 and 2 Timothy 1:7-9 suggest, this involves embracing the call to spread the Gospel and impact the world for Christ. A mission-driven life is characterised by clarity of purpose, a commitment to serve, and a reliance on the Holy Spirit for strength and guidance.

Prayer Point:

Heavenly Father, inspire and equip us to live mission-driven lives, aligned with Your purpose and calling.

Thursday November 14

Topic: Biblical Teachings on Compassion and Empathy

Memory Verse: "Therefore, as God's chosen people, holy and dearly loved, clothe yourselves with compassion, kindness, humility, gentleness, and patience." - **Colossians 3:12**

Bible Reading: Luke 10:25-37

Read & Learn:

The Parable of the Good Samaritan in Luke 10:25-37 is a powerful illustration of compassion and empathy in action. In this story, a Samaritan, considered an outsider and enemy by Jews, shows compassion to a beaten and robbed Jewish man, while others, including a priest and a Levite, pass by without helping. This Samaritan not only provides immediate assistance but also ensures the man's continued care. Jesus used this story to redefine the concept of 'neighbour' and to illustrate that compassion and empathy should cross cultural and societal boundaries. The parable challenges believers to see everyone as their neighbour and to extend compassion and empathy, even to those who are different from them or with whom they might disagree.

Biblical teachings on compassion and empathy emphasise the importance of understanding and sharing the feelings of others, especially those who are suffering or in need. As Colossians 3:12 suggests, believers are called to embody compassion and empathy as fundamental aspects of their Christian character. This involves more than just feeling sorry for someone; it requires taking action to alleviate their suffering.

Prayer Point:

Lord, fill our hearts with Your compassion and empathy, that we may see others as You see them and respond to their needs with Your love.

Friday November 15

Topic: The Importance of Christian Accountability

Memory Verse: "Carry each other's burdens, and in this way, you will fulfil the law of Christ." - **Galatians 6:2**

Bible Reading: James 5:16

Read & Learn:

Nathan's confrontation of King David after his sin with Bathsheba (2 Samuel 12:1-14) is a poignant example of Christian accountability in action. Despite David's power as king, Nathan, the prophet, courageously holds him accountable for his actions. Nathan's approach—telling a story that allows David to recognise his own wrongdoing—demonstrates the importance of truthfulness and love in accountability. David's response of repentance shows the effectiveness of godly accountability in leading to confession, repentance, and restoration. This story highlights the necessity of having people in our lives who are willing to speak the truth in love, helping us to stay on the path of righteousness and to grow in our faith.

Christian accountability involves mutually supporting one another in living according to God's standards. As Galatians 6:2 and James 5:16 suggest, it includes confessing sins to one another, praying for each other, and bearing each other's burdens. This practice is important for personal growth, preventing isolation, and providing a safeguard against temptation and spiritual drift. Accountability in a Christian context is not about judgment or control but is a form of discipleship that helps individuals to live in a way that honours God. It requires vulnerability, trust, and a commitment to spiritual growth.

Prayer Point:

Heavenly Father, guide us in fostering relationships of accountability that reflect Your love and grace.

Saturday November 16

Topic: Navigating Relationships with Non-believers

Memory Verse: "To the weak I became weak, to win the weak. I have become all things to all people so that by all possible means I might save some." - **1 Corinthians 9:22**

Bible Reading: 1 Peter 3:15-16

Read & Learn:

The relationship between Daniel and King Nebuchadnezzar in the Book of Daniel provides an insightful look into navigating relationships with non-believers. Daniel, a devout believer in God, found himself serving a pagan king in a foreign land. Despite their different beliefs, Daniel served the king with excellence and integrity. Through his respectful and wise approach, Daniel was able to positively influence Nebuchadnezzar without compromising his own faith. His interactions with the king demonstrate the balance of being true to one's faith while engaging respectfully and meaningfully with those who do not share the same beliefs. Daniel's life is an example of how believers can maintain their Christian witness and values while building positive relationships with non-believers.

Navigating relationships with non-believers is a significant aspect of Christian life. As stated in 1 Corinthians 9:22 and 1 Peter 3:15-16, Christians are called to engage with those outside their faith in a way that is respectful, loving, and considerate. This involves being a witness to the love and truth of Christ through one's actions and words. Christians are encouraged to build genuine relationships, listen empathetically, and share their faith in a way that is sensitive and appropriate to the context.

Prayer Point:

Lord, give us wisdom and love as we navigate relationships with those who do not share our faith.

Sunday November 17

Topic: The Challenge of Spiritual Warfare

Memory Verse: "For our struggle is not against flesh and blood, but against the rulers, against the authorities, against the powers of this dark world and against the spiritual forces of evil in the heavenly realms." - **Ephesians 6:12**

Bible Reading: Ephesians 6:10-18

Read & Learn:

Spiritual warfare is a reality that every Christian must face. In Ephesians 6:10-18, the apostle Paul describes the spiritual armour that believers should put on to stand against the schemes of the devil. This passage reminds us that our battles are not against mere human opponents but against the spiritual forces of evil. Just as the early church faced persecution and opposition, we too encounter spiritual challenges in our journey of faith. However, by putting on the full armour of God, we can be equipped to withstand and overcome these spiritual battles. The early church's unwavering faith and reliance on God's protection in the face of adversity serve as an inspiration for us as we confront the challenges of spiritual warfare.

Spiritual warfare is a topic that can be daunting, but it's essential for every believer to understand and engage in. Ephesians 6:10-18 teaches us that we are not wrestling against flesh and blood but against unseen spiritual forces. The early church faced persecution and opposition, often driven by spiritual opposition to the spread of the Gospel. Just as they relied on God's strength and spiritual armour, we must do the same.

Prayer Point:

Heavenly Father, we acknowledge the reality of spiritual warfare in our lives. Help us to put on the full armour of God daily.

Monday November 18

Topic: Understanding the Epistles of Paul

Memory Verse: "All Scripture is God-breathed and is useful for teaching, rebuking, correcting and training in righteousness, so that the servant of God may be thoroughly equipped for every good work." **- 2 Timothy 3:16-17**

Bible Reading: 2 Peter 3:15-16

Read & Learn:

The Epistles of Paul, found in the New Testament, are a significant part of the Christian canon. Paul's letters provide deep theological insights, practical guidance for Christian living, and valuable lessons for the church. In 2 Peter 3:15-16, the apostle Peter acknowledges the wisdom found in Paul's writings but warns that some find them difficult to understand, twisting their meaning to their own destruction. This emphasises the importance of studying and interpreting Paul's letters with care and understanding. The early church grappled with these writings, seeking to apply Paul's teachings to their unique contexts.

Paul's Epistles, including letters to churches and individuals, offer a wealth of spiritual and practical guidance. They address issues such as theology, ethics, Christian living, and the role of the church. These letters were written to specific communities and individuals but contain timeless principles that apply to all believers. Understanding the Epistles of Paul requires studying the historical and cultural context in which they were written and discerning the underlying theological messages.

Prayer Point:

Heavenly Father, thank you for the wisdom and guidance found in the Epistles of Paul. Help us to approach them with humility and a desire for understanding.

Tuesday November 19

Topic: The Power of Hope in Difficult Times

Memory Verse: "May the God of hope fill you with all joy and peace as you trust in him so that you may overflow with hope by the power of the Holy Spirit." - **Romans 15:13**

Bible Reading: Psalm 42:11

Read & Learn:

Hope is a powerful force that sustains us in the midst of life's trials. In Psalm 42:11, the psalmist expresses his soul's thirst for God, even in times of trouble and despair. Yet, he does not lose hope. The psalmist acknowledges that hope in God is the source of his strength and his reason to praise. Throughout history, people have found strength and resilience in moments of adversity by holding onto hope. The story of the early Christians, who faced persecution and challenges, demonstrates the transformative power of hope. Their unwavering faith and hope in Christ enabled them to endure hardships and continue spreading the Gospel. In our own difficult times, we can draw inspiration from their example and allow the power of hope to sustain us.

Hope is more than just optimism; it is the confident expectation of good things to come, rooted in faith. In Romans 15:13, we are reminded that God is the source of our hope, and through the Holy Spirit, we can overflow with hope even in challenging circumstances. The story of the early Christians reminds us that hope is not dependent on our circumstances but on our trust in God. In difficult times, hope can be our anchor, providing us with joy and peace that surpass understanding.

Prayer Point:

Heavenly Father, we thank you for being the God of hope. Fill us with your joy and peace as we trust in you.

Wednesday November 20

Topic: Navigating Family Challenges

Memory Verse: "Be completely humble and gentle; be patient, bearing with one another in love. Make every effort to keep the unity of the Spirit through the bond of peace." **- Ephesians 4:2-3**

Bible Reading: Genesis 37:3-4

Read & Learn:

Family dynamics can be both beautiful and challenging. In Genesis 37:3-4, we see the story of Joseph, who faced significant family challenges. He was his father's favourite son, which caused jealousy and strife among his brothers. Their envy led them to sell Joseph into slavery, creating deep pain and division within the family. Despite the hardships he endured, Joseph maintained his faith in God and eventually forgave his brothers, leading to reconciliation and restoration. Joseph's story teaches us that even in the most challenging family situations, God's grace and forgiveness can lead to healing and unity. It reminds us that navigating family challenges requires humility, patience, and a commitment to maintaining the bond of peace within our families.

Families often face difficulties, whether it's conflicts, misunderstandings, or strained relationships. In Ephesians 4:2-3, the apostle Paul encourages us to approach family challenges with humility, gentleness, patience, and love. Joseph's story illustrates the importance of forgiveness and reconciliation in family relationships. When we face family challenges, it's an opportunity to apply these principles, just as Joseph did. Navigating family challenges requires us to prioritise unity and peace, Recognising that God's grace can bring healing even in the most broken family situations.

Prayer Point:

Heavenly Father, we lift up our family challenges to You. Grant us the wisdom, humility, and love to navigate them with grace.

Thursday November 21

Topic: Christian Perspectives on Health and Healing

Memory Verse: "Is anyone among you sick? Let them call the elders of the church to pray over them and anoint them with oil in the name of the Lord. And the prayer offered in faith will make the sick person well; the Lord will raise them up." **- James 5:14-15**

Bible Reading: Mark 5:25-34

Read & Learn:

In Mark 5:25-34, we encounter a woman who had been suffering from a bleeding condition for twelve years. She had spent all her money on physicians but only grew worse. However, her faith in Jesus led her to believe that if she could just touch His garment, she would be healed. When she did, Jesus felt power go out from Him, and she was instantly healed. This story demonstrates the powerful connection between faith, healing, and Jesus' compassion. It teaches us that healing, whether physical or spiritual, is possible through faith in Christ. As Christians, our perspective on health and healing is rooted in trust in God's sovereignty, the power of prayer, and the belief that Jesus is the ultimate healer.

Christian perspectives on health and healing are multifaceted. While we acknowledge the importance of medical science and healthcare, our ultimate trust is in God's providence and healing power. James 5:14-15 highlights the role of prayer and the community in seeking healing. It also underscores the importance of faith in the process. The story of the woman with the bleeding condition emphasises the significance of faith in Jesus as the source of healing.

Prayer Point:

Heavenly Father, we thank You for being the ultimate source of healing. We lift up those who are in need of healing today, trusting in Your mercy and grace.

Friday November 22

Topic: The Importance of Jesus' Birth

Memory Verse: "Today in the town of David a Saviour has been born to you; he is the Messiah, the Lord." **- Luke 2:11**

Bible Reading: Luke 2:1-20

Read & Learn:

The birth of Jesus is a pivotal moment in human history. In Luke 2:1-20, we read about the humble circumstances surrounding His birth in Bethlehem. He was born in a manger, surrounded by Mary and Joseph, shepherds, and angels. This event marks the fulfillment of Old Testament prophecies and God's promise to send a Saviour into the world. Jesus' birth is not just a historical event but a divine revelation of God's love and redemption plan for humanity. It is a reminder of God's willingness to enter into our world, identify with our humanity, and offer us salvation through His Son. The importance of Jesus' birth cannot be overstated; it is the beginning of God's redemptive work and the foundation of our faith.

Jesus' birth is significant for several reasons. It represents the incarnation, God taking on human form, demonstrating His deep love for us. His birth fulfils numerous prophecies, confirming His identity as the Messiah. It is a message of hope, as the angels declared "good news of great joy" to the shepherds. Jesus' birth signifies the beginning of God's plan for our salvation, ultimately leading to His sacrificial death and resurrection. His life, teachings, and ultimate sacrifice on the cross are all rooted in His birth in Bethlehem. As Christians, we celebrate Jesus' birth not just as a historical event but as the dawning of God's light in a dark world.

Prayer Point:

Heavenly Father, we thank You for the gift of Your Son, Jesus Christ, whose birth we celebrate. Help us to understand the profound significance of His coming into the world.

Saturday November 23

Topic: The Dynamics of Christian Discernment

Memory Verse: "But test everything; hold fast what is good. Abstain from every form of evil." **- 1 Thessalonians 5:21-22**

Bible Reading: Acts 17:10-12

Read & Learn:

In Acts 17:10-12, we encounter the Berean believers who were commended for their approach to discernment. When they heard the teachings of Paul and Silas, they didn't accept everything at face value but examined the Scriptures daily to see if what they were hearing aligned with God's Word. Their discerning attitude led to a deeper understanding of the truth and a strengthening of their faith. The example of the Bereans illustrates the importance of Christian discernment - the ability to distinguish between truth and error, wisdom and deception. In a world filled with diverse teachings and ideas, Christian discernment is crucial for maintaining a firm foundation in the faith.

Christian discernment is the ability to recognise and evaluate spiritual truths and deceptions, aligning one's beliefs and actions with God's Word. It involves testing everything against the standard of Scripture, as advised in 1 Thessalonians 5:21-22. The Bereans in Acts 17 exemplify this process by searching the Scriptures daily to confirm the teachings they received. Christian discernment is not about cynicism or scepticism but a thoughtful and prayerful examination of what we encounter in our faith journey. It is a safeguard against false teachings, distortions of the Gospel, and spiritual pitfalls.

Prayer Point:

Heavenly Father, we seek Your guidance and wisdom in the practice of Christian discernment.

Sunday November 24

Topic: The Role of Faith in Overcoming Prejudice

Memory Verse: "There is neither Jew nor Gentile, neither slave nor free, nor is there male and female, for you are all one in Christ Jesus." **Galatians 3:28**

Bible Reading: Acts 10:9-34

Read & Learn:

In Acts 10:9-34, we witness a powerful transformation in the life of the apostle Peter. He had grown up with cultural and religious prejudices that separated Jews from Gentiles. However, through a divine vision and encounter, God challenged Peter's biases. He learned that God does not show favouritism and that the message of salvation was for all people, regardless of their background. This experience led Peter to visit the Gentile Cornelius and share the Gospel with him and his household. Peter's journey illustrates the role of faith in overcoming prejudice. When we allow our faith in God to shape our perspective, it can break down barriers, challenge stereotypes, and lead to unity and reconciliation.

Faith plays a pivotal role in overcoming prejudice because it leads us to see others through the lens of God's love and grace. Galatians 3:28 reminds us that in Christ, there is no distinction based on ethnicity, social status, or gender; we are all one. The story of Peter and Cornelius demonstrates that faith can transform our hearts and minds, enabling us to embrace diversity and reject discrimination. As Christians, our faith calls us to love our neighbours as ourselves and to extend God's grace to all, regardless of their background.

Prayer Point:

Heavenly Father, we confess any prejudices or biases that may hinder our relationships with others. Transform our hearts through faith and love.

Monday November 25

Topic: The Importance of Building a Strong Faith Foundation

Memory Verse: "Therefore, everyone who hears these words of mine and puts them into practice is like a wise man who built his house on the rock. The rain came down, the streams rose, and the winds blew and beat against that house; yet it did not fall because it had its foundation on the rock." - **Matthew 7:24-25**

Bible Reading: Luke 6:46-49

Read & Learn:

In Luke 6:46-49, Jesus tells the parable of the wise and foolish builders. The wise builder listens to Jesus' teachings and puts them into practice, building his house on a solid rock foundation. When the storms come, the house stands firm. In contrast, the foolish builder hears Jesus' words but does not obey them, building his house on the sand. When the storms come, the house collapses. This parable illustrates the importance of building our lives on the firm foundation of faith in Christ and His teachings. When we do so, we can withstand the trials and challenges that inevitably come our way.

Building a strong faith foundation is essential for the Christian journey. Just as a house needs a solid foundation to withstand storms, our faith requires a firm footing in Christ's teachings and the Word of God. The memory verse from Matthew 7:24-25 emphasises that hearing God's Word and putting it into practice is like building on a rock foundation. This foundation enables us to stand strong when life's storms, trials, and doubts arise. Building a strong faith foundation involves daily study of the Scriptures, prayer, obedience to God's commands, and a personal relationship with Christ.

Prayer Point:

Heavenly Father, we acknowledge the importance of building our lives on the solid foundation of Your Word and the teachings of Jesus.

Tuesday November 26

Topic: The Role of Prayer in Spiritual Warfare

Memory Verse: "And pray in the Spirit on all occasions with all kinds of prayers and requests. With this in mind, be alert and always keep on praying for all the Lord's people." **- Ephesians 6:18**

Bible Reading: Ephesians 6:10-18

Read & Learn:

In the book of Daniel, we find a powerful illustration of the role of prayer in spiritual warfare. Daniel, a faithful servant of God, faced a decree that prohibited him from praying to anyone but the king for 30 days. Despite the danger, he continued to pray to the Lord as he always had. His unwavering commitment to prayer led to his arrest and his subsequent encounter with the lions in the den. However, God miraculously delivered Daniel from harm, demonstrating the victory of prayer in the face of opposition. This story reminds us that prayer is not only our communication with God but also a potent weapon in the spiritual battles we face.

Ephesians 6:18 encourages us to pray in the Spirit on all occasions, emphasising the vital role of prayer in spiritual warfare. The passage also describes the armour of God, highlighting the necessity of being equipped with truth, righteousness, faith, and the Word of God. Prayer is the means by which we put on this spiritual armour and engage in the battle against spiritual forces. Our prayers are not just words; they are powerful tools for seeking God's guidance, protection, and intervention in the midst of trials and challenges. Through prayer, we align our hearts with God's will and invite His strength into our lives, ensuring victory in our spiritual battles.

Prayer Point:

Heavenly Father, teach us to pray fervently, knowing that prayer is a mighty weapon in spiritual warfare.

Wednesday November 27

Topic: Biblical Insights on God's Character

Memory Verse: "The Lord is compassionate and gracious, slow to anger, abounding in love." - **Psalm 103:8**

Bible Reading: Exodus 34:6-7

Read & Learn:

In the book of Jonah, we find a compelling story that illustrates God's character. Jonah, a reluctant prophet, was sent by God to the city of Nineveh, known for its wickedness. Jonah initially resisted and tried to flee from God's call. However, God's relentless compassion for the people of Nineveh was evident. When Jonah finally delivered God's message of impending judgment, the people of Nineveh repented, and God showed His compassion by relenting from the disaster He had threatened. This story highlights God's desire for repentance and His willingness to show mercy even to those who have gone astray.

Psalm 103:8 and Exodus 34:6-7 reveal essential insights into God's character. These passages describe God as compassionate, gracious, slow to anger, abounding in love, and forgiving. God's character is marked by His unfailing love and mercy. He is patient with our shortcomings and desires reconciliation rather than judgment. The story of Jonah further demonstrates God's character in action. Despite Jonah's reluctance and the city's wickedness, God's compassion prevailed, leading to repentance and salvation. Understanding God's character encourages us to approach Him with humility, knowing that He desires our repentance and offers forgiveness to those who turn to Him.

Prayer Point:

Heavenly Father, thank you for your boundless compassion and grace.

Thursday November 28

Topic: Understanding the Ministry of Jesus

Memory Verse: "For even the Son of Man did not come to be servedbut to serve, and to give his life as a ransom for many."

Mark 10:45

Bible Reading: Luke 4:16-21

Read & Learn:

In Luke 4:16-21, Jesus begins His earthly ministry by declaring His mission in the synagogue at Nazareth. He reads from the scroll of Isaiah, proclaiming that He is anointed to bring good news to the poor, freedom to the prisoners, sight to the blind, and to set the oppressed free. This profound statement encapsulates the heart of Jesus' ministry – to bring hope, healing, and salvation to all. His ministry was marked by compassion, miracles, and teaching that touched the lives of countless people. As we delve into the ministry of Jesus, we see a Saviour who came not to be served but to serve, ultimately giving His life as a ransom for humanity.

Mark 10:45 reminds us of Jesus' central mission: to serve and give His life as a ransom for many. The passage in Luke 4:16-21 reveals Jesus' purpose and ministry by quoting Isaiah's prophecy. Jesus came to proclaim good news, bring freedom, and offer hope to those in need. His ministry was characterised by compassion and a desire to heal and restore broken lives. This devotional invites us to understand the ministry of Jesus as a model of selfless service and an embodiment of God's love for humanity. As we reflect on His mission, we are encouraged to follow His example by serving others and sharing the good news of salvation.

Prayer Point:

Heavenly Father, thank you for the ministry of Jesus, which brings hope and salvation to the world.

Friday November 29

Topic: The Power of Christian Generosity

Memory Verse: "In everything I did, I showed you that by this kind of hard work we must help the weak, remembering the words the Lord Jesus himself said: 'It is more blessed to give than to receive.'"

Acts 20:35

Bible Reading: 2 Corinthians 9:6-8

Read & Learn:

The story of the widow's mite in Mark 12:41-44 demonstrates the power of Christian generosity. In the temple, Jesus observed a poor widow who offered two small coins, all she had to live on. While others gave large sums of money, Jesus commended the widow's offering as more significant because she gave sacrificially out of her poverty. This story teaches us that Christian generosity is not measured by the size of the gift but by the heart's willingness to give. It reminds us that God values the motives behind our giving, and even the smallest acts of generosity can be profoundly meaningful in His sight.

Christian generosity, as depicted in 2 Corinthians 9:6-8 and illustrated by the widow's mite, is rooted in the principles of sowing and reaping. When we give generously with a cheerful heart, we are sowing seeds of blessing, not only for ourselves but also for others. God loves a cheerful giver because generosity reflects His own character. He blesses us not only materially but also spiritually when we share what we have with others. Generosity is an act of worship and a way to demonstrate our trust in God's provision.

Prayer Point:

Heavenly Father, teach us to be cheerful givers, reflecting Your generous nature.

Saturday November 30

Topic: The Role of Faith in Overcoming Depression

Memory Verse: "The Lord is close to the broken-hearted and saves those who are crushed in spirit." **- Psalm 34:18**

Bible Reading: Psalm 42:11

Read & Learn:

The story of Elijah's struggle with depression in 1 Kings 19 provides insight into the role of faith in overcoming this emotional battle. After a powerful victory against the prophets of Baal, Elijah faced severe discouragement and despair. He even asked God to take his life. In his darkest moments, an angel of the Lord came to him, provided food and water, and encouraged him to continue his journey. Elijah's faith in God's care sustained him. Overcoming depression often requires leaning on God's promises, as David did in Psalm 42:11, and seeking His presence even when circumstances are overwhelming. Elijah's story reminds us that faith in God's love and care can be a powerful source of hope in the midst of depression.

Depression can be a formidable struggle, but faith plays a crucial role in overcoming it. Psalm 34:18 assures us that the Lord is near to those who are broken-hearted, offering comfort and salvation. In Psalm 42:11, the psalmist acknowledges the downcast spirit but chooses to put hope in God. This reveals the power of faith in shifting our focus from despair to trust in God's character and promises. Faith doesn't eliminate the challenges of depression, but it provides a lifeline to God's presence and a source of hope.

Prayer Point:

Heavenly Father, draw near to those who are struggling with depression and grant them your comfort.

Sunday December 01

Topic: The Role of Scripture in Spiritual Formation

Memory Verse: "Your word is a lamp to my feet and a light to my path." - Psalm 119:105

Bible Reading: 2 Timothy 3:16-17

Read & Learn:

The story of the Ethiopian eunuch in Acts 8:26-40 illustrates the transformative role of Scripture in spiritual formation. Philip, guided by the Holy Spirit, encountered the eunuch who was reading from the book of Isaiah but did not fully understand its message. Philip explained the Scripture to him, focusing on Jesus as the fulfilment of Isaiah's prophecy. As a result, the eunuch believed in Jesus, was baptised, and went on his way rejoicing. This encounter highlights how Scripture, when illuminated by the Holy Spirit and shared by believers, can lead to profound spiritual transformation. It reminds us of the importance of studying God's Word for guidance, growth, and the formation of our faith.

Scripture plays a vital role in the spiritual formation of believers. As 2 Timothy 3:16-17 tells us, all Scripture is God-breathed and serves various purposes, including teaching, rebuking, correcting, and training in righteousness. The Word of God equips believers to live out their faith and be prepared for good works. It acts as a lamp, guiding our steps and enlightening our path (Psalm 119:105). Studying Scripture helps us understand God's character, His will, and His plan for our lives. It transforms our minds, shapes our values, and deepens our relationship with Him.

Prayer Point:

Heavenly Father, thank You for the gift of Your Word. May it continue to guide and transform us.

Monday December 02

Topic: The Power of the Gospel in Everyday Life

Memory Verse: "For I am not ashamed of the gospel, because it is the power of God that brings salvation to everyone who believes: first to the Jew, then to the Gentile." - Romans 1:16

Bible Reading: Romans 1:16-17

Read & Learn:

The story of the woman at the well in John 4:1-42 demonstrates the power of the gospel in everyday life. Jesus, tired and thirsty, encountered a Samaritan woman at a well. Despite cultural barriers and her past, Jesus offered her living water, symbolising eternal life through Him. The woman believed, her life was transformed, and she became a powerful witness to her community. This narrative illustrates how the gospel, when shared with authenticity and compassion, can break down barriers, bring salvation, and transform ordinary lives. It reminds us that the power of the gospel is not confined to church walls but has the potential to impact our daily interactions and relationships.

The gospel, as proclaimed in Romans 1:16-17, is the power of God for salvation. It reveals God's righteousness and is received by faith. This gospel is not a distant or theoretical concept but a living force that can change lives. The story of the woman at the well exemplifies how the gospel intersects with our everyday encounters, offering hope, forgiveness, and transformation. Just as Jesus engaged with the Samaritan woman, we are called to share the gospel in our daily lives, breaking down barriers and leading others to salvation

Prayer Point:

Heavenly Father, thank You for the power of the gospel that brings salvation. Help us to share it boldly in our daily lives.

Tuesday December 03

Topic: Christian Views on Authority and Submission

Memory Verse: "Submit to one another out of reverence for Christ." Ephesians 5:21

Bible Reading: Ephesians 5:21-33

Read & Learn:

In Acts 4:19-20, when the religious authorities told Peter and John not to speak or teach in the name of Jesus, their response was, "Which is right in God's eyes: to listen to you or to him? You be the judges! As for us, we cannot help speaking about what we have seen and heard." This story illustrates the Christian view on authority and submission to God's higher authority above all human authorities. While Christians are called to submit to governing authorities (Romans 13:1), they must always prioritise obeying God's commands, even if it means respectfully challenging earthly authorities when they conflict with divine principles. This story exemplifies the balance of submission to earthly authorities while Recognising the supreme authority of God.

Christian views on authority and submission are rooted in biblical principles. Ephesians 5:21 emphasises mutual submission out of reverence for Christ. It sets the tone for healthy relationships within the family, the church, and society. The passage goes on to highlight the roles of husbands and wives, illustrating the concept of servant leadership for husbands and respectful submission for wives. This model mirrors the relationship between Christ and the Church, where Christ, the head, demonstrates sacrificial love, and the Church responds in loving submission.

Prayer Point:

Heavenly Father, help us to understand and live out the principles of mutual submission and servant leadership in our relationships.

Wednesday December 04

Topic: The Significance of Personal Devotion and Quiet Time

Memory Verse: "He says, 'Be still, and know that I am God; I will be exalted among the nations, I will be exalted in the earth.'"

Psalm 46:10

Bible Reading: Mark 1:35-39

Read & Learn:

In Luke 10:38-42, we find the story of Mary and Martha. While Martha was busy with preparations and serving, Mary sat at the feet of Jesus, listening to His teachings. When Martha complained to Jesus about Mary's lack of help, Jesus gently replied, "Mary has chosen what is better, and it will not be taken away from her." This story highlights the significance of personal devotion and spending quiet time with the Lord. In our fast-paced lives, it's easy to become like Martha, busy with many things, but we must remember the value of choosing the "better" thing—spending time with Jesus.

Personal devotion and quiet time with God are vital aspects of a believer's life. Mark 1:35-39 illustrates how Jesus Himself practiced this discipline. He withdrew to a solitary place to pray, seeking communion with the Father. In today's world filled with noise and distractions, finding moments of stillness and reflection with God is essential. Psalm 46:10 reminds us to "be still" and know that God is God. Personal devotion allows us to draw closer to Him, gain spiritual strength, and receive guidance, just as Jesus did before His ministry's busy day. It's in these quiet moments that we hear God's voice, find renewal, and develop a deeper relationship with Him.

Prayer Point:

Heavenly Father, help us prioritise personal devotion and quiet time in our daily lives.

Thursday December 05

Topic: Biblical Teachings on God's Sovereignty

Memory Verse: "Remember the former things, those of long ago; I am God, and there is no other; I am God, and there is none like me. I make known the end from the beginning, from ancient times, what is still to come. I say, 'My purpose will stand, and I will do all that I please.'" - **Isaiah 46:9-10**

Bible Reading: Romans 8:28-30

Read & Learn:

The biblical story of Joseph in the Book of Genesis is a powerful illustration of God's sovereignty. Despite facing adversity, betrayal by his brothers, and years of hardship, Joseph trusted in God's ultimate plan. In the end, God used Joseph's journey to save his family and fulfil His purpose. Joseph's words to his brothers in Genesis 50:20 reflect his understanding of God's sovereignty: "You intended to harm me, but God intended it for good to accomplish what is now being done, the saving of many lives."

The Bible is filled with teachings on God's sovereignty, emphasising His supreme authority and control over all things. Isaiah 46:9-10 declares that God's purposes will always prevail, and nothing can thwart His plans. Romans 8:28-30 reassures believers that God works all things, even the challenges and hardships of life, for the good of those who love Him and are called according to His purpose. Understanding God's sovereignty brings comfort and peace, knowing that He is in control, and His plans are for our ultimate good.

Prayer Point:

Heavenly Father, we acknowledge Your sovereignty over all things and trust in Your perfect plan.

Friday December 06

Topic: The Power of Community in the Christian Life

Memory Verse: "And let us consider how we may spur one another on toward love and good deeds, not giving up meeting together, as some are in the habit of doing, but encouraging one another—and all the more as you see the Day approaching." **- Hebrews 10:24-25**

Bible Reading: Acts 2:42-47

Read & Learn:

The early Christian community described in Acts 2:42-47 is a remarkable example of the power of Christian fellowship and community. They were devoted to learning, fellowship, breaking bread, and prayer. This unity and shared devotion allowed them to experience awe-inspiring wonders and signs. They cared for each other's needs and met regularly, both in the temple and in their homes. This deep sense of community and fellowship not only strengthened their faith but also attracted others to the faith, leading to the continuous growth of the church. This story demonstrates the transformative impact of Christian community on the lives of believers and the expansion of God's kingdom.

The Christian life is not meant to be lived in isolation but in the context of a loving and supportive community of believers. Hebrews 10:24-25 encourages us to consider how we can spur one another on toward love and good deeds and not neglect meeting together. Acts 2:42-47 illustrates how the early church practiced this principle, resulting in a vibrant and growing community. Christian community provides accountability, encouragement, and opportunities for spiritual growth.

Prayer Point:

Heavenly Father, thank You for the gift of Christian community. Help us to actively engage and support one another.

Saturday December 07

Topic: The Role of Christians in Promoting Social Harmony

Memory Verse: "And above all these put on love, which binds everything together in perfect harmony." **- Colossians 3:14**

Bible Reading: Ephesians 4:1-6, 11-16

Read & Learn:

In the early 19th century, John Newton, a former slave trader turned Anglican clergyman and hymn writer, exemplified Christian transformation and social harmony. After his profound conversion to Christianity, Newton became an ardent abolitionist, advocating against the slave trade. His most famous hymn, "Amazing Grace," reflects his personal journey from despair to faith. Newton's life demonstrates how a heart changed by Christ can impact society, promoting love, repentance, and ultimately, social harmony. His partnership with William Wilberforce in the abolition movement underscores the Christian's role in societal change, rooted in the Gospel's transformative power.

Today's devotional focuses on the Christian's role in fostering social harmony, guided by Colossians 3:14, emphasising love as the unifying bond. The Bible reading from Ephesians 4 encourages believers to live in unity and grow in spiritual maturity, recognising that diverse gifts are meant for building up the church in love. Christians are called to embody Christ's love and humility, promoting peace and understanding in a fractured world. This mirrors the life of John Newton, whose transformation led him to oppose the injustices he once supported.

Prayer Point:

Lord, help us to embody Your love, bringing unity and harmony in our communities.

Sunday December 08

Topic: The Importance of Christian Witness

Memory Verse: "In the same way, let your light shine before others, that they may see your good deeds and glorify your Father in heaven." - **Matthew 5:16**

Bible Reading: Acts 1:6-11

Read & Learn:

In the 18th century, George Whitefield, a key figure in the Great Awakening, exemplified the power of Christian witness. Whitefield, known for his passionate and charismatic preaching, travelled extensively, sharing the Gospel and impacting countless lives. His open-air sermons attracted large crowds, transcending denominational boundaries. Whitefield's deep conviction and eloquent preaching stirred many hearts, leading to numerous conversions. His ministry illustrates the profound effect that a dedicated Christian witness can have, encouraging believers to share their faith boldly and authentically, impacting society and leading others to Christ.

The importance of Christian witness is central to the faith, as highlighted in Matthew 5:16. Christians are called to be the light of the world, showcasing the love and truth of God through their actions and words. The Bible reading from Acts 1 emphasises Jesus' command to be His witnesses, starting from our immediate surroundings and extending globally. George Whitefield's life is a testament to the impact of such witness. He utilised his gifts to spread the Gospel, affecting many lives and sparking a spiritual revival.

Prayer Point:

"Lord, grant us the courage to be Your faithful witnesses in our daily lives."

Monday December 09

Topic: Understanding the Mercy of God

Memory Verse: "The Lord is compassionate and gracious, slow to anger, abounding in love." - Psalm 103:8

Bible Reading: Luke 15:11-24

Read & Learn:

The parable of the prodigal son in Luke 15:11-24 beautifully illustrates God's mercy. A young man squanders his inheritance on reckless living but, in his despair, decides to return home to his father. Even while he was still far away, the father sees him, runs to embrace him, and throws a lavish celebration. This parable shows that God's mercy is abundant and available to those who turn back to Him. It reveals the Father's compassion and love, even for those who have gone astray. Through the prodigal son's story, we see the depth of God's mercy and His desire to welcome us back into His loving embrace when we repent and return to Him.

Understanding the mercy of God is central to our faith. Psalm 103:8 tells us that the Lord is compassionate and gracious, slow to anger, and abounding in love. God's mercy means that He withholds the punishment we deserve for our sins and instead offers forgiveness and reconciliation. The parable of the prodigal son mirrors God's mercy in action. No matter how far we've strayed, God's arms are always open, ready to receive us with love and forgiveness when we turn back to Him. His mercy is not earned but freely given out of His great love for us. It's a reminder that no one is beyond the reach of God's mercy, and it is available to all who seek it through repentance.

Prayer Point:

Heavenly Father, we thank You for Your boundless mercy and love. Help us to fully grasp the depth of Your compassion.

Tuesday December 10

Topic: Christian Views on the Afterlife

Memory Verse: "In my Father's house are many rooms; if it were not so, would I have told you that I go to prepare a place for you?"

John 14:2

Bible Reading: 1 Corinthians 15:50-58

Read & Learn:

In the early 5th century, Augustine of Hippo, a theologian and philosopher, profoundly influenced Christian thought on the afterlife. In his seminal work, "The City of God," Augustine contrasts the earthly city with the heavenly city, emphasising the eternal nature of the Christian's ultimate home. He argued that while Christians live in the world, their true citizenship and hope lie in the heavenly city, where they will enjoy eternal life with God. Augustine's reflections on the afterlife reassured believers of the promise of resurrection and the continuity of life beyond death, offering comfort and hope in the promise of eternal communion with God.

Christian views on the afterlife are rooted in the promise of resurrection and eternal life with God. The memory verse from John 14:2 speaks of a prepared place in the Father's house, symbolising the believer's eternal home. The Bible reading in 1 Corinthians 15 emphasises the transformation of believers, affirming the resurrection and the victory over death through Christ. Augustine's insights offer a deeper understanding of these truths. He highlighted that our current existence is transient compared to our eternal destiny in God's presence.

Prayer Point:

Heavenly Father, help us to anchor our hope in the promise of the afterlife with You.

Wednesday December 11

Topic: Navigating Christian Ethics in a Diverse World

Memory Verse: "Do not conform to the pattern of this world, but be transformed by the renewing of your mind. Then you will be able to test and approve what God's will is—his good, pleasing and perfect will." **- Romans 12:2**

Bible Reading: 1 Peter 2:11-17

Read & Learn:

In the late 19th century, William Booth, founder of The Salvation Army, demonstrated how Christian ethics could be lived out in a diverse and challenging world. Booth and his organisation worked in the slums of London, helping the poor, the homeless, and the addicted. His approach was revolutionary, combining evangelical work with social action. Booth's vision was driven by his deep Christian faith and his understanding of God's love for all people, regardless of their social status. His work exemplifies how Christians can navigate ethical challenges, showing compassion and justice in a diverse society, and addressing physical and spiritual needs simultaneously.

Navigating Christian ethics in a diverse world requires understanding and applying biblical principles in various cultural contexts. The memory verse from Romans 12:2 reminds Christians to be guided by God's will, rather than societal norms. William Booth's life is a practical example of this teaching. He demonstrated that Christian ethics involve not only preaching the Gospel but also actively loving and serving those in need.

Prayer Point:

Lord, guide us to live out our Christian ethics with love and wisdom in a diverse world.

Thursday December 12

Topic: Christian Perspectives on the Sanctity of Life

Memory Verse: "For you created my inmost being; you knit me together in my mother's womb. I praise you because I am fearfully and wonderfully made; your works are wonderful, I know that full well." - **Psalm 139:13-14**

Bible Reading: Genesis 1:26-28

Read & Learn:

In the mid-20th century, Mother Teresa, known for her compassionate ministry to the poorest of the poor, embodied the Christian belief in the sanctity of life. She founded the Missionaries of Charity in Kolkata, India, to serve those whom society often neglected or abandoned, including the sick, the dying, and orphaned children. Her relentless dedication to preserving and honouring life, especially in its most vulnerable forms, was rooted in her deep conviction that every person is made in the image of God and deserves dignity and care. Mother Teresa's life and work powerfully demonstrate how the Christian perspective on the sanctity of life can be lived out in practical, loving service to others, regardless of their status or condition.

The Christian perspective on the sanctity of life is based on the belief that all human life is sacred because it is created by God. The memory verse from Psalm 139 expresses awe at God's intimate involvement in the creation of life. The Bible reading in Genesis 1 highlights that humans are made in God's image, affirming the unique value and dignity of every life. Mother Teresa's ministry exemplifies this belief in action.

Prayer Point:

Heavenly Father, help us to see and honour Your image in every person we meet.

Friday December 13

Topic: Navigating the Ethical Challenges of Faith

Memory Verse: "If any of you lacks wisdom, let him ask God, who gives generously to all without reproach, and it will be given him." **James 1:5**

Bible Reading: Matthew 7:12

Read & Learn:

Dietrich Bonhoeffer, a German pastor and theologian during the Nazi regime, stands as a profound example of navigating ethical challenges in faith. Confronted with the moral atrocities of his time, Bonhoeffer actively opposed Hitler's tyranny, believing that the Christian faith demanded a response to injustice. He was involved in the resistance movement and spoke vehemently against the persecution of Jews. Bonhoeffer's decision to resist evil, despite the immense personal risk, demonstrated his commitment to living out Christian ethics, even in the face of overwhelming opposition. His legacy reminds believers that faith sometimes calls for courageous action in defence of justice and truth.

Navigating the ethical challenges of faith involves applying biblical principles to complex real-world situations. The memory verse from James 1:5 highlights the need for divine wisdom in making ethical decisions. Dietrich Bonhoeffer's story illustrates the application of these principles under extreme circumstances. His actions during the Nazi era show that faith is not passive but requires active discernment and sometimes difficult choices, especially when confronting injustice or oppression.

Prayer Point:

Lord, grant us wisdom and courage to face ethical challenges with faith and integrity.

Saturday December 14

Topic: Navigating Faith in a Pluralistic Society

Memory Verse: "But in your hearts revere Christ as Lord. Always be prepared to give an answer to everyone who asks you to give the reason for the hope that you have. But do this with gentleness and respect." **- 1 Peter 3:15**

Bible Reading: Romans 12:2, 17-21

Read & Learn:

n the early centuries of the church, the Apostle Paul's missionary journeys, as recorded in Acts 17:22-34, provide a compelling example of navigating faith in a pluralistic society. When Paul visited Athens, a city known for its diverse beliefs and philosophies, he skilfully engaged with the local thinkers at the Areopagus. Instead of outright condemning their beliefs, Paul acknowledged their religious sentiments and used a local altar inscription, "To an unknown god," as a starting point to introduce them to the God of Christianity. Paul's approach demonstrates the importance of understanding and respectfully engaging with different worldviews while confidently sharing one's own faith.

Navigating faith in a pluralistic society requires Christians to understand and respect different beliefs while maintaining their commitment to Christ. The memory verse from 1 Peter 3:15 highlights the importance of being ready to share one's faith, but doing so with gentleness and respect. Romans 12 advises Christians not to conform to the world but to live out their faith authentically and peacefully.

Prayer Point:

Heavenly Father, give us wisdom to navigate our faith with grace and truth in a diverse world.

Sunday December 15

Topic: Understanding the Historical Context of the Bible

Memory Verse: "Do your best to present yourself to God as one approved, a worker who does not need to be ashamed and who correctly handles the word of truth." - **2 Timothy 2:15**

Bible Reading: Luke 24:27

Read & Learn:

In the 4th century, Saint Jerome, a Christian scholar and translator, undertook the monumental task of translating the Bible into Latin, known as the Vulgate. Jerome's dedication to understanding the historical and cultural context of the Scriptures was revolutionary. He moved to Bethlehem, living in a cave near Jesus' birthplace, immersing himself in the land and languages of the Bible. His translation and commentaries provided a clearer understanding of biblical texts in their original context. Jerome's work reminds us of the importance of comprehending the historical setting of the Bible to grasp its true meaning and apply it accurately in our lives.

Understanding the historical context of the Bible is crucial for accurate interpretation and application. The memory verse from 2 Timothy 2:15 urges believers to handle the word of truth correctly, which includes appreciating the cultural, geographical, and historical background of biblical events. Our Bible reading in Luke 24 shows Jesus himself explaining the Scriptures in their historical context. Saint Jerome's life exemplifies this pursuit of understanding

Prayer Point:

Father, guide us to understand Your Word in its historical context for deeper insight.

Monday December 16

Topic: Understanding the Role of Angels in Scripture

Memory Verse: "Are they not all ministering spirits sent out to serve for the sake of those who are to inherit salvation?" - **Hebrews 1:14**

Bible Reading: Psalm 91:11-12

Read & Learn:

The biblical story of the angel Gabriel visiting Mary in Luke 1:26-38 is a profound example of the role of angels in Scripture. Gabriel, a messenger of God, was sent to Mary to deliver the extraordinary news of the birth of Jesus. This encounter highlights how angels act as God's messengers, delivering crucial information and guidance. Gabriel's visitation to Mary shows the significance of angels in God's plan, serving as divine messengers to humans, especially in moments of great importance and change.

Angels, as depicted in the Bible, play a vital role as God's messengers and servants. The memory verse from Hebrews 1:14 speaks of angels as ministering spirits sent to serve those inheriting salvation. Psalm 91:11-12 reflects on their protective role. Angels are often seen as intermediaries between God and humans, delivering messages, offering guidance, and providing protection. The story of Gabriel and Mary illustrates these roles clearly. Understanding the function of angels in Scripture helps us appreciate the many ways God communicates and intervenes in human affairs. It reminds us of the supernatural dimension of God's interaction with the world, assuring us of His continued presence and activity in our lives.

Prayer Point:

Heavenly Father, thank You for Your ministering spirits, the angels, who serve Your purposes and help guide and protect us.

Tuesday December 17

Topic: Christian Perspectives on Self-Care and Self-Love

Memory Verse: "The second is this: 'Love your neighbour as yourself.' There is no commandment greater than these."

Mark 12:31

Bible Reading: 1 Corinthians 6:19-20

Read & Learn:

The biblical account of Elijah's experience in 1 Kings 19:1-8 provides a valuable lesson on the importance of self-care and self-love in a Christian context. After a significant spiritual victory, Elijah faced exhaustion and despair. God's response was not immediate action or further commands, but rather providing Elijah with rest, food, and care. This moment of nurturing allowed Elijah to regain his strength for the journey ahead. This story highlights how physical and emotional self-care is vital in sustaining one's spiritual journey and service.

Christian perspectives on self-care and self-love emphasise the importance of caring for oneself not out of selfishness, but as a reflection of God's love and as an act of stewardship. The memory verse, Mark 12:31, implies that loving oneself is integral to loving others effectively. 1 Corinthians 6:19-20 reminds believers that their bodies are temples of the Holy Spirit, and honouring God includes taking care of themselves. Self-care in a Christian sense involves physical, emotional, and spiritual well-being.

Prayer Point:

Heavenly Father, help us to understand the importance of caring for the body, mind, and spirit You have entrusted to us.

Wednesday December 18

Topic: Biblical Wisdom for Healthy Relationships

Memory Verse: "Be completely humble and gentle; be patient, bearing with one another in love. Make every effort to keep the unity of the Spirit through the bond of peace." **- Ephesians 4:2-3**

Bible Reading: Colossians 3:12-14

Read & Learn:

The story of Ruth and Naomi, as depicted in the book of Ruth, offers profound insights into healthy relationships. Despite being from different generations and cultures, and facing immense loss and hardship, Ruth's loyalty to Naomi is exemplary. Ruth's words, "Where you go, I will go, and where you stay, I will stay," reflect deep commitment and love. This story teaches the value of loyalty, kindness, and selflessness in relationships. Ruth and Naomi's relationship, strengthened by mutual respect and love, stands as a testament to the power of strong bonds in overcoming life's challenges.

Healthy relationships, according to the Bible, are built on foundations of love, kindness, humility, patience, and forgiveness. The memory verse from Ephesians emphasises the importance of humility and patience, while the Bible reading from Colossians encourages believers to clothe themselves with virtues that nurture unity and peace. The story of Ruth and Naomi showcases these principles in action. It illustrates how relationships can thrive even under difficult circumstances when they are grounded in mutual respect, compassion, and commitment.

Prayer Point:

Lord, guide us to build our relationships on the principles of Your Word, cultivating love, patience, and humility.

Thursday December 19

Topic: Biblical Perspectives on Personal Growth

Memory Verse: "Being confident of this, that he who began a good work in you will carry it on to completion until the day of Christ Jesus." **- Philippians 1:6**

Bible Reading: 2 Peter 1:5-8

Read & Learn:

The transformation of the Apostle Paul, from Saul the persecutor to a principal figure in the spread of Christianity, is a striking example of personal growth in the Bible. Initially, Saul was known for his zealous persecution of Christians. However, after a profound encounter with Jesus on the road to Damascus (Acts 9), his life took a dramatic turn. He grew from being a fierce opponent of Christians to one of the most influential apostles, spreading the Gospel across the Roman Empire. Paul's journey of growth, which involved deep reflection, repentance, and learning, illustrates the transformative power of God in personal development.

Biblical perspectives on personal growth emphasise continual development in faith and character, guided by God's hand. The memory verse from Philippians 1:6 reassures believers that God is actively involved in their growth process. 2 Peter 1:5-8 outlines a pathway for growth, starting with faith and culminating in love, suggesting a progression that involves adding various virtues to one's life. The story of Paul's transformation demonstrates how personal growth can lead to significant changes in beliefs, behaviours, and actions.

Prayer Point:

Heavenly Father, guide us in our journey of personal growth, that we may develop qualities that reflect Your love and goodness.

Friday December 20

Topic Point : The Role of Faith in Personal Decision Making

Memory Verse: "Trust in the Lord with all your heart and lean not on your own understanding; in all your ways acknowledge him, and he will make your paths straight." **- Proverbs 3:5-6**

Bible Reading: James 1:5-6

Read & Learn:

The story of Abraham being called to leave his homeland in Genesis 12:1-4 serves as a powerful example of faith in personal decision-making. Abraham, then Abram, was called by God to leave his familiar surroundings and go to a land that God would show him. This decision required immense faith as Abraham was stepping into the unknown based on God's promise alone. His obedience to God's call, without knowing the outcome, demonstrates the profound role that faith can play in decision-making - trusting in God's guidance, even when the path is not clear.

Faith plays a crucial role in personal decision-making for believers. The memory verse from Proverbs 3:5-6 encourages trusting in God rather than solely relying on personal understanding. James 1:5-6 highlights the importance of seeking wisdom from God in decision-making processes and doing so with unwavering faith. Abraham's story is a testament to this principle. It shows that faith involves relying on God's promises and direction, even when the future seems uncertain. When making decisions, believers are called to seek God's wisdom, trust in His leading, and step forward in faith, knowing that God's plans are for their good and His glory.

Prayer Point:

Heavenly Father, grant us the faith to trust in You as we make decisions, seeking Your wisdom and guidance in every step.

Saturday December 21

Topic: Reflecting on your Personal Faith Journey

Memory Verse: "The steadfast love of the Lord never ceases; his mercies never come to an end; they are new every morning; great is your faithfulness." **- Lamentations 3:22-23**

Bible Reading: Psalm 77:11-12

Read & Learn:

The life of King David, as chronicled in the Psalms, particularly in Psalm 77, presents a rich tapestry of personal faith journey. David often reflected on his life, acknowledging both times of triumph and periods of despair. Through battles, moral failures, and moments of great victory, David consistently turned to God, reflecting on His faithfulness throughout his journey. David's psalms provide a model for personal reflection, demonstrating the importance of remembering and meditating on God's presence and work in our lives, in both good times and bad.

Reflecting on one's personal faith journey is an important spiritual practice, as it helps to recognise God's steadfast love and faithfulness throughout different seasons of life. The memory verse from Lamentations and the Psalm reading both emphasise the importance of remembering and meditating on God's past deeds. This reflection can bring comfort, perspective, and renewed faith. Just as David recalled God's past faithfulness, believers today can gain strength and encouragement by looking back at their own faith journeys. Reflecting on how God has guided, provided for, and stayed faithful in various circumstances can deepen one's trust in Him and provide motivation to continue growing and walking in faith.

Prayer Point:

Heavenly Father, help us to reflect on our faith journey, Recognising Your constant love and mercy in every chapter of our lives.

Sunday December 22

Topic: God's Redemption Plan

Memory Verse: "In him we have redemption through his blood, the forgiveness of sins, in accordance with the riches of God's grace." - **Ephesians 1:7**

Bible Reading: Romans 5:6-11

Read & Learn:

The biblical account of the Passover in Exodus 12 represents an early foreshadowing of God's redemption plan. The Israelites were instructed to mark their doorposts with the blood of a lamb, signifying their obedience and faith. This act led to their salvation from the final plague and their eventual freedom from slavery in Egypt. This event not only signified God's power to redeem and save but also pointed forward to the ultimate act of redemption through Jesus Christ, the Lamb of God, who takes away the sins of the world.

God's redemption plan, as revealed in the Bible, is a profound demonstration of His love and grace towards humanity. The memory verse in Ephesians speaks of redemption and forgiveness available through Jesus Christ. Romans 5:6-11 further elaborates on this theme, emphasising that Christ's sacrifice was an act of love for a fallen humanity. The Passover story in Exodus, as a symbol of salvation, prefigures the greater redemption that comes through Christ. Understanding this plan helps believers appreciate the depth of God's love and the magnitude of Christ's sacrifice. It's a reminder that redemption is not just a historical event but a continual process that offers hope, transformation, and a new beginning in Christ.

Prayer Point:

Heavenly Father, we thank You for Your redemption plan, showing Your immeasurable love through the sacrifice of Jesus Christ.

Monday December 23

Topic: Why Mankind Needs Redemption

Memory Verse: "For all have sinned and fall short of the glory of God." - **Romans 3:23**

Bible Reading: Isaiah 59:1-2

Read & Learn:

The parable of the Prodigal Son in Luke 15:11-32 vividly illustrates why mankind needs redemption. In this story, a young man squanders his inheritance in reckless living and finds himself in destitution. Realizing his folly, he returns to his father, expecting rejection. Instead, he is welcomed with open arms and forgiveness. This parable mirrors humanity's condition—lost in sin and unable to save ourselves. It highlights our need for redemption and the loving, forgiving nature of God, who welcomes sinners back and restores them to Himself.

The need for redemption arises from humanity's inherent sinful nature, as stated in Romans 3:23, and the resulting separation from God, as described in Isaiah 59:1-2. Sin has created a chasm between mankind and a holy God, necessitating a bridge to restore this broken relationship. The parable of the Prodigal Son not only reveals the consequences of sin but also the depth of God's grace and willingness to forgive and redeem. Redemption is essential because it reconciles us with God, offering forgiveness, a fresh start, and the promise of eternal life. Understanding our need for redemption is the first step towards accepting God's offer of salvation through Jesus Christ, the ultimate expression of God's redeeming love for mankind.

Prayer Point:

Heavenly Father, we acknowledge our sinfulness and our profound need for Your redemption. Thank You for Your mercy and forgiveness.

Tuesday December 24

Topic: The Concept and Principle of Redemption

Memory Verse: "Christ redeemed us from the curse of the law by becoming a curse for us, for it is written: 'Cursed is everyone who is hung on a pole." **- Galatians 3:13**

Bible Reading: Ephesians 1:7-10

Read & Learn:

The Old Testament story of Boaz and Ruth beautifully illustrates the principle of redemption. Boaz, as a kinsman-redeemer, willingly stepped forward to marry Ruth, a Moabite widow, thereby preserving her deceased husband's lineage and property. This act of redemption not only provided security and protection for Ruth and her mother-in-law, Naomi, but also demonstrated a profound sense of duty, love, and kindness. This story foreshadows the greater redemption found in Christ, who, as our ultimate kinsman-redeemer, redeems us from sin and its consequences.

The memory verse in Galatians highlights how Christ redeemed humanity from the curse of the law. Ephesians 1:7-10 explains that redemption is possible through Christ's sacrifice, which brings forgiveness of sins and unifies all things under Him. The story of Boaz and Ruth is a powerful example of the redemption theme in the Bible, showcasing how redemption involves restoration, protection, and love. It's a reflection of Christ's redemptive work, which not only reconciles us with God but also restores our true identity and purpose in Him. Understanding this principle helps believers appreciate the depth of God's love and the transformative power of redemption in their lives.

Prayer Point:

Lord Jesus, we thank You for redeeming us through Your sacrifice, offering us forgiveness and new life in You.

Wednesday December 25

Topic: Embracing the Joy of Christmas

Memory Verse: "Today in the town of David a Saviour has been born to you; he is the Messiah, the Lord." **- Luke 2:11**

Bible Reading: Isaiah 9:6-7

Read & Learn:

On the first Christmas, the birth of Jesus Christ in a humble stable in Bethlehem marked a pivotal moment in history. This event, foretold by prophets like Isaiah, was not heralded in palaces or among the elite but announced to shepherds in the fields. The shepherds, upon hearing the angelic proclamation, hurried to see the newborn King and were filled with awe. Their response to the news of Jesus' birth - one of joy, wonder, and sharing the good news with others - encapsulates the true spirit of Christmas. It reminds us that the heart of Christmas is the celebration of God's incredible gift to humanity: His Son, Jesus Christ, who brings hope and salvation to all.

Christmas Day is a time of joyous celebration for Christians around the world, commemorating the birth of Jesus Christ. Isaiah 9:6-7 prophesied the coming of a child who would bring peace and establish an everlasting kingdom. This prophecy was fulfilled in the birth of Jesus, who is Wonderful Counsellor, Mighty God, Everlasting Father, Prince of Peace. Christmas is more than a historical event; it's a reminder of God's love and the hope that Jesus brings into our lives. It's a time to reflect on the humility and simplicity of Jesus' birth and the profound impact of His life and teachings

Prayer Points:

Heavenly Father, on this Christmas Day, I celebrate the birth of Your Son, Jesus Christ, and the hope and salvation He brings.

Thursday December 26

Topic: Success is a Journey

Memory Verse: "Keep this Book of the Law always on your lips; meditate on it day and night, so that you may be careful to do everything written in it. Then you will be prosperous and successful" - **Joshua 1:8**

Bible Reading: 2 Samuel 7:8-16

Read & Learn:

Consider the life of Joseph, detailed in Genesis 37-50. His journey from a young dreamer, sold into slavery by his brothers, to becoming the second most powerful man in Egypt, is a remarkable story of perseverance, faith, and divine orchestration. Despite facing betrayal, false accusations, and imprisonment, Joseph remained faithful to God. His success was not an overnight event but a journey filled with trials and triumphs. Joseph's story teaches us that true success is a process shaped by our faith, character, and God's timing, not just the achievement of goals.

Success, from a biblical perspective, is about more than achieving worldly goals; it's a journey of growing closer to God and fulfilling His purpose for our lives. Philippians 4:13 reminds us that our strength to overcome challenges and achieve success comes from Christ. Proverbs 16:3 encourages us to commit our work to the Lord to establish our plans. Success in God's eyes is not measured by our societal status but by our obedience, faithfulness, and perseverance. It's a journey that involves trusting God's plan, even when it differs from our own, and Recognising that every step, whether forward or backward, is an opportunity for growth and deeper reliance on God.

Prayer Point:

Heavenly Father, guide me on my journey to success, anchoring me in Your strength and wisdom as I navigate life's challenges.

Friday December 27

Topic: Count Your Blessings

Memory Verse: "Always giving thanks to God the Father for everything, in the name of our Lord Jesus Christ." **- Ephesians 5:20**

Bible Reading: Psalm 103:1-5

Read & Learn:

The story of the ten lepers in Luke 17:11-19 beautifully illustrates the importance of Recognising and being thankful for our blessings. After Jesus healed them, only one returned to express gratitude. This man, a Samaritan, recognised the magnitude of what Jesus had done and returned to give thanks. His act of gratitude set him apart and received Jesus' commendation. This story reminds us to be mindful of the blessings in our lives, both big and small, and to express our gratitude to God, who is the source of all good things.

Counting our blessings is an essential practice in the Christian life. It involves acknowledging God's goodness and expressing gratitude for all He has done. Psalm 103:1-5 encourages us to praise God and remember all His benefits, including forgiveness, healing, and redemption. This practice shifts our focus from our problems and challenges to God's provision and faithfulness. It fosters a positive outlook and a heart of contentment, reminding us of God's presence and activity in our lives. Counting our blessings is not just about acknowledging what we have received, but also Recognising who God is and His love for us.

Prayer:

Heavenly Father, help me to recognise and count my blessings each day, cultivating a heart of gratitude for all You have done.

Saturday December 28

Topic: Letting Go and Letting God

Memory Verse: "Trust in the Lord with all your heart and lean not on your own understanding; in all your ways submit to him, and he will make your paths straight." **-Proverbs 3:5-6**

Bible Reading: Matthew 11:28-30

Read & Learn:

The biblical account of Abraham being asked to sacrifice Isaac in Genesis 22 is a profound example of letting go and trusting God. Abraham, faced with the unimaginable task of sacrificing his son, chose to trust in God's promise and goodness. His willingness to surrender what was most precious to him demonstrated his complete trust in God. At the moment of ultimate surrender, God provided a ram as a substitute, showing His faithfulness and provision. Abraham's story teaches us the power of letting go of our deepest fears and uncertainties and fully entrusting them to God's hands.

Letting go and letting God is about relinquishing control and trusting in God's plan and timing. It involves surrendering our worries, plans, and desires to God, as emphasised in Proverbs 3:5-6. This act of trust acknowledges that God's wisdom and understanding surpass our own. Matthew 11:28-30 invites us to find rest in Jesus, who offers relief from our burdens. Letting go is not a sign of weakness but of strength and faith, Recognising that God is sovereign and His plans for us are for good. It's about finding peace in the assurance that God is in control and His love for us is unending.

Prayer Point:

Lord, help me to let go of my worries and fears, trusting in Your perfect plan and timing for my life.

Sunday December 29

Topic: Peace that Transcends Understanding

Memory Verse: "And the peace of God, which transcends all understanding, will guard your hearts and your minds in Christ Jesus." **Philippians 4:7**

Bible Reading: John 14:27

Read & Learn:

Consider the story of Daniel in the lion's den (Daniel 6). Faced with the threat of death for praying to God, Daniel remained steadfast in his faith. In the den, surrounded by lions, Daniel experienced a peace that transcends human understanding. This peace was not a denial of danger, but a profound trust in God's protection and sovereignty. Daniel's story is a powerful testament to the peace that God provides in the midst of life's most terrifying trials, a peace that is not dependent on circumstances but on the unchanging character of God.

The peace that transcends understanding is a unique gift from God, as described in Philippians 4:7. It's a peace that doesn't make sense in the natural realm, especially in the face of trials and difficulties. John 14:27 emphasises that this peace is given by Christ, different from what the world offers. It's not the absence of trouble, but a calm assurance in the midst of it. This peace guards our hearts and minds, keeping us anchored in Christ despite the chaos around us. It's a result of trusting in God's promises and His control over our lives, allowing us to rest in His care regardless of our circumstances.

Prayer Point:

Heavenly Father, grant me the peace that transcends understanding, keeping my heart and mind secure in You amidst life's storms.

Monday December 30

Topic: Looking Forward to New Beginnings with Faith

Memory Verse: "See, I am doing a new thing! Now it springs up; do you not perceive it? I am making a way in the wilderness and streams in the wasteland."- **Isaiah 43:19**

Bible Reading: 2 Corinthians 5:17

Read & Learn:

Reflect on the story of Noah after the flood (Genesis 8-9). After enduring the flood, Noah stepped into a world that was essentially a new beginning for humanity. With faith in God's promises, symbolized by the rainbow, Noah embarked on this new chapter of life. This story is a powerful reminder that new beginnings often follow challenging times and that with faith in God's promises, we can embrace these new starts with hope and courage. Noah's experience encourages us to look forward to our own new beginnings, trusting in God's faithfulness and His ability to make all things new.

New beginnings are an integral part of the Christian journey, as seen in 2 Corinthians 5:17, which speaks of becoming a new creation in Christ. This scripture reassures us that our past does not define us; rather, we are continually renewed through our faith in Jesus. Isaiah 43:19 encourages us to be attentive to the new things God is doing in our lives, even in places that seem barren. Embracing new beginnings with faith means trusting in God's plan, believing that He is working for our good, and being open to change and growth. It's about seeing every new chapter as an opportunity to deepen our relationship with God and to witness His transformative work in our lives.

Prayer Point:

Lord, as I face new beginnings, fill me with faith and hope, trusting in Your promise to make all things new and guide my path.

Tuesday December 31

Topic: Reflecting on God's Faithfulness at Year's End

Memory Verse: "Because of the Lord's great love we are not consumed, for his compassions never fail. They are new every morning; great is your faithfulness." - **Lamentations 3:22-23**

Bible Reading: Psalm 90:12-17

Read & Learn:

As the year draws to a close, the story of Joshua leading the Israelites to set up twelve stones as a memorial at Gilgal (Joshua 4:1-7) serves as a poignant reminder. These stones were a physical representation of God's faithfulness in leading them across the Jordan River into the Promised Land. Just as the Israelites looked back on God's past deeds with gratitude, the end of the year is a time for us to reflect on how God has been present in our lives, guiding, providing for, and protecting us throughout the year.

The last day of the year is a significant time for reflection and thanksgiving. Psalm 90:12-17 encourages us to count our days wisely, acknowledging God's sovereignty over our lives. Lamentations 3:22-23 reminds us of God's unfailing love and faithfulness, which are as constant as the rising sun. As we look back on the year, we can see God's hand in both the challenges and the blessings. This reflection leads to a deeper appreciation of God's presence in our lives and prepares our hearts for the year ahead, trusting in His continued faithfulness.

Prayer Point:

Lord, as I reflect on this year, I thank You for Your unwavering faithfulness and love in every moment of joy and challenge.

Inspiring Books by Pastor Femi & Pastor Dotun OYEWOPO

Get your copy on Amazon TODAY! Looking for life transforming gift ideas? Get copies and give as gifts to bless other.

Scan QR Code to buy book on Amazon.

Scan QR Code to buy book on Amazon.

Scan QR Code to buy book on Amazon.

Scan QR Code to buy book on Amazon.

Scan QR Code to buy book on Amazon.

Scan QR Code to buy book on Amazon.

www.ingramcontent.com/pod-product-compliance
Lightning Source LLC
Chambersburg PA
CBHW062045290426
44109CB00027B/2735